ENGLISH FOR MATURITY

By the same author

POETRY

Imaginings	Putnam, 1961
Against the Cruel Frost	Putnam, 1963
Object Relations	Methuen, 1967

FICTION

Lights in the Sky Country	Putnam, 1962
Flesh Wounds	Methuen, 1966

CRITICISM

Llareggub Revisited	Bowes and Bowes, 1962
The Quest for Love	Methuen, 1965

EDUCATION

English for the Rejected	Cambridge, 1964
The Secret Places	Methuen, 1964
The Exploring Word	Cambridge, 1967
Children's Writing	Cambridge, 1967

COMPILATIONS

Children's Games	Gordon Fraser, 1957
Iron, Honey, Gold	Cambridge, 1961
People and Diamonds	Cambridge, 1962–6
Thieves and Angels	Cambridge, 1962
Visions of Life	Cambridge, 1964
The Broadstream Books	Cambridge, 1965

Shortened editions of novels for school use:

Oliver Twist, by Charles Dickens
Childhood, by Maxim Gorki
Roughing It, by Mark Twain
Pudd'nhead Wilson, by Mark Twain

I've Got to Use Words	Cambridge, 1966
The Cambridge Hymnal	Cambridge, 1967
with Elizabeth Poston	

Mr Weston's Good Wine, by T. F. Powys	
with an Introduction	Heinemann, 1966

Plucking the Rushes	
Chinese poems in translation	Heinemann, 1967

ENGLISH FOR MATURITY

ENGLISH IN THE SECONDARY SCHOOL

by

DAVID HOLBROOK, M.A.
Sometime Fellow of King's College, Cambridge

SECOND EDITION

CAMBRIDGE
AT THE UNIVERSITY PRESS
1967

Published by the Syndics of the Cambridge University Press
Bentley House, 200 Euston Road, London, N.W. 1
American Branch: 32 East 57th Street, New York, N.Y. 10022

Library of Congress Catalogue Card Number: 67–26068

First printed 1961
Reprinted 1961, 1964, 1965
Second edition 1967

Printed in Great Britain
at the University Printing House, Cambridge
(Brooke Crutchley, University Printer)

For Geoffrey Thorp and Lance Harris
and to the memory of Nugent Monck:
they taught me what matters

Preface

Any culture worth having depends, at its best, on words. Everything of importance, from the techniques whereby we exist to our attitudes towards life, is shared and handed on by words. Our feelings about things that matter—birth, love, death—are moulded by words and their associations, words with a charge of meaning, increased and renewed by their use in poetry and song. This richness and vitality and precision of the English language form a kind of capital accumulated by words over centuries of active use.

The literature that took life in words and in turn gave them life was never the creation or possession of one class. But that is likely to be its fate for a time—to exist mainly as an object of study by the exam-taking classes. (We may deplore examinations in English, but they keep literature in the curriculum.) The cause of this neglect is the crowding-out of words by pictures, in the familiar forms—visual aids, comics, newspapers and T.V. Words will continue to be used, but for technical and utilitarian wants, and not much else. Literature, the feeder of the imagination that is needed so much in public and private life, will be shelved and not understood. Pictures are a coarse medium, and as Sir George Barnes has noted, 'in a picture age the use of language must be coarsened'.

Things will be worse before they are better. On the one hand the entertainment industry expands its empire; on the other, English in schools is sometimes viewed as a matter of filling up forms correctly. There will be no upward trend without some vigorous action in schools, especially through music, drama and English. Much is being done; there are many devoted and effective teachers in modern schools who do spark off something in their pupils; the battle for literacy is on. Enough is being achieved to show that 'putting children in touch with their cultural heritage' can be something more than an educational cliché. I am sure Mr Holbrook's book will not only arm and encourage those who are already teaching; it will also implant spirit and purpose in many a teacher-in-training who might otherwise have drifted into cynicism.

It is sometimes said that children in modern schools are incapable of anything better than the poor diet they often receive. One answer is that their forebears not so long ago were producing the music that was the making of Vaughan Williams and Gustav Holst; they were essentially educated people. Because he knows this—and he demonstrates it beyond cavil—Mr Holbrook aims high and writes without condescension. Though English in schools is for him a matter of teaching literature (and that is crucially important), not of filling up forms, he provides an abundance of lively practical help that will be welcomed by teachers at any stage of their career.

DENYS THOMPSON

Note on the Second Edition

This book was originally written in 1956, and when I came to revise it ten years later I had behind me five further years' work with adult students and teachers, two years' further work with children, and five years' study and writing about education. I had also learned much from student teachers, who had used *English for Maturity* and who gave parts of it a thorough thrashing in seminar work. After all this I felt at times gloomily that nothing short of complete re-writing would do. I had come to distrust the self who made such sweeping statements about the beneficial relationship between English work and personal growth, yet on the other hand I wasn't prepared to give ground to those who wished to cling to beliefs that the English teacher's work had nothing to do with the development of individual personality, but with a subject or 'structure'. At first, in the throes of revision, I produced pages which looked like a palimpsest.

Then I came to see that the whole grain of my thinking and writing about English teaching had changed: the old and new wouldn't fit, and so all I could do was to try to put right passages where I now felt I was wrong or badly misguided. Where I had exaggerated my readers would, I hoped, be provoked into correcting me in disagreement: or my wilder generalisations could be taken to be modified by my later books. Certain material amendments were obviously necessary: the American Library which was so useful a source in the fifties had been axed, and all gramophone records had been changed to long playing categories. There had been considerable changes in interest in folksong, both positive and negative. Many more useful books on teaching English, and for classroom use, have appeared since 1961.

There has also been something of a break-through by the movement with which this book was associated, a culmination of the work of Denys Thompson and *The Use of English* journal. The formation in England of the National Association for the Teaching of English has consolidated the sense of professional coherence among English teachers organisationally, though it has thrown up further problems, by what seems to me the confusion of its aims, and the unevenness of its publications. But the arrival of NATE has perhaps helped a little to counteract inimical developments such as that of the new examination, the Certificate of Secondary Education. Here the inevitable tendency for an examination to generate mediocrity and stereotypes is having its deadly effect, as can be seen by examining the generally dreary and tawdry syllabuses. But even here there is a gleam of hope. For instance, the first syllabuses for East Anglia (North) CSE were largely influenced by the Report of the Working Party published by the Cambridge Institute of Education and the University Press. This Report in its turn was manifestly influenced by *English for Maturity*—inevitably since the drafting was done by the same author.

Thus there is satisfaction to be felt in that thousands of children in East Anglia, and maybe elsewhere, are reading *Where Angels Fear to Tread*, *An Outpost of Progress*, *Oliver Twist*, *Childhood*, *Goodbye to All That*, *Huckleberry Finn* and *Pudd'nhead Wilson*, rather than 'second-class fiction' by such writers as Nevil Shute, Nicholas Monsarat, and Margery Allingham (all of whom appear elsewhere as set books for second class citizens), because this book was published in time to influence syllabus committees.

There is much to do yet, to reconsider and develop the whole range of English teaching, and especially the teaching of literature. From this book have developed the schemes of provision represented by *Iron*, *Honey*, *Gold*, *People and Diamonds*, *Visions of Life*, *Thieves and Angels*, *The Cambridge Hymnal*, and the Broadstream series of books cut to the dimensions of reading stamina of the secondary school child. One's work also takes its place among other books such as Mr Frank Whitehead's *The Disappearing Dais*, and Mr J. H. Walsh's *Teaching English*, while other books available to support the enthusiastic English teacher are now richly proliferating. In such a situation the campaigning note of this book will no doubt come to seem dated in another ten years' time. One does not have to travel far, however, to find situations in which even its insistent tone still feels appropriate—as it certainly does if one travels as far as the United States and Canada. There, as still in darkest Britain, the emphasis I put here on the need to consider language development in relation to the 'culture of the feelings' is still felt to be radical. So even if we need to go on reconsidering exactly what goes on between the word and the person, I hope this book may still be found to have its uses, in raising the central issues about what the use of English teaching may be and how aims are best served in practice.

DAVID HOLBROOK

Contents

Acknowledgements

Acknowledgements appear in general in the text, particularly to those who have kindly allowed me to use material from *The Use of English*, Miss Susie I. Tucker, Mrs Sybil Marshall, Mr Kenneth Fell, Mr G. G. Urwin, Mr W. Worthy and Mr Eric Austen. I would also like to acknowledge encouragement and material given by Mr T. C. Pryor, Mr Geoffrey Hawkes, Mr John Brigham and other colleagues, including teachers in scattered groups with whom I have worked, through the Institute of Education, in Cambridge, Oxford, Leicester, Cardiff, Monmouthshire, Northamptonshire, Downham Market and Clacton. Above all I wish to acknowledge the value of the liberal atmosphere at Bassingbourn Village College in Cambridgeshire where I have been Tutor during the time of writing. This atmosphere, created by my Warden Mr F. W. P. Thorne, his humane relationship with the children, and his encouragement of me and his young staff were to me an earnest of what secondary modern education can, at its best, be. Happily, I was later able to test my completed volume in his school. I am also grateful to friends who have allowed me to use their private letters and diaries.

The author's thanks are due to the following for permission to quote copyright material:

The Estate of the late Mrs Frieda Lawrence and Messrs William Heinemann Ltd (*Last Lesson of the Afternoon* and *A Snowy Day in School* from *Collected Poems*, *The Rainbow* and *Lady Chatterley's Lover* by D. H. Lawrence); Messrs Faber and Faber (*The Cocktail Party* and *Murder in the Cathedral* by T. S. Eliot, and *The Entertainer* by John Osborne); Mrs Edward Thomas and Messrs Faber and Faber (*Thaw*); the Literary Trustees of Walter de la Mare and The Society of Authors as their representative (*Peacock Pie*); Messrs Macmillan and Co. Ltd (*The Molecatcher* by Edmund Blunden); Messrs Cassell and Company (*The Story of Esther Costello* by Nicholas Monsarrat); Southern Music Publishing Co. Ltd (*Till the End of the World* by Vaughn Horton); Michael

Acknowledgements

Joseph Ltd (*Lord Hornblower* by C. S. Forester); Mrs Sybil Marshall and Messrs Chatto and Windus Ltd (*Idiom in the Primary School* from *The Use of English*); Messrs Novello and Co. Ltd (*I Sowed the Seeds of Love*: Collector/Arranger, Cecil J. Sharp).

I am grateful to Mr Maurice Howarth for preparing the notes on folksong recordings given on pp. 106–12 and in Appendix G, pp. 244 ff. I am grateful to Mr Brian Hankin for help with revising my lists of recommended reading, and to Mr J. Gibson and the Editor for permission to make use of his notes on recorded poetry from *The Use of English*.

Every normal man,—that is, every uncivilised or civilised human being not of defective mentality, moral sense, etc., has, in some degree, creative insight (an unpopular statement) and an interest, desire and ability to express it (another unpopular statement). There are many, too many, who think they have none of it, and stop with the thought or before the thought. There are a few who think (and encourage others to think) that they and they only have this insight, interest, etc....and that (as a kind of collateral security) they and they only know how to give expression to it, etc. But in every human soul there is a ray of celestial beauty (Plotinus admits that), and a spark of genius (nobody admits that).

If this is so, and if one of the greatest sources of strength,—one of the greatest joys, and deepest pleasures of men, is giving rein to it in some way, why should not every one instead of a few, be encouraged, and feel justified in encouraging everyone including himself to make this a part of every one's and his life,—a value that will supplement the other values and help round out the substance of the soul?

CHARLES IVES (the American composer),
note to *114 Songs*, Redding, Conn., 1922

PART I

ENGLISH IN THE SECONDARY SCHOOL

Introduction

...unattractive as the raw Englishry is, it is good stuff...
always supposing it not to deteriorate but to improve...
MATTHEW ARNOLD, *Letters*, vol. II, p. 154

I remember once being shown round a huge new secondary modern school. The architecture was an achievement of the spirit. The airy grace of the building, at one with the original use of light steel frame, prefabricated walls, and glass, put to shame the meanness of the stock jobbing-builders' fancies in the streets round about. No-one could help being stirred by that building: the gay colours in the corridors and class-rooms; the way the architect had scaled his rooms and all the furniture to the stature of the children; its convenience, and warmth, and generosity. In the great gymnasium the yellow pine bars and rails, the red glow of the sprung floor, made one feel an urge to leap and dance. And in the grounds there was a pool, and a fine family group in bronze by a great contemporary sculptor.

The acoustics were perfect; in the classrooms one could be heard in an undertone. The hall, the kitchens, the workshop—perfection! Nothing had been spared, not even the thought to plant flowering shrubs and trees. And splendid curtains by the best present-day designers.

The headmaster took me into his large, wall-papered study.

'Of course,' he said, 'we only get the duds here.' I can't remember my reactions now: I probably giggled, or blushed, or looked knowing, in the terrible cynical way we, the educated of the world, do when we chat about our work among the populace: always trying to knock some sort of sense into the duds, the heel-kickers, who don't want to be educated.

But the more one meets other teachers the more one finds that this disease of cynicism (for it is a disease, and 'There's many on's have the disease and feel it not') is a form of defensiveness indicating unease. It may be partly explained by the emotional and

3

nervous strain of developing relationships with groups which are too large: work with children is always emotionally taxing:

> All the long school-hours, round the irregular hum of the class
> Have pressed immeasurable spaces of hoarse silence
> Muffling my mind, as snow muffles the sounds that pass
> Down the soiled street. We have pattered the lessons ceaselessly—
>
> But the faces of the boys, in the brooding, yellow light
> Have been for me a dazed constellation of stars,
> Like half-blown flowers dimly shaking at the night,
> Like half-seen froth on an ebbing shore in the moon.
>
> Out of each face, strange, dark beams that disquiet...
> —How can I answer the challenge of so many eyes?...
> A voice
> Falters a statement about an abstract noun—
> What was my question?—My God, must I break this hoarse
>
> Silence that rustles beyond the stars?—There!—
> I have startled a hundred eyes, and now I must look
> Them an answer back; it is more than I can bear...
>
> And all things are in silence, they can brood
> Alone within the dim and hoarse silence.
> Only I and the class must wrangle; this work is a bitter rood!

The teacher who has served his apprenticeship will perhaps smile at the hypersensitivity of D. H. Lawrence in those poems of his about teaching: one couldn't go on with the job if one allowed oneself to feel it so deeply. One has to adjust oneself: and Lawrence shows magnificently, in his account of the young woman Ursula's school teaching experience in *The Rainbow* that he knew what sort of adjustment is involved:

So there existed a set of separate wills, each straining itself to the utmost to exert its own authority. Children will never naturally acquiesce to sitting in a class and submitting to knowledge. They must be compelled by a stronger, wiser will. Against which they will always strive to revolt. So that the first great effort of every teacher of a large class must be to bring the will of the children into accordance with his own will. And this he can only do by an abnegation of his personal self, and an application of a system of laws, for the purpose of achieving a certain calculable result, the imparting of certain knowledge. Whereas

Introduction

Ursula thought she was going to become the first wise teacher by making the whole business personal, and using no compulsion. She believed entirely in her own personality. So that she was in a very deep mess. In the first place she was offering to a class a relationship which only one or two children were sensitive enough to appreciate, so that the mass were outsiders, therefore against her...

And so inevitably, in the necessary 'abnegation of his personal self', the teacher suffers a strain, and even the best teacher is bound to become somewhat mechanical: 'Tomorrow was Monday. Monday, the beginning of another school week! Another shameful, barren school-week, more routine and mechanical activity...' That is from the later novel by Lawrence, *Women in Love*: he calls teaching 'mechanical', and 'mechanical' is what teaching is bound to be in our age in which, as Matthew Arnold said, 'knowledge is very largely become mechanical'.

But Lawrence also calls the school week 'shameful': and I think the word may help explain some of the uneasy self-defensive air of teachers. Even the most efficient people who enjoy their teaching work are touched, at times, by the feeling that the repetitive tasks of teaching are 'shameful'. This even more so in an age when the whole environment seems to be alien to creativity. So one finds people like the headmaster of that magnificent new school, establishing tone with an educated stranger by saying: 'Of course, we only get the duds here.'

It drives the administrators, who provide the buildings and handle the huge public fortunes spent on education, into a black rage, naturally, the grumbling cynicism of a staff-room. But it's a real feature of our public education, particularly among those who work in the new secondary modern schools, some of whom still protest that all that's been done is to give the old senior schools a new name, and hang them.

Yet the cynicism has some justification in the lack of any robust and adequate aims in secondary education outside the scramble, in the grammar schools, for certificates and university places. 'Secondary education for all' as a social and political intention implies that the thick and chunky marmalade of grammar school education is now to be thinly spread over the whole population.

There aren't any longer to be any education have-nots: all men are to be educationally equal. Yet, inevitably, to use George Orwell's ironical slogan, 'Some are to be more equal than others'. The cream goes to the grammar school, while the parents of the rest are to be appeased by giving them a 'secondary education', which everyone knows *really* to be a second-best: 'We only get the duds here.' And the poor secondary modern teacher languishes, with his crowds of unruly unintelligent children, who might just as well be kicking about the streets, or sitting in the cinema, while his luckier colleagues in the grammar schools enjoy special responsibility allowances and social prestige. Now, to avoid all this snobbery and cantankerousness, social and political thought have invented the comprehensive school as a solution. It seems to have been forgotten that the mere organisational change did not provide the secondary modern school with aims.

The time-tables, the content of work, in many schools reflect the belief that what the secondary modern school should offer is a watered-down imitation of grammar school education. The academic Parnassus of the grammar school is the 'blessedness in the meridional height' (to use John Donne's words for heavenly light), of many a disappointed secondary school teacher. Only with one's eyes on that, they believe, can one hope to combat, or raise one's head above the relentless pressure of the environment, the popular press, the cults of alienated indolence, the fatuous love-lyric, the gum-chewing couldn't-care-less attitudes of present-day youth in the mass. And out of this belief that you can't convert these 'duds' to Shakespeare springs the protective cynicism: 'We've got the dull louts, and have to make the best of it we can.'

These aren't the attitudes of the best teachers in the secondary schools, certainly not those of the sort of people who are likely to read this book. Yet we are all touched by it, and its atmosphere can undermine one. There are schools where to imply in the staff-room that you enjoyed a lesson, that you like your work, is to be met by a frosty silence. Some cynicism soon reaches the new young struggling teacher fresh from his training: one too often meets its effects.

This book is offered to those who profess to teach English, or who have to teach English, in the secondary modern school, to help them consider their work as part of all English teaching—whether in the university, in the grammar school, primary school, or secondary modern school—and as of equal value. They are helping train the sensibility of three-quarters of the nation: and they are helping create its capacities for living and its potentialities as an audience for new forms of popular culture. And it is for the English teacher because his subject must be at the centre of all education, the subject by which substance may be given to aims throughout.

Sensibility is undoubtedly linked with intelligence. But responsiveness of feelings, with which we as English teachers are primarily concerned, isn't measured by the kind of tests which decide whether or not a child is fit for an academic training in a grammar school and a professional career. Vocation, class, status have little to do with the need for every individual to be equipped to meet the large and small crises of every life. Snobbery—and the attitude of the headmaster about the 'duds' is essentially snobbish—snobbery is out of the question when we come face to face with love or death, to seek the satisfactions derived from life, and to try to maintain some sense of order in our lives.

'Knowledge is very largely become mechanical.' A senior mistress in a secondary modern school once said to me, 'There's so much knowledge to impart these days that there's no time for all this poetry and imagination.' And in this spirit, in the grammar school, children are paced through a remarkable range of subjects and devote their lives to acquiring an unnecessary amount of fact, much of this acquired to no purpose since it may always be found, when needed, in books of reference or tables. Many grammar schools neglect entirely the development of their pupils' sensibilities, and are thereby failing to foster inner resources, deeper literacy, and thus the capacity to deal effectively with the world.

One can hardly believe that Charles Dickens' *Hard Times* was written over a hundred years ago, as a dreadful warning to the Gradgrinds and M'Choakumchilds of education.

Without that drive for examination results, and places in a

technological society—without that mill-like grinding drive, what a chance for the secondary modern teacher! Free, to put his pupils in touch with anything in the whole range of English literature he likes! To spend all his time, if he wishes, reading with children just the novels, stories and poetry which he likes himself. He doesn't have to accept the academic standards of 'Eng. Lit.' and suppose that because these are unattainable with his non-academic pupils he is thereby cut off from 'literature' forever. He will have to look at his classics again. Is there anything for them in (say) *Paradise Lost*, among all the other classics in the cupboard? To question established works thus is valuable in itself. Even of *Paradise Lost* Dr Johnson said, 'Its perusal is a duty rather than a pleasure. We read Milton for instruction, retire harassed and overburdened, and look elsewhere for recreation: we desert our master and seek for companions.' Can't we be as honest as Johnson? Not only about that classic, but about many more, the tattered and ink-stained copies of which lie in the cupboards of our modern schools? Not only lie, but are used, out of a sense of painful duty, because we feel that the children ought to be given that thinly spread marmalade which looks like the education their brighter brothers and sisters are receiving at the grammar school? Can't we even develop, as secondary modern teachers with a new freedom, a sense of superiority over our unlucky colleagues in the grammar schools? And show them, even, where they are failing?

Let's have done with it, this feeling of inferiority, 'we've only got the duds here', of humbly imitating the grammar school curriculum. Even though, through CSE, much of our work is now bound to the deadening requirements of examinations there is some flexibility left (as by the opportunity for schools to submit their own syllabuses). The point of English in secondary education is still being thrashed out from new beginnings.

First of all, I suggest, we should consider what kind of life we would like to lead, now we approach the age of automatic machines, less drudgery in work and greater leisure. What kind of society is our ideal? For it seems to me that the lack of assurance in the work of the secondary modern school is the index of a prevailing uncertainty about life itself. We feel less sure than our ancestors about what we live for. Our culture is too thin to give us much help in constructing positive attitudes to life. But as English teachers we ought to be better off than most: our work is with poetry, the pondering of life by metaphor. And it is the poet who asks, How to live? The more we read literature ourselves, the better sense we should gain of how rich life may and could be.

When we have some inkling of possible aims and our duty as teachers towards those aims, then we may consider the aims of teaching English. I have tried to make my way through these stages in writing this book, and in preparing anthologies to go with it. I had in mind the three-quarters of the population on the quality of whose lives the fibre of England as a nation depends. England needs the opportunities for creativity that folk culture once supplied—that which may be seen in the shape of our villages, craft traditions, in folk-song, and in such works as the Authorised Version of the Bible and Shakespeare's last plays, which had their roots in popular modes of speech and life. The writer and the teacher can help make the English people into the audience it needs to be for a sound verbal culture: needs to be, not only for the sake of the greatest literature in the world, but for the sake of those who inherit one of the finest traditions of civilisation. I have tried to keep my feet on the ground, and have not, I think, been unpractical. Indeed there is practical work enough here for a lifetime, if one does the real work.

Can the real work, given the present conditions, be done? I will end this introduction by quoting from a friend's letter. If he is right—and I do not think he is—how futile is our belief in education! But in so far as he is right he indicates something terribly wrong with teachers' training, and suggests the need for radical changes in the running of our secondary schools—those impressive buildings in which those serving there can say, 'We only get the duds here':

An ex-pupil of mine now teaching in a grammar school, with thirty-six to a class, gets very few free periods, is occupied through the lunch hour, and takes home with her three hours' worth of marking every night—eighteen hours of it each week. I suspect she's being over-conscientious, and that she's imposed on, but she assures me it's not so. Three years of that and she'll be as embittered as the rest of the staff. Class teaching is very exhausting. I fear, therefore, that at any rate some teachers would start taking short cuts—you can't assume a high level of effort and seriousness on the part of the teacher...but this is an argument that would stultify all effort if pursued far...

CHAPTER I

Feet on the ground

LETTERS FROM A FRESH YOUNG TEACHER

I

I find I am teaching Art this week! There seems to be no system —for the staff at any rate: the little rotters just arrive and begin to break up the furniture. The poor art master is in the Army for his two weeks Reserve training—he's apparently a neat, brutal man (was once fined for breaking a chair-leg over a boy's back) and all his art stores are in tidy little dollops. The only thing I know about art teaching is from the illustrations to the Ministry of Education pamphlet *Story of A School* by L. A. Stone, where they seem to have had unlimited paper and paint, so this is what they get. I tried reading a Chinese poem to them—translated of course.

I asked them to illustrate it and write a story to go with their picture.

The results, when I collect them from the sodden floor at the end, are so far gratifying—three or four interesting pictures and stories; a large number of neurotic diagrams (these I find very interesting: one boy draws a double-dannatt barbed wire fence round his paper before he starts); a quarter of the output just dull and backward; and a few really queer. The latter I watch, fascinated: one boy painted his paper bright yellow, then emptied his water jar over his palette and fell off his chair into the mess. All this was done very carefully and deliberately, and he washed his hands between episodes.

At the moment I'm only experimenting, rather bewildered by it all. But it seems to me that any formal methods—even the simplest forms of comparison between poems or passages from the newspaper—are pretty well useless with the great range of children we have to deal with, and their backgrounds. Though some of my experiments (e.g. correction by the class of individual efforts) have worked. But I can see why you get exhausted—I've only had three days of this.

II

The governors consist of the local grocer (to whom we owe so much it's an embarrassment to meet the man), a local business man who, I gather, finances hire purchase and has something to do with a garage, and others who have no status to speak of unless they are all members of some mysterious organisation, the Buffaloes or Masons or Frothblowers.

They enforce the pattern which the Bull maintains. School life must be orderly (quiet, sound accounts for the auditors, stocks of pencils kept up, no disorderly behaviour such as farm walks or project work); noble (patriotic, decently Christian, healthy, hygienic, and not dirty [no love poetry]); and it must be of an improving social quality (i.e. go through the public school motions and carry aloft the public school totems). Some inspectors, headmasters, teachers actively work against the ethos, but it's a lie that hangs over both children and teachers.

Can you imagine a school so well trained in critical sense that the speech day speaker perceives an ironic glint in the eyes of the whole school as he ploughs through his false analogies, cheap emotional appeals, and sees the whole school blush as he reads out *He Fell Among Thieves* for their improvement?

Not that the university was much better, come to think of it—it's two or three years after one has left that one realises that behind all the bull there are only one or two people with anything significant to offer. When you're there the dark wainscot, the 'brasses black and red', the 'dais serene' and all the snobbery is such an encouragement to think otherwise.

III

I'm not going mad yet, though I can understand now why ushering is so exhausting. I find it very difficult to work, read or think in the evenings. I need to get the chalk-dust out of my hair, so most of my time's spent patching up boats and pottering about on the river in them.

The children I imagine are cleaner and brighter than in some industrial towns. We have some very backward ones, though, with no proper special schooling or psychiatric care, as far as I can discover. And while the staff has possibilities the headmaster is such an old fool that even the bright ones are becoming cynical and clock watchers.

Some of the rules are fantastic: no borrowing of books between teachers (sets of books, that is: it hardly matters as they're all pre-1890); no books to be taken out of the library except for a few belonging to the County Library stock; separate common rooms for men and women teachers; no classes to be taken out-of-doors (high summer!) and so on. I'm on supply and he's abjectly impressed by my degree, so I can afford to break the rules: what it's like for those whose bread and butter depend on working here, Lord knows.

Even I was reprimanded the other day. I'd got the fourth year boys interested in planning an outing by motor-boat by promising trips to the best pupils. After borrowing a nice set of 1″ ordnance survey maps for this *twice*, I was told I was *using them too much*. He's a stock-preserver—rubbers, pens, etc.—which I suppose is a common type. The school, as you might expect, loses about six of its staff of twenty, each year.

I take the fourth year boys a good deal (two of them can't write more than their own names) and the second year 'A' stream. The latter are very good: but it would be a joy to have a really bright pupil sometimes. I feel I'm getting dull myself and I certainly can't spell any more. What I find delightful is the pleasant loyalty of some of the staff to their backward pupils—and if only collaboration was *allowed* between departments we could do so much more. (It isn't—I'm doing folk-songs in collaboration with the music mistress, and the art teacher is getting the 2nd year to make covers and illustrations for a book they're writing for me—but such eccentricities aren't encouraged.)

IV

We've been asked for detailed syllabuses! The intention (I have been tipped off) is to have a piece of paper in the drawer which is

shown to H.M.I.s and no-one else. (The staff aren't allowed to
see a complete arithmetic syllabus for the whole school prepared
some years ago. Nor, by the way, are they told anything of the
contents of reports on their pupils by the authority's psychologist
or probation officers.) I have insisted on meetings to discuss
syllabuses, but I haven't much hope of their being successful—
some of the teachers are so tired of frustration that they've
settled for just 'keeping them busy and quiet.'

What a farce most of the English must be, with a teacher with
no training in English, working through a text-book 20 or 30
years old—just exercises! Some of my children are flabbergasted
to find anything enjoyable. One boy this week learned a piece of
nonsense poetry by heart (I'd asked them to learn a piece they
liked—most chose little pieces, naturally,) and recited it in a
defiant way as if he expected a flogging for it. He nearly fainted
when I gave him a merit mark.

The disturbing thing is the *down* on enjoyment among the old
hands—raised eyebrows if they see anything unconventional
going on in your class room. Though I'm surprised how some of
the young teachers do good work (and how good it is)—you
have to find out about such things by stealth, as both teachers and
children conspire to conceal them from 'Authority'. Did I tell
you one teacher who wanted to take contemporary poetry with
her class and read them short stories had to have the geography
books on the table to deceive the Bull? He came in to find her
reading them D. H. Lawrence's *Snake* one day and ridiculed it—
and her—in front of the class, and forbade her to read 'modern
stuff'. He knows the whole of *The Ancient Mariner* off by heart,
and recites it in such a way as to reveal that he hardly under-
stands any of it. Of course the friendship between a teacher and
the children under such a ban is a lovely thing, though it makes
discipline complicated.

When the Bull has been unjust to one of my children we have
a little weeping-by-the-streams-of-Babylon together about it, yet
I feel I oughtn't to side with them against him.

V

I never knew how much shop-front there is behind—or rather in front of—teaching. We're compiling syllabuses. The lists some of the teachers send in, when asked what books they use! Hakluyt's *Voyages* with 3B. The fourth year, *Hamlet, Macbeth, The Deserted Village.* 2B, *Dr. Faustus.* What can they mean? 'Those books are what we ought to be doing if we're showing parity of esteem by being like the grammar school'—that's about it.

And when an H.M.I. steps off the train at the station (perhaps to visit a junior school) telephone messages are passed to the Bull from his spies, notes are sent round, the library (a show piece which is never used properly, only as an extra classroom), tidied up. And, just as you've encouraged your class to speak up in their 'conversation practice' the Bull rushes in and roars at them to keep quiet. He rushed in and abused one of my pupils' drawings: a red cow. As soon as he left the boy drew large black bars down the paper and put his cow in prison—those are my sentiments, only it would be a Bull I'd put behind bars. On another occasion —a noisy play-reading outside (mark you)—I saw him peering at us through the boys' lavatory window, like the Owl of the Remove. I wonder how many schools are like this? My own school became like it when I was in my VIth form: the City Fathers appointed a man who believed in the commercial values, another owl, concerned to seek 'results'. When I feel this is a mad-house, if a lively and cheeky boy says something outspoken to me I'm alright (sometimes they say, 'Never mind 'im, Sir'!); but if I catch sight of a dull boy with a cast in his eyes abusing himself under the desk I'm not sure I can go on. I wasn't cut out to be a male orderly in a lunatic asylum, and it's when you're not sure who is sane that you begin to be worried.

CHAPTER 2

Aims: for Living or Earning a Living?

The safety of the world and the future of civilisation depend
upon the character and intelligence of the multitude.

GEORGE SAMPSON, *English for the English*

Our society today would seem to have plenty of 'drive': but—to
use the words of one of D. H. Lawrence's characters in *Women in
Love*—'where does its go go to?' Except for a few catch phrases
such as 'an even higher standard of living', 'a world of plenty', a
'bright future', it is impossible to discover what kind of life is the
ideal to the representative present-day imagination: and yet the
busy activity of industrial directors, trade-union officials and
political leaders implies that we are all working towards some ideal
goal. What kind of life are we working towards? The 'better
living' that manufacturers and political parties promise, remains,
as in optimistic works of literature such as J. B. Priestley's *They
Came to a City*, off-stage, in the wings.

In pessimistic works, which seem less deceived, such as Aldous
Huxley's *Brave New World* or George Orwell's *1984* our ideals
are denied or ridiculed. We believe fervently in 'progress' while
the motive power of our life seems mostly to be greed. Our real
problem is inward weakness, but the popular mind preoccupies
itself largely with activity not on earth at all, but on the surface
of some other planet, or round the moon, and remote from the
conditions of normal life.

I have suggested, in my Introduction, that we need to postulate
a possible ideal future in human terms. Our concepts of what life
might be like can only be given substance by our culture. And we
need more adequate concepts before we can decide what we are
educating our population *for*. The dilemmas in which we find
ourselves in discussing the place and function of the secondary
modern school derive largely from our having hardly any positive

concepts of what human life might be, if it is to be different from the life we live now. And while we are not satisfied with the life we lead—to some extent because we accept it merely as a passage towards a 'brighter future'—we are surprisingly unable to conceive of a life that is successfully different from the one we lead. And surprisingly, as our living becomes 'better living' in the advertisement sense, we see signs of a fear of leisure and material wealth: nothing is more disturbing than the plight of young people with both of these, and yet no sense of how to put their time and money to civilised living; the representative personality of James Dean was symbolic of a suicidal distraction from the terrors of normal quiet, positive, living. But James Dean was just one of 40,000 Americans killed on the roads in the New World every year. Meanwhile, through 'image-living' we seek to make our hallucinations larger than life: *Playboy* is now one of the biggest-selling papers in the western world.

I wish to avoid discussion of 'educating against the environment'. It may be part of our work: but to contemplate teaching in such terms seems to me dangerously negative. We must first know why we educate at all—and it is not by any means simply to make our pupils dissatisfied with their environment. Of such dissatisfaction, addiction, 'teenage' hooliganism and 'pop' cults of futility are indicative in a minority. What is missing from the music of our young people, from their entertainment, and from their social life together is the germ of positive vitality. They have few cultural sources of succour, to develop positive attitudes to life, and develop human sympathy. The home is afflicted by the influence of the mass-media, by the pressure of advertising and by the new illiteracy. As Richard Hoggart points out, such traditions as standing by one another, or of passing on traditional wisdom, have declined in working people's lives under these influences. Thus it remains to the school—and mainly the secondary modern school—to supply new positives.

By what human activities can such positives be supplied? By those which, in any society of the future I can imagine, would occupy our major effort in living: activities devoted to the 'something' outside the individual. Not, that is, to the 'fulfilment of the individual', or the 'individual's fullest self-expression'—filling the personal sack—which is how our acquisitive society spends its time, but to the development of that richness of the individual being which releases sympathy and creative energy in community.

This is achieved by the arts: and it was to them civilised and leisured communities of the past gave their effort—to coming together in submission to embodiments of the human spirit. It is by these that men come to possess their traditions and values— possess them in their thought and feeling, rather than as acquired fragments of knowledge about them. And we possess our traditions largely through and in *the word*. What D. H. Lawrence called 'spontaneous-creative fullness of being' is, paradoxically, achieved only by what Mr T. S. Eliot has called the obtaining of tradition: 'It cannot be inherited, and if you want it you must obtain it by great labour.' The obtaining of tradition is largely a matter of possessing our native language, using it responsibly, and maintaining its vitality. The Englishman develops a fullness of being only in so far as he possesses the English language more deeply and extends his responsiveness to it. Keeping the English word alive, therefore, is crucial to any future flowering of English civilisation: and crucial to our own need for positive attitudes to life. As Keats said, 'English ought to be kept up.'

The implications for English in the secondary modern school would seem to be plain. But they are often not plain when one begins to ask, among a group of other teachers, why we teach English. What do we reply to D. H. Lawrence's cry, 'The great mass of the population should never be taught to read and write. Never.'?

The answer lies, I think, in the insistence, such as that of George Sampson in his very fine book *English for the English*, on education which is 'a civilising and humanising practice', 'part of the act of living', rather than a preparation for life or, worse still, for 'earning a living'.

The best of the primary schools, certainly at the infant stage, have made their work accord to these requirements: where the selection examination casts the shadow of the world of greed over the school perhaps the primary schools are less successful.

But in the earlier years they have converted school into the embryonic experience of civilised life which it should be. The public is often angry (or guilty) about the degree to which infant pupils enjoy themselves, 'playing about'. But the primary schools have demonstrated that at the centre of education there needs to be that pleasure which propagates sympathy and is the basis of civilisation: the pleasure of organising experience in art. The primary school concentrates on the development of beings: the secondary schools have to turn their attention to pupils as workers, intellectuals and technologists. A minority are groomed for the best places and academic achievements: the rest follow as best they can, and every pupil's sensibility, his civilisation, is left to take care of itself. Our education begins by being one thing and ends by being another: the result is too often the inarticulate scientist, the illiterate workman, the immature being.

Let me try to put together, as simply and positively as I can, the aims of education in the secondary modern school, as I feel they should be, and the aims of English as the central and dominating subject, as it must needs be. My argument derives a good deal from that book which I cannot hope to emulate, *English for the English*, and I hope the reader who is irritated with my inadequate statement will turn to George Sampson's distinguished essay.

Most of the skills and capacities our pupils will require when they leave school will be learnt after they leave, in the factory, shop, or office. A few special skills, such as the ability to type, they can learn quickly, if they need them, at evening classes after they are fifteen: or they may go on to a technical college after they complete their secondary education. We have no need, therefore, to concern ourselves, even if it were correct to do so, with education for 'earning a living': we educate for living.

It is impossible for the most intelligent man, who is subjected to education of one form or another for twenty years or more, to acquire more than a very tiny proportion of what goes to make up human knowledge of facts. Since universal education has been developed, it has been conceived too much in terms of the acquiring of facts. The possession of very few facts is necessary for anyone's existence and work: they can be acquired according to one's needs and interests from books (so long as we know how to use a book). The concern to fill children with facts goes naturally with the examination system, as the examination can only measure, with any accuracy, the possession of factual information.

The primary schools have learnt that it is not, for instance, the acquiring of numerical facts that develops a child's powers, but the growth of a sense of number, and of the ability to deal with numerical concepts. In the modern school, perhaps we should save time by teaching the means of access to facts rather than the facts themselves. An academic child who is to work in, say, medicine, may need to carry many facts in her head, and the acquiring of them does her little harm, if she has mental capacity. By the less 'brainy' child we often mean the child who cannot easily acquire more than a smattering of information: it would seem to be sufficient to train such a child to know how to seek what it finds hard to store for itself. And saving thus time and energy we may spend it on developing, through the arts subjects, powers of being, rather than knowing: if we accept this the artificial barriers between subjects, devised for the purposes of speed of training necessary in grammar school work, and for specialist training up to university level, are no longer required in the secondary modern school. The capacity to begin to think scientifically must, of course, be related to empirical experiment and observation in the laboratory: but it can also be developed by a simple training in argument, or by oral or written accounts of something observed in life, on a farm or in a factory. Far more important than being told what happens when iron filings and sulphur are heated together is that each child shall at some time have had the experience of thinking objectively and deductively about some such phenomenon which he or she has observed. The old type of farm-worker had this faculty—his work depended on it being for him an almost unconscious habit: but it is a faculty seldom found in our own time.

Again, mathematics can become tangible experience in studying music, or simple astronomy and physics, in calculation of area, seed and quantities in agriculture. (I am thinking of a letter from a scientist to the *Manchester Guardian* who had timed sparrows eating grass seed on his new lawn, and calculated how many extra seeds he needed to provide for the sparrows: the cost of these was less than the cost of protection. Such a calculation seems to me to be of the kind our children's minds should be trained to embark on: most of the mathematics we were taught was unnecessary if we have a ready-reckoner in the house or adding machine in the office.) A sense of history, the capacity for imagining lives different from our own, derived from a good book or play, is of far more value than a detailed knowledge of the names of the kings of England, or the dates of stages in the English constitution. The experience of a regulated discussion is of more value than a detailed knowledge of parliamentary procedure.

Significantly, while not all the capacities I have mentioned above could be developed by a training in English, all of them depend upon their being taught in English, and by being enlarged by English training. For instance, the empirical habit, the scientific approach, goes with the use of language for deduction and argument—one supplements the other, and the science teacher whose English is bad, whatever else he may be doing, is not teaching science. The link between the formula and the world is made in English words. In all 'subjects' which tend towards abstraction, the faculty for which belongs to the minority, the teacher will inevitably use more words in dealing with the modern school child. A grammar school child will see the connection between πr^2 and a circle: his brother in the modern school, less capable of abstractions, will only grasp it if he needs to deal with an actual circle of wood or stuff: and he will need it explained to him carefully in clear English rather than in algebra, or by geometrical theorems. (Not, of course, that we can truly put π into words!)

With the modern school child, then—which is the same as saying most children—it is worth repeating the truism that *every teacher is a teacher of English because every teacher is a teacher in English*; that 'through the English language the pupils learn all other subjects'; that 'English cannot wait'; that English is not a subject, but 'a condition of school life'. All four of which phrases are not mine, but George Sampson's, and I see no reason to try to improve on them.

There is something more implied in this than giving a child, by the time he has left school, the ability to use his language as a tool for reading and writing merely because in a complex industrial era we need universal literacy. Of course we must have universal literacy, at the level of practical living, in an age which is liable to confront us with such notices as 'Police dogs patrol this area', or 'Danger: radioactivity', or with more complicated requests, such as for instance: 'What alterations, if any (including change of colour, type of engine and/or propelling fuel), have been made affecting the registration particulars since the last declaration?' Of course, too, as George Sampson insists 'the person who cannot make a correct, concise, lucid and intelligible statement in writing is an uneducated person', and if we produce such persons we are not doing our work efficiently as English teachers.

But, and here is a point which should indicate complete revision of the syllabus: the use of English for normal practical purposes cannot be developed for most pupils by exercises alone. It can only be developed culturally—that is, from the pleasure of the organised word in imaginative writing. The three-quarters of the population we take in the secondary modern school descends from ancestors whose culture was subtle, vigorous and fine, though it was oral and unwritten, and they were uneducated. For most people, writing things down and reading written statements are specialised tasks; speaking and listening are not. For many, reading and writing are difficult acts of abstraction, less so when they render emotional satisfactions: listening and speaking come to them 'by nature'. Certainly the act of writing something about practical matters which do not exist in the concrete, and then examining that abstract writing itself to see what is wrong with its grammatical construction, is a very special function of the mind, and only a very small proportion of the population can gain any benefit from it.

That teachers regard this latter kind of work as being of such importance in English teaching seems to me to be based on several mistaken assumptions. (And, alas, too much English teaching is given up to this meaningless and useless work.) First, of course, it appears to produce tangible results, and to be *real* work, a *real* discipline. The exercises are numbered: the answers are either right or wrong, the children and teacher recognise the game they are playing, and authority, seeing the children kept quiet, nods approvingly. Secondly, it is a kind of 'grammar' teaching, and grammar schools is what schools were always called before we had universal education. Thirdly, the teacher's own education contained more than enough of this kind of abstracting function, particularly if he learnt other languages, and so he feels it contains the essence of education : he fails to remember that he is a person who is more capable than the majority of thinking in the abstract (or he would not have become a member of one of the professions).

Grammar for learning languages is merely a short-circuiting method for the abstracting mind, to enable it to acquire other languages more quickly than by living with them. We often take the short-cut method as being the *only* way to acquire mastery of a language. The way to develop one's mastery over English is to live within a rich context of its lively use, by reading, listening, and talking.

Children sometimes cannot write or read because of emotional disturbances or preoccupations: this is recognised in the primary school, and, in general, in the secondary school. But what is not perhaps so well recognised is the converse: that the pupil or man who cannot speak or write clearly, who cannot read, listen or understand correctly, is suffering from inadequate development of his sensibility, of his capacities for thought and feeling. Even to write a recipe for making tea clearly requires all the powers of a man's sensibility. And his powers of sensibility grow in his culture.

We must recognise here, while dealing with the practical use of English, that acquiring English 'within the context of its lively use' means acquiring it within the context of its *imaginative* use, largely; even to write the instructions for making tea is an exercise in imagination. I am thinking of the complaints now made by science faculties at the university, that their students cannot read, précis, write. Science dons ask the English dons what can be done about it and receive the reply that at that stage it is very unlikely that this can be corrected by any exercises in English. The inability to write goes with an inability to think, and the inability to think goes with weaknesses in the whole sensibility, of which capacities for feeling are a significant part. A scientist, then, who has never developed his maturity by imaginative works of literature, music, drama, painting, who has made no contact with the liberal studies, who has never pondered the questions 'What for?' and 'How to live?' has very limited capacities as a scientist. And this would seem to me to be as true of the man who is to be the skilled or semi-skilled worker in the ranks of the trade union as it is of the scientist and professional man. The automatic factory, the richer and more leisured working class which goes with it, the middle class that is losing its definition in the processes of a mass-production society—these will bring a dangerous instability to a society weakened in its popular culture unless we train the majority of our school-leaving pupils in the ability to use English in the simple observing of experience and making orderly deductions from it, such as a recipe for making tea. A competent writer might write the recipe thus:

Have ready a teapot (holding about two pints of liquid for four people), tea, milk, sugar, and sufficient cups, saucers and spoons for the company. Some people like their tea strained, so you may need a strainer. Fill the kettle with fresh water and bring it to the boil. Pour a little boiling water into the teapot to warm it: when the pot is warm, throw this water away. Put into the warmed pot a teaspoonful of tea for each of the company, and one spoonful extra 'for the pot'. (Of course you may vary the amount when you know how your family likes its tea.) Pour on the water while it is still boiling, and put the lid on the pot.

Let the filled pot stand for about one minute, to 'draw'. Meanwhile put milk and sugar into the cups of those who take them. Then pour out the tea, remembering to refill the pot with hot water from the kettle in case anyone should ask for a second cup.

There is a model recipe in the Ministry of Food pamphlet *The ABC of Cookery* (most of this Ministry's pamphlets are very well written): mine is perhaps more informal, and a bright child would produce an amusing and more human account. But does the reader realise how difficult it is to write such a recipe? How much it is an act of imagination, for which one is trained by imaginative word-use? How specialised a function of the mind it is, so to abstract and order processes, selecting those which are relevant and organising a sequence which is logical and omits nothing? How much such a task draws on our feeling for the language gained by reading? It is an accomplishment we should only demand from our pupils in recognising its difficulty: and such difficulties in writing are not those of science, history or domestic science, but of the English by which these subjects are taught and learnt. It goes without saying that unless the teacher of such subjects is himself equipped with sound English in talking and writing, he can only add to the difficulties.

In some subjects there is a kind of skill and understanding for which language is not only unnecessary, but which cannot be imparted in words: and such skills were once part of a way of life for a large proportion of the population with whom we are dealing:

It is by no means easy to tie a knot effectively in straw, and the younger generation of labourers are often impatient of the intractability of the stuff and prefer, when they can, to provide themselves with pieces of twine. Their fathers and mothers, having learnt the old sheaf-knots almost in infancy, tie them with inimitable rapidity and deftness, though they are often unable to do it deliberately or in material other than straw and are nearly always totally incapable of explaining the process in words.[1]

For this reason perhaps much of our work in the secondary modern school should be oral work—not written at all, and English, in so far as it is practical English, should be the responsibility of subject teachers, particularly of the practical subjects. But these teachers should only demand written matter when this is an essential part of the task in hand—making a record of a recipe or experiment, explaining a map or diagram, for instance. Even in the other subjects the teacher should aim above all at developing the child's facility for giving a clear spoken account of something he has seen or heard or done: that would seem to one to be the

---

[1] T. Hennell, *Change on the Farm* (quoted by Adrian Bell in *The Open Air*).

primary aim in training children in English as a tool. Here, then, we may allow ourselves to state our minimum and maximum *practical* aims in teaching English.

✎ Our minimum aim will be this: every child on leaving school should be able to read well enough to understand written public instructions, and simple newspaper articles which directly concern his safety and rights as a citizen. He should be able to understand a letter and answer it, and write a letter asking for information. He should be able to give simple instructions in speech, and a clear account of something he has seen, heard or done. He should be able to keep notes of simple recipes and other instructions.

Our maximum aims will include these: the best of our pupils will be able to:

1. Give by word of mouth a summary of something he has read, heard or seen or an account of something he has done. He will be able to converse, give a talk on a subject, tell a story, answer questions, read and recite clearly and remember poems and songs. He should be able to give an account of himself at an interview.
2. Read and answer a letter, write a letter of application, a letter to a friend giving news, offering condolence, congratulation and so on. He should be able to send a telegram, give instructions over the telephone, take down messages correctly, read instructions correctly, fill in forms correctly, and send a post-card efficiently.
3. Take a part in a play, spontaneous charade or sketch, or a mime.
4. Read a newspaper, and give by word of mouth or in notes a summary of its contents in some sort of order of importance, and have opinions on the news and the way it is presented.
5. Write a note on a practical or technical subject clearly, putting observed phenomena, or instructions, in correct sequence. He should also be able to write a note on the general significance of such practical and technical matters—i.e., not only on how a petrol engine works, but on the difference it has made to, say, farming. In practice this means the ability to organise material from notes and from sources, and write it up. (This is a most difficult achievement, and we should expect it of only a few in writing: though everyone should be able to do it to a degree in speech—for instance, tell their neighbour how to treat a septic wound.)
6. Understand how to use a book (including how not to use it); how to use a library. He should understand the use of dictionaries, encyclopedias, directories and indices.

Most of these, as I have insisted, should be given to the secondary modern child by the teachers of other subjects than English. What then is the function of the English teacher?

If we consider the capacities outlined above, we can see that they cannot be learnt mechanically. Even observing and recording phenomena in the correct sequence involves capacities for patience, for deduction from experience, making patterns or shapes out of experience which belong to what Yeats called 'the whole man, blood, imagination, intellect, running together'. It is the development of 'whole' men and women, without which the practical tasks cannot be done well, which is the special province of the English teacher. So now we may consider our larger aims: the minimum and maximum aims in English as a means to achieving wholeness:

Our minimum aim is to develop powers of imagination in every child so that the school leaver has had some experience, in phantasy, of the major adult problems of living, (he is, of course, already beginning to face them outside school). Every child should gather thereby that such problems are common to all mankind, and are met with varying degrees of moral quality. Even the weakest pupil should have at one time or another felt deeply about a story or a poem, so that the experience provides a sense of balance, the enlargement of sympathy, and a grasp of values.[1]

And here are our maximum aims:

1. The school-leaver should be able to read easily and should enjoy reading.
2. He should have read, or have had read to him, in each year of his school life some 50 first-rate stories and poems.
3. He should have read, or joined in the reading, in 'low gear' of a number of poems, short stories and longer works of fiction of the best quality at the direction of a teacher who delights in literature.
4. He should know a number of poems and songs by heart.
5. He should have had the experience of creating poems, stories and plays (or what I call below 'programmes').
6. He should have gained sufficient pleasure in drawing on the wisdom of all forms of verbal culture to feel, as he lives on, the need to read

---

[1] The need for the child to explore inner reality by phantasy has since been examined at length by the present writer in *English for the Rejected.*

something of English literature. And here I include under literature ballad, folksong and all forms of popular culture: I have tried to make their wisdom about life the criterion for selecting poems and songs for the anthology which accompanies this book.

7. He should have some sense of discrimination. He should know what he likes to read, and choose one book rather than another by inspecting the quality of a few pages, or by making use of reviews, and the opinions of librarians and others, in relation to his own taste.

8. He should feel that the celebration of possible ways of living in song, poetry, drama, and other forms of literature is a primary activity of civilised man.

And this work in the secondary modern schools is at one with the recreation of a sound and active popular culture, for our pupils are the common audience and in them, chiefly, the English tongue lives.

CHAPTER 3

Some Enemies

A man cannot plough a field well, or vote satisfactorily, or take part in the social context of his factory adequately, or raise a family competently unless he is to some degree a mature and civilised creature. How does he achieve that civilisation? Largely through his language: if he speaks the English language his will be an English civilisation. And his civilisation largely depends not upon his use of his language in a practical, 'non-fictional' way, but upon the complex flux of language to and fro in his life in fictional and imaginative ways. From his mother's first nonsense-words, through nursery rhymes, proverbs, chatter with other children, hymns, game-rhymes, arguments, nicknames, songs, stories, comic-strip balloons and poetry his capacities to be a whole- or half-man are being established. This is not yet sufficiently understood: it is memory, consciousness and their indissoluble links with the word that make us different from, if not superior to, the beasts. Weakness in the word is weakness in our life itself.

So we must concern ourselves, in all education, even when acquiring fact and technological skills, with the whole range of the word, and not least with the word's imaginative power.

This is not yet understood by many. And, indeed, the need for training in language to be based on the use of words to their fullest range has many enemies. Some of these enemies represent the present-day interest in simplifying human life in terms of quantity, often because someone wants to make money out of large numbers of people. Thus mass-production, in order to sell huge quantities of goods, demands standardisation, and reduces human life to easily manageable formulae, as by sales research and readership surveys. Then there are the people who fear the very complexity and subtlety of life itself, and would wish life to be reduced to a limited and manageable state. Both these impulses, the commercial and the over-simplifying, converge on language and on English. The teaching of English in some technical colleges for instance, even tends to be based on such suppositions.

One of the chief representatives of the commercial forces creating children's reading habits, Mr Marcus Morris, complained at the British Association conference in 1958 that schools were not producing pupils 'literate in science': the influence of the educational system should be 'reversed', and children's curiosity fed by scientific information. He went on to say that, 'however charming Kipling's *Just So Stories* might be, they could do damage to a child's outlook'. Mr Morris was thereby denying that to be literate in science requires imagination: the *Manchester Guardian*, in reporting his address, pointed out that why a giraffe's neck is long (children demanded to know such things, said the speaker), is still a subject of dispute between the Darwinians and the Lamarckians: that is, still the proper subject of scientific imagination, to be later checked against available evidence. Appropriately at the same Conference a professor of psychology said that the result of a study of the imagination of school children between the ages of 10 and 15, 'revealed a lack of cultivation of the imagination in schools, and this neglect could seriously impair the quality of training in science technology...It was a mistake to suppose that the scientific intelligence operated autonomously: in its higher flights it was greatly dependent on metaphorical imagination.'[1]

That precision and effectiveness in the use of words depend upon responding to and using words in imaginative ways is implicitly denied by experts in 'communications', by semanticists, and by less reputable people who believe that in a 'modern age' with new apparatus for transmitting messages, the schools are wasting time in handling poetry, stories and such fancy, out-of-date, gear. I feel it is necessary to deal briefly with these enemies because their representatives are active in the schools themselves.

First perhaps I should deal briefly with the 'communications' experts. Their assurance comes from finding their preoccupations effective in the practical world, particularly the world of industry and commerce. In their world, the transmission of information is

[1] Professor John Cohen, *Manchester Guardian* 30 Sept. 1958.

one of the major problems of human life: the solving of complicated data by electronic computers, the control of rockets and automatic processing machines, the direction of aeroplanes, the running of a works, the ordering of sales campaigns, even the solving of international disputes and the direction of our personal lives—all these are problems only of communication. If messages came through clear and strong, all the difficulties of life would be made straight, and the rough places plain.

No doubt much waste and anxiety would be removed from our life if communications were improved. Yet it is not the wires that are crossed, but complexities in human nature. No two people are alike, to the despair of the commercial mind. Each human being has infinite capacities and infinite variations of spirit—and each life in time is a unique mystery. The communications experts really seem to act as if human beings are a form of rather inefficient thinking machine: the fundamental assumptions of communications experts and enthusiasts for the 'new technology of education' often fail to see the mystery of the flesh that can think and be aware of its existence. For our purposes the main objection to the 'communications' preoccupation is that it is related to the concern to make education serve practical ends—to be for 'earning a living'. Short-sightedly, too, for the more effective organiser or workman, the more effective 'communicator', will be the man who is trained in his whole sensibility, trained not only to use language but to live wholly. The quality of feeling, of perception, of conceptual thought in each of us, and our sense of order in experience—all these depend upon our language habits in a much more complex way than is covered by the term 'communications'. For much of the communications experts' expertise, their slick jargon, their analogies with computers, and their mechanical talk about brains cells and impulses, merely hides their intolerance of the infinite intractability of language and personality. What they too often leave out of account is our communication with ourselves, in the inward world with which we must first learn to deal, before we can deal with the outside world.

Some of the irritation with life's intractability emerges in the useful and admirable concern to check meaning. In this way such writers as Mr Stuart Chase have done much to help reduce the amount of nonsense talked in public, perhaps. But even the semanticists have been misled by their own conception of themselves as scientists of meaning. The response of the human brain and being to language can never be anything more than complex and intangible, because it is a living process. If it could be tidied up we should become morons, or die. We live much by hunches, by making suppositions from inadequate evidence and acting on them (as came out recently in the trial of a railway signalman: the court decided he was being tried for doing what a living human being *must* do in order to live at all), and by motives which belong to emotion and bodily metabolism.

Semanticists such as Mr Chase sometimes naively yearn for human beings to be robots. Here is a representative passage from a book of his, *The Power of Words*. He is describing a scientific book:

The thesis of [W. Ross Ashby's] book is stated twice, once in standard English, once in mathematics, and is arranged that the reader can turn from the English to the mathematics, and vice versa. Thus we have the story in *two* languages, expertly cross-referenced—which must be some kind of landmark in semantics. The mathematics act as a stern judge of the prose, allowing nothing to be said which cannot be restated in the form of a rigorous equation. A better way to get rid of hunches and opinions would be difficult to imagine.

I am not here concerned with Mr Ashby's book, which I have not read: his method indicates one problem of language—for the scientist, concerned to argue out facts, quantities, it needs a 'stern judge'. For rational scientific argument and exposition a one-word-one-thing relationship is desirable. If one is proving that, say, proteins have the most complicated molecular structure known to man, then it is appropriate to 'get rid of hunches and opinions'. But Mr Chase implies that human relationships, society, international politics, would be better if we could 'get rid of hunches and opinions'.

Another definition of science might be, 'knowledge which makes common sense obsolete,'... science, through its dynamic force, is sweeping the world. As it sweeps, its terminology is gradually modified, becoming more inter-cultural...we have seen how one's mother tongue may shape one's world view...If an understanding of nature is to go forward some method must be found of correcting these distortions...

Against the excitement of Mr Chase's emotional and most unscientific acceptance of progress ('sweeping the world', 'dynamic', 'to go forward') stands his irritation that human beings are human beings, complex, different, and that their cultures tend to conserve themselves and to be indigenous.

Now, in fact, you can only endeavour to 'get rid of hunches and opinions' and 'correct distortions' in people and cultures by one means: the gas chamber. No Inquisition ever did it. But if you are willing to leave people alive, then you must accept that all human activity—even 'scientific progress'—depends upon 'hunches and opinions'. Nearly every great scientific discovery came not by accident but through imagination. The work from which 'hunches' needed to be rigorously excluded followed, until the imagined conclusion was reached and proven. The scientist has to be prepared to disprove his hunch. But remove 'hunches' and 'opinions' and there would be no science, no political life, no culture. Indeed it is impossible, as Mr Chase himself should have realised, for he himself points out that 'some fifteen billion interaction points in the brain give humans great powers of flexibility and adjustment'...'the mathematical sum of theoretically possible interactions between fifteen billion units...is rather more than all the molecules in the universe'.

'Great powers of flexibility and adjustment', says Mr Chase patronisingly, giving God a 'highly commended' certificate for Man's brain. There seems to be in this a too mechanical attitude, going with a dangerous lack of awe. The mind is just a complicated machine: so is society. If only we could get rid of life! If only we could pretend that the barrier at the end of physics weren't a metaphysical one! If only we knew all and could manipulate all! Mr Chase is one of the latest of the Fausts.

I have dealt with popular semantics at some length because they represent a sentimental tendency in our industrial society. A desire, that is, to ignore the inescapable conditions of man's life by believing in 'science'. And their intentions for language, in the end, go with fantasies about space-travel or a Wellsian future life, as a way of avoiding feeling and thought about actual living on this earth. This is not to say that semantics has not some value at times or that Mr Chase's *The Tyranny of Words* wasn't valuable for its challenging of political slogans and for its rule for careful writing: 'find the referent'. Though even there, one must say that although the referents, for, say, 'honour', 'grace', 'evil' aren't easily found, that doesn't invalidate them; in a play like Shakespeare's *Macbeth*, they are given form and body.

Which brings me to say that there is a kind of precise definition which poetry can make, of a kind which does not lend itself to paraphrase or translation into mathematics, and which depends upon the very aura of uncertainty and ambiguity that surrounds every word. Training people in responding to this kind of definition is a very real discipline, and it is the discipline of English teaching. Far more universal in its application than the discipline of semantics, it can give substance and exactness to the very 'hunches' and 'opinions' which Mr Chase would like to cut away but obviously can't, because life depends upon them. (On the other hand, if Mr Chase wanted his appendix cut out he would depend on the 'hunches' and 'opinions' of a surgeon who would *imagine* the offending organ inside Mr Chase before he cut his abdomen open, and the surgeon's imagination would help him find the referent to 'patient Chase's appendix'.) For the kind of definition of experience that poetry can give I refer the reader to my chapter on poetry below, p. 63.

The semanticist's fear of being misled is based upon a demand for an impossible degree of certainty in communication. Less reputable are the modernists. These share, with the semanticists and communications experts, a good deal of respect even in institutes of education. They are not even deceived by their own theories: they represent mere compromise with the industrial age: like the semanticists their ambition is to bring what Yeats called 'all the complexities of mire and blood' of human life into schemes and catalogues, but knowingly for the purposes of commerce. And as secondary modern teachers particularly are dealing with 'educative units' (i.e. boys and girls) who will spend all their lives in the mechanical surroundings of the factory, trolley-bus, cinema, television, internal combustion engines, atomic power stations and guns, let us, they say, relate their training to that environment. Let us use contemporary means for our work: the traditional teaching methods are out of date in a world of competition from mechanical toys. But what happens to the ends of education when they are made 'contemporary' in the same way too? 'In real life the unsuccessful man is usually the one who has not trained himself for a worthwhile job, and to remedy the position he has to take off his jacket and get down to some hard work.' That is from a textbook of English for the secondary modern school. It is bad English (cf. Sir Ernest Gowers in *Plain English*, p. 63, on 'the position miasma'). It is unsuccessful as communication: when the 'unsuccessful man' has 'remedied the position' by hard work, does he still remain the unsuccessful man? Because he has to work hard? Despite the presence of the sickly word 'worthwhile' the implications are immoral; that hard work is a deserved punishment for people who are 'unsuccessful'; success, it is implied, is the avoiding of hard work: hard work is what one puts in to 'remedy the position' of being unsuccessful only. These are the limited values of manufacture and commercial organisation: the terms by which industry keeps its 'go' going. But they are not adequate for us.

Such attitudes to what is valuable in life are picked up from sources in our industrial society—those sources which believe that the way of life based on acquisitiveness represents the best in man. This attitude is found in such advertising matter as the *British Trades Alphabet*—an atrociously written, printed and produced magazine which is distributed to the schools, free (1,200,000 copies a year):

We continue to receive letters from teachers telling us of their appreciation...they find that children who enter the competitions become keener, more self-reliant and in general, alive to the world around them...Team Spirit in Action...[1]

Nowadays, as we often say, the world has become a very small place.

[1] Editorial comment.

You can breakfast in New York and have tea in London, and you can read about something which happened on the other side of the world today in your newspaper tomorrow...the impulse behind these changes...has been the growth of industry and trade...the more you discover (about these) the richer your own life becomes.[1]

These excerpts reveal the factitious values of commerce: team-spirit, keenness, self-reliance, belief in progress (somehow related to increase in speed and telecommunication) which by material benefits makes life 'richer'. The more you know about 'things' the richer your life becomes.

When the 'modernists' come to English we find this (from a book called *English for Citizens*): 'So it seems rather absurd that English books should give so much attention to plays, novels and poetry and so little to the most popular form of art in our age—the cinema. If we can make ourselves intelligent cinema-goers we shall become better citizens.' That is, the word is out of date. It is a visual age, so we must have strip cartoons, films, film-strips, charts, *visual aids*. Language is superannuated.

Some teachers fall for the argument. Modern life changes so rapidly, the invention rate has gone up so sharply, we enter the age of automation: so communication machines must replace books. The teacher, at least, has something to play with. And Something Is Going On. Progress is Happening. If a visiting Governor looks in, he won't see the same old business of pupils with dog-eared books in their hands. He'll see a shining new machine with knobs on, a machine which cost £150, showing children a film of cocoa cultivation by the United Africa Company, emphasising the virtues of self-reliance and keenness, which industry—and cocoa cultivation—require.

Unfortunately, when the children grow up and work for the visiting Governor, he finds these qualities lacking. They can't write, or read much. Perhaps they are emotionally unstable, so they don't stay long in one job. Their attitudes to work, life, leisure, seem to him immoral. Why is this? Blame it on the teachers, who with their new-fangled ideas have let the children grow up good-for-nothings. Little does this businessman realise

[1] Foreword by J. Longland, Director of Education for Derbyshire.

how much the teacher may have struggled against the whole disruptive pressure of an environment created by commerce and the sales drive. In the administration of education and governing of schools, the pressure towards respectability exerted by parents, the examination system, the ideals exhorted in textbooks, the limited values of English commercial pressures exert powerful forces. Learning and the Muses would have fled long ago had it not been that the best members of the teaching profession have cherished and used that independence which English tradition leaves them, despite all 'the business world' can do.

We must never give way: we are teachers of responsiveness to the word, in an age when it is possible for even quite intelligent people to believe that a concern for words, for language, is 'out of date'. The new illiteracy of the cinema, television, comic strip, film-strip and popular picture paper they accept as the dawn of a new era. Many schools are even buying comic-strip books of classics, and many see films and television as the bases of new forms of teaching, whereby a deep impression can be given of some aspect of the world with the minimum use of words. In so far as this is believed, and is not a disguised acclaim for a mechanisation of teaching to solve the mere organisational problem of education—shortage of good teachers—it is believed in as an aspect of educational progress. In televised science, for example, every pupil has a front seat. Without denying the value of any medium properly used, I think we may accuse some enthusiasts for visual aids of seeing them as a means to avoid the real work. In science the real work is giving the experience of setting up an experiment, observing it, using the experiment to verify a concept or formula: giving the experience of empirical activity, in fact. If this is experienced, then the visual reproduction of other experiments will be effective. But the giving of the true experience of empiricism is to a great extent a matter of using language.

And, in a not unrelated way, the giving of the experience of a work of dramatic fiction, say, is a matter of giving it through the substance of, and in the control of, the words. A 'classic' in terms of strip-cartoon or film version is no longer the classic. And in living as in education the word can never be dispensed with: the talk of lover to lover, the advice of father to son, our dealings with the world, our expressions of anger, prayer, persuasion, and condolence, will always be in words: and the refining agent of words is poetry. Words are our chief source of insight.

When we are weary of dealing with pupils from an environment which has given up reading and in which the word is so badly damaged by popular media, there is a great appeal in the 'visual theory'—that words no longer matter to a world with television: or that the way to literature is through illustrated strip-books.

The word—the complex, sinewy, subtle and evasive word is at one with our life. 'In the beginning was the word, and the word was made flesh': let them illustrate that, if they can.

CHAPTER 4

The Very Culture of the Feelings

We are all aware of a troubling difference between how we live and how we would like to live, an ideal and an actual. As we grow older we may, if we allow ourselves, come to believe that the 'actual' is a second-best, humdrum or even wretched existence—we say we have lost our youthful dreams, our ideals. Much of our literature nowadays, particularly drama, from T. S. Eliot's *The Cocktail Party* to John Osborne's *Look Back In Anger*, seems to be saying that life is hardly worth living, and that our relational goal, of man and woman finding fulfillment in love in marriage, for instance, is impossible or at best a second best:

> Two people who know they do not understand each other
> Breeding children whom they do not understand
> And who will never understand them.

Mr Eliot's repugnance (evident in the placing and use of the word 'breeding') has led him to an un-Christian negativeness. Mr Osborne's play ends with the whimpers of self-pity, in a squalor of undefined emotion. Yet both are representative works of literature in our time, and they are our 'serious' culture's equivalent to the emotional blur of the cinema and the hopeless sensationalism of the daily press (cf. its use of the word 'tragedy'): in both there is a fashion for schizoid futility.

Our language culture, on the whole, offers little content, little to celebrate. At the popular level the ethos of the 'pop' cults expresses, as in the ostinato beat that drowns personal contact, an off-hand contempt for courtesy, the hysteria of pseudo-events, and a tendency to pointless violence—all marking false solutions to the quest for a sense of identity.

Much utterance, whether popular or minority, is now largely conceived in terms of exploiting the cosy emotion of helplessness. D. H. Lawrence defined sentimentality as 'working out on yourself feelings you haven't really got': the new forms of sentimentality are a substitute for true creativity. We call it 'anger' but in fact it is the softest throw-away sentimentality—its cosiness going with a moral abrogation, the failure of any attempt to 'construct something upon which to rejoice'. Here, for example, is Archie Rice, the figure from John Osborne's play *The Entertainer*, who represents the worn-out vitality of English music-hall, of English culture, of the representative English sensibility. But as with Mr Eliot's Harcourt-Reilly in *The Cocktail Party* the character is a thin disguise for the author's sermonising:

Archie Rice. And do you know why? Do you know why? Because we're dead beat and down and outs. We're drunks, maniacs, we're crazy, we're bonkers, the whole flaming bunch of us. Why, we have problems that nobody's ever heard of, we're characters out of something that nobody believes in. We're something that people make jokes about, because we're so remote from the rest of ordinary every-day, human experience.

But we're not really funny. We're too boring. Simply because we're not like anybody who ever lived. We don't get on with anything. We don't ever succeed in anything. We're a *nuisance*, we do nothing but make a Godalmighty fuss about anything we ever do. All the time we're trying to draw someone's attention to our nasty, sordid, un-likely little problems...

This is where the naturalistic and 'realistic' theatre ends—in the histrionic wallow of self-pity, the cosy sense of waste: compare the end of Granville Barker's play *Waste*:

No, I don't know why he did it...and I don't care. And grief is no use. I'm angry...just angry at the waste of a good man. Look at the work undone...think of it! Who is to do it? Oh...the waste...!

Here is the original 'anger': and there ends the drama which pretends to be portraying the 'real' and refuses to attempt to celebrate positives, or rather, possible creative attitudes to life by which life may be lived.

By contrast we may consider the work of Shakespeare; not only because he is so great a figure but because he is the touchstone when we discuss literature—we may dispute the value, say, of Pope or Milton, but we can all agree that Shakespeare is a great poet and thus he may be more easily used in discussion about what the writer should do—what writing *is*, in fact. And when we consider what the experience of Shakespeare's work means to us we can easily see that it is a constructive achievement, a 'making' (the Scots still call a poet a 'makar'), a celebration of life's possibilities. And when we consider this constructive aspect of Shakespeare's work we will find that many of our present fashionable habits of thought about literature and life are unusually negative.

Shakespeare's constructive achievement as an artist is a great one because of his 'terrifying honesty' (a phrase Mr Eliot used of William Blake, who also saw many terrifying things in human life that ordinary people dare not allow themselves to see). Often, when, as I have said, we are cynical about our ideals, or our poetry or drama is cynical, we say it is because 'we have seen so much', 'we know so much', and say 'after such knowledge, what forgiveness?' (this phrase is a line from Mr Eliot's poem *Gerontion*). But much would seem to depend on whether a preoccupation with human evil and wickedness is unbalanced or balanced. In Shakespeare's tragedy *King Lear* the hideous depths of human proclivities to seek perverted satisfactions from power, from torture, from deceit, the sexual brutishness under the 'robes and furr'd gowns'—all are uncovered. And in Shakespeare's tragedies we have poetry whose impulse is a deep realisation of the irreconcilable difference between what we would be, what we would seem, and what we are: they ask, given man's nature, and the conditions of his life, his weakness, his lust, his being exposed to hostile nature within himself and outside in the world, his being subject to time and death—by what can he live?

Nothing could be more terrible than Shakespeare's vision of how unwarranted the agents of human justice and punishment are: here the Earl of Gloster is blinded and turned out on the heath where the King, mad, spurned, wanders:

Lear. Thou has seen a farmer's dog bark at a beggar?
Gloster. Ay, sir.

Lear. And the creature run from the cur? There thou mightst
behold the great image of authority: a dog's obeyed in office—
>   Thou rascal beadle, hold thy bloody hand!
>   Why dost thou lash that whore? Strip thine own back;
>   Thou hotly lusts to use her in that kind
>   For which thou whipst her. The usurer hangs the cozener.
>   Through tatter'd clothes small vices do appear;
>   Robes and furr'd gowns hide all. Plate sin with gold
>   And the strong lance of justice hurtless breaks;
>   Arm it in rags, a pigmy's straw does pierce it...

In this close-textured poetry we experience the pain of physical
assault mingled with lust and a bitter sense of injustice: the whole
horror of human physical, sensual weakness hidden under robes
of office, yet of every man being the 'bare fork'd animal': this is
given us as we read the lines. Yet, though Lear is mad, there is a
moral control exerted—the language is close to that of the common people, the metaphorical and proverb-like balance of the
phrases belonging to popular saw, to the liturgy, the Authorised
Version and the popular sermon. A positive concern is holding in
order almost ungovernable feelings, provoked by the poet's
'terrifying honesty'. And this is done by the muscularity and controlled movement of the words. Few writers are able to dare to
see and feel so much. Jonathan Swift saw much, but his awareness
of the human condition provoked a fierce agitation of disgust:
'Their skins appeared so coarse and uneven, so variously coloured
when I saw them near, with a Mole here and there as broad as a
Trencher, and hairs hanging from it thicker than pack-threads; to
say nothing further concerning the rest of their persons...'
Here the writing is on the verge of unbalance, of a schizoid
rejection of our humanity. Shakespeare's creativity is able to
bring him to the simple verse of the end of *King Lear*—to a
simplicity which is not that of innocence, but of having plumbed
all human experience, of having dissolved all values, and then
found life still good, having reconstructed and being bent on
celebrating possible attitudes to life. This verse gives us the
triumph of love and 'grace'. It sounds like innocence—it is really
the deepest self-knowledge: beside it the spirit of our age's

pretence of 'knowing what things are really like' seems the self-flattering pride of Chanticleer, the cock in a dirty farmyard:

Lear.   Pray, do not mock me:
I am a very foolish fond old man,
Fourscore and upward, not an hour more nor less;
And, to deal plainly,
I fear I am not in my perfect mind.
Methinks I should know you, and know this man;
Yet I am doubtful: for I am mainly ignorant
What place this is; and all the skill I have
Remembers not these garments; nor I know not
Where I did lodge last night. Do not laugh at me;
For, as I am a man, I think this lady
To be my child Cordelia.
Cordelia.   And so I am, I am.

'I am ignorant'...'as I am a man'...'I know not'...'I am': *Lear* is a poem about the essentials of being: the poet has organised his experience to such a fine degree that he is able later to offer the significance of the lovers in *The Winter's Tale* against the 'vast' of time and the winds:

when you do dance, I wish you
A wave o' th' sea, that you might ever do
Nothing but that; move still, still so,
And own no other function

Writing poetry *is* the ordering of experience. *Lear* gives us the experience of Shakespeare bridging the gap between mediaeval and modern attitudes to life: by experiencing his work we may come to have a renewed grasp on life, to understand how to live in this post-Renaissance era, fully recognising our own feeble natures, and accepting the conditions of our lives which are dominated by Time and Death. His courage serves to succour us in our modern age: to ignore his work, or regard him as 'old fashioned', or to fail to see all poetry, not only his, as a present spiritual force, an essential means to our dealing with life in our time, is virtually to deny the advances the human spirit has made since Shakespeare's birth. As part of 'the mind of Europe' Shakespeare cannot be 'superannuated'.

In his tragedies, and particularly in his later plays, we have answers in terms of organised poetic experience to the question, How to live? While much of our fashionable writing today seeks to claim that we have given up trying to put together answers to that question because of the horrors of our time, our writers have never, of course, seen one fragment of the horror which Shakespeare, in his 'terrifying honesty', saw. The lack of constructive effort in writing in our time derives not from a Christ-like awareness of human evil, but rather from an arrogant spiritual laziness, or accidie, as they called it in mediaeval times: our representative figure might be Tittivillus, a minor devil, rather than Christ, or even Faustus.

Of course, in one significant matter our writers have a disadvantage as compared with Shakespeare in his time; he had a public which shared a rich and figurative language and a natural delight in creative symbolism. We have lost these language habits in an age of standardised literacy, and of mechanical amusements through mass-media. But this alone does not explain our universal abrogation of a concern for creativity and celebration. In our own time poetry, drama, literature, music and song, entertainment, painting, are almost universally deficient in offering possible positive answers to the question, How to live? In the primitive tribe one of the most important conservative and creative functions of the elder members is to preserve rituals, ceremonies and other lore so that the growing youth in that tribe may acquire a sense of belonging to his tribe, of its place in the world, and of its moral patterns, the meaning of life as held in the tribe, its mythology. In our society we feel we can live without this activity, if it ever enters our heads to question whether we can or not.

The fact is that we cannot live without symbolism. Yet both popular and educated culture are declining in many ways in England, despite the rapid development of mechanical means of providing the shadow of those satisfactions which cannot be given mechanically. Our live theatre is gradually being wound up and many, in any case, live beyond range of one good theatre; local music-making declines; while the environment is deficient in creative opportunities. Instead of the magnificent baroque roundabout rides we have the factory-produced juke-box.[1] We depend for our cultural satisfactions on the mere ingestion of experiences through the gramophone, television set, wireless or cinema: there is no giving to something beyond individuals, no *entente* between audience and performer or artist, or between members of the audience—our essential cultural experiences are not celebrative, they are, rather, manic. Hence the negative qualities, the impotence, of so many of our works of art—they are less an engagement with experience than a manic assertion that we are still alive. In these strictures I include both serious and popular works of art and amusement: the schizoid negativeness of the London theatre and the plays of the bed-sitter schools; much contemporary poetry, not least the Beats; widely acclaimed novels such as *Lucky Jim*—these are essentially as hollow of real creativity as *Salad Days*, or the latest film version of a classic, or the *Daily Mirror*. What is everywhere lacking is a culture for what Yeats called 'the whole man—intellect, blood and imagination all running together'. One seldom finds in our culture true compassion, commitment on the larger themes of life and death, or real tenderness. What we are forgetting and abandoning is 'the culture of the feelings'. This phrase comes from John Stuart Mill's *Autobiography*.

The instability of the typical identity in our Western society becomes manifest in startling ways from time to time. For instance, in the *Manchester Guardian* of 25 November 1957 appeared a remarkable account of a report (first published in the *New Yorker* by Mr Eugene Kinkead) on what happened among American prisoners-of-war in Korea. Leaving aside questions of 'collaboration' in a war whose purpose might for many have been difficult to understand, we read:

The death rate among prisoners—38 per cent—was higher than in any other war that America has been engaged in, the Revolution included . . . The men needn't have yielded . . . they needn't have died in such great numbers . . . Prisoners abandoned wounded comrades by the roadside.

[1] Many of the craftsmen of fair-ground construction are now, significantly, working in film and television set construction.

Men ill with dysentery were rolled out into the cold to die...some died of what was called 'give-up-itis' (in primitive societies it would be 'turning one's face to the wall') and were not shaken out of it in time by their fellows. In contrast (a group of) 229 Turkish prisoners though half of them were wounded at the start, they lost not one man...A doctor blames 'some new failure in...childhood and adolescent training...a new softness'. The American soldier...'seemed lost without a bottle of pills and a toilet that flushed'.

I don't offer toughness in war as a high value: but such a crisis does surely test inner resources and the strength of community impulses. It was these that broke. Yet we urge on our patterns of life in the same American direction. There even such a humane educationalist as J. S. Bruner still sees the culmination of evolution in technological advance—so that education must be concerned with skills—while yet perceiving that, even because of technology, suburban life has 'lost touch with tragic issues' and is deficient in inner satisfaction. In our education and culture we are not yet sufficiently positively active in providing for 'the culture of the feelings'.

In order to understand fully the role of English in education we should read Mill's *Autobiography*. Mill's father, he tells us, 'had scarcely any belief in pleasures.. He deemed very few of them worth the price which, at least in the present state of society must be paid for them...Temperance...was with him...almost the central point of educational principle;...he thought human life a poor thing at best, after the freshness of youth and of unsatisfied curiosity had gone by'. Mill's father preferred the 'real' to the 'imaginary'. The severity of his education of his child of course went with this attitude: it is recorded in the *Autobiography*. Mill had no contact with childhood lore of the nursery and back street ('I have no remembrance of the time when I began to learn Greek...I have been told that it was when I was three years old') and his early life lacked contact with works of imagination suitable for a child. In consequence, at the age of thirty he underwent a crisis in his mental history: 'I seemed to have nothing left to live for; I felt that the flaw in my life must be a flaw in life itself; that the question was, whether, if the reformers of society and government could succeed in their object and every person in the community were free and in a state of physical comfort, the pleasures of life, being no longer kept up by struggle and privation, would cease to be pleasures.' Mill, that is, had no adequate attitudes to life, answers in the blood, to the question How to live? He had immense intellectual power, but insufficient powers of being.

Mill's way out of his crisis was by way of reading Wordsworth's poetry for the first time. 'What made Wordsworth's poems a medicine for my state of mind was that they expressed, not mere outward beauty but states, of feeling, and of thought coloured with feeling, under the excitement of beauty. *They seemed to be the very culture of the feelings, which I was in quest of*' (my italics). What does Mill mean by 'the very culture of the feelings'? It is necessary for us to be careful here, because of the disabling attitude of some that culture is a matter of possessing certain rich experiences like eating so many Chinese figs, and the kind of petrified cultivation of the feelings that once led the late Sir Albert Richardson to live in eighteenth-century costume in a house full of 'art treasure', by candlelight. We cannot live by the order and pattern imposed on life by the eighteenth century alone, however beautiful we find it: we need to relate that order, and the disturbances beneath its surface, to the order we endeavour to impose on our own disturbances. To see Mozart's music or Jane Austen's novels as mere means to elegant surface self-cultivation is to fail to see their greatness, their beauty, which depend upon the presence in them of awareness of deeply disturbing inward problems. If these are not seen, then the relevance of Mozart's and Jane Austen's order to our own attempts to ask 'How to live?' is not seen either.

What Mill intends by his phrase 'the very culture of the feelings' can perhaps be best shown by turning to a poem by Wordsworth. Of course only a full possession of the poem can give 'culture of the feelings'—a gloss cannot provide a short cut—and here I can only discuss the poem in such a way as to help myself—and, if I can, the reader—to possess its experience better.

English for Maturity

Catherine Wordsworth
(died June 4, 1812)

Surpris'd by joy—impatient as the wind
I turned to share the transport—Oh! with whom
But Thee, deep buried in the silent tomb,
That spot which no vicissitude can find?
Love, faithful love, recalled thee to my mind—
But how could I forget thee? Through what power
Even for the least division of an hour,
Have I been so beguiled as to be blind
To my most grievous loss?—that thought's return
Was the worst pang that sorrow ever bore,
Save one, one only, when I stood forlorn,
Knowing my heart's best treasure was no more;
That neither present time, nor years unborn
Could to my sight that heavenly face restore.

In reading this poem we experience in fantasy what Worsdworth, at one unhappy moment, experienced. By writing the poem Wordsworth put in order, or came to terms with, his sorrow—if we can experience the ordering we will be helped to order ourselves. We find pleasure in the ordering, in the poem, although we do not enjoy grief in real life ourselves. And this pleasure 'propagates sympathy' by making us more aware of the inward life of others.

Without discussing the whole poem let me try to show how it *does what it says* in the opening lines, and thus re-enacts the experience in us. Rhythm and movement follow first the turning-to-the-child recreated in the hurried 'surpris'd' opening. 'Transport' is an important word—the poet is so 'transported' out of the real moment by his joy that he forgets the child is not standing beside him, but is dead. He turns as the wind does, 'impatient', not to be constrained by any consideration of living beings. But the impatient movement of the first two lines is arrested by a pause, a groan, and a question:—'Oh! with whom...' And the 'p's' and 'b's' of the following lines emphasise the bitterness in the pursed lips at the realisation: one has in saying the line the feel in the mouth of sorrow, followed by the even more bitter hiss of 'vicissitude'—the line seems to mean, 'never more by a chance moment shall I come upon you, like this joy which surprises: the tomb is not visited on us like one of these chance coincidences: it is final, and I cannot come to you there by any visit from which it is possible to return—we find the tomb only by leaving for ever the sequence of changes of fortune which life is'. 'Vicissitude' is the only 'difficult' word in the poem: and its strangeness goes with its advantages in its contribution to the texture and movement of the line, with its meaning in terms of enactment.

Again, at the end of the poem the rhythm of 'save one, one only' is that of resignation to the recognition that nothing relieves the finality of the first knowledge of her death: he has experienced that and 'stood forlorn'—the final tribute has been paid ('forlorn!—the very word is like a bell'—to invoke Keats' line seems appropriate here: a bell almost seems to toll with the 'one, one only...forlorn' behind the image of the father who 'stood' helpless at the pang).

So indulgence in the disbalancing turmoil of remorse and counter-assertion seems unnecessary: the rhythm seems to brace its shoulders and walk on; the death is *known*:

> Knowing my heart's best treasure was no more;

The firm rhymes go with the assured rhythm:

> That neither present time, nor years unborn
> Could to my sight that heavenly face restore.

The poem is a poem of great emotional sincerity and courage, and one which, in its simplicity, can give us the experience of these things, can give us 'the very culture of the feelings'.

In Wordsworth's poem this movement of the experience is registered in the movement of the poetry: it is 'felt in the blood and felt along the heart'. This is important for my argument, because I contend that you cannot make 'the whole man' a civilised being by ratiocinative means alone—it isn't what he *knows* that makes him able to live without giving up, but what he *is*—deep down in his being. This poem gives us little that requires our thought: it provokes no philosophical activity and is thus at the other extreme of poetry from Mr Eliot's marvellously philosophical poems *Four Quartets*. What it gives us is largely there in rhythm and movement; we experience the rhythm of a surge of feelings, and their being put in order, by symbolic creative effort.

Surprisingly we find these qualities too in the best language products of the old English popular culture: 'What the people want' in the pre-industrial society was what embodied an anonymous sincerity. Cecil Sharp, the great collector of folksongs, wrote in his *English Folk-song—Some Conclusions* that 'the unconscious output of the human mind, whatever else it may be, is always real and sincere'—and he also wrote that the songs were formed by first of all being made up by some one person, and then handed down, in which process people '*changed what they did not like*'. Thus the English folksong embodies the attitudes to life of the English rural community from the Middle Ages to the coming of our industrial life. Here is an example of such a song:

The Turtle Dove

O say do you see yonder turtle dove
Sitting under a mulberry tree?
See how that she doth mourn for her true love
As I, my love, will mourn for thee, my dear,
As I, my love, will mourn for thee.

If you must suffer grief and pain
'Tis for a little while.
Though I roam far away I will surely come again
Though I go ten thousand mile, my dear,
Though I go ten thousand mile.

Ten thousand mile is very far
For me to bide alone,
With a heavy sign and a bitter cry
No one to hear my moan, my dear,
No one to hear my moan.

The tide shall cease to beat the shore,
The stars fall from the sky,
Yet I will love thee more and more
Until the day I die, my dear,
Until the day I die.

Then let the seas run dry, my love,
The rocks melt in the sun;
Yet here I will stay nor ever from thee part,
Till all these things are done, my dear,
Till all these things are done.

The extraordinary thing is that a communally-produced song, moulded and formed by being handed down in an oral tradition from singer to singer, should preserve felicities of poetic expression which seem to guarantee sincerity: the words 'beat', 'seas run dry', for instance, and 'rocks melt', which latter makes the movement in the mouth of pledged constancy. These felicities come from two things—first from a habit of metaphorical speech in rural life which goes with habits of moral 'placing', and second from the related recognition by the folk of grief, pain, transience and death in human life—most folksongs, and children's game rhymes for that matter, are about love and death.[1] Here are some old rural saws: one can see how the poetry of folksong (and of the Bible) is as natural to these language habits as walking:

He married the midden for the muck and now he's poisoned by the stink.
He's singing Hallelujah to the dead nettles.
Thou'll never be satisfied till thou gets thy mouth full of mould.
You're the right man to send for sorrow: you're so long upon the road.
If the hen don't prate, she won't lay.

The language habits embody a felt wisdom: the folksongs embody a felt wisdom too, a shared common experience. The embodiment is in the rhythm:

> Then let the seas run dry, my love,
> The rocks melt in the sun;

—the lines have an insistent rhythm that urges the constancy against a real apprehension in concrete imagery of eternity and the brevity of life. They follow 'until the day I die, my dear' and strike a relationship to the words 'nor ever' which follow.[2]

The song provides an experience which enacts, as Wordsworth's sonnet does, the coming to terms with the increased awareness of Time that human love brings. To say this of it is not

[1] See the present author's *Children's Games* (Gordon Fraser, 1957).
[2] Readers should hear the lovely recording of the song by Isla Cameron on an H.M.V. gramophone record: the poetic rhythm and movement are indivisible from the music with which they grew. *Celui qui perd ses mots perd son air*—the folksingers were incapable of dividing words from music and we must always bear this is mind in considering folksong.

to crush it with comment—the heart of a folksong, worn down by centuries of use, is as tough as granite—but to pay it a tribute —and to pay a tribute to 'what the people want'—when they are not preyed upon by mass media. They want a delightful song, delight of the order of that lilting

> As I, my love, will mourn for thee, my dear

—and a pleasure, too, which enlarges sympathy by its *unique*, un-cliché departures from the expected: these—such phrases as 'rocks melt'—seem to guarantee the quality of an individual experience, though in fact we have in the song nothing of the kind. Once all English people would know some of the great folksongs such as *Foggy Dew*, *The Seeds of Love*, *O Waly Waly*, and these had all a quality of emotional 'sincerity'.

Here we see something of the essential difference between the popular songs of the old rural England, and the highly accomplished popular songs written for commercial distribution nowadays, and by analogy the difference between all indigenous culture and all commercial culture. The 'experience'—if one can call it that—in the latter has to be manufactured to fit a lowest common denominator of popular 'wisdom'. The tendency is not towards what seems unique although it is universal, but towards the more than universal or too common (demand must just exceed supply to make commercial culture work) and the non-unique. We live therefore by a 'wisdom' which is clichéd and inadequate.

And so—and this is the point of my chapter—the young person growing up today, searching adult popular culture to ask 'what is adult life, love, like?' learns this mostly from a commercial culture whose quality is steadily running down. His newspapers become less and less *news*papers; commercial television drives out the cinema and undermines the advertisement-supported popular press: jazz becomes reduced to a mere dead beat, a more stubborn ostinato, its harmony ever less interesting than that of its nineteenth century origins, and so on. Our young people are driven to seek vitality, in rock and cha-cha, for instance, in a hypnotic and distracted dance movement. On this food they starve. The worst failure in commercial popular culture is that it gives no help, offers no wisdom 'felt in the blood and felt along the heart', as 'culture of the feelings'. So we all suffer from inadequate holds on life, because our capacities for symbolism are undernourished.

The deficiency of felt wisdom, culture for the feelings, in popular culture is evident as teachers will know at the level of children's reading matter: the stories and poems in the Hulton *Robin* or in Enid Blyton's books, for instance, are deficient in the rhythms and imagery of experienced difficulty: in nursery rhymes there are real terrors, real pain and real difficulties, in the rhythm and texture of the verse:

> Can you reap it with a sickle of leather,
> Parsley, sage, rosemary and thyme,
> And bind it up with a peacock's feather?
> And you shall be a true lover of mine.
>
> She went a little farther and she calls to a dog,
> Dog, dog, bite pig,
> Pig will not go,
> And I should have been at home two hours ago!
> But the dog would not.

One of the chief virtues of the experience of such trying difficulties in fantasy is that they become more and more inevitable in real life as we grow older. So children in their games provide complex and taxing rules and taboos to simulate the difficulties of living with other people: they try themselves out against the conditions of hop-scotch, without realising that they are training themselves to deal with troubling feelings within their own breasts, and with the often bizarre and frightening demands which adults make on them. For our growing up and becoming mature is as much a matter of resisting other people's selfish claims as of anything else: in their games children practise flouting authority:

> Mother: Who do you care for?
> Children: *Not for you! (all run off:* Mother *chases*)

So our children will be the less developed in 'the very culture of the feelings' if they give over their nursery rhymes and game rhymes to the tedious violence of Wild West television, or pulp writing lacking in symbolic content. As we all know from experience in school, the testing time, even with a bright and sound pupil, is when the child begins to mature: as the voice deepens and the beard or the breasts grow, so does the 'weight of this unintelligible world' crowd in. At this stage the young person needs to revolt, in order to put away childish things and become an individual adult being. Then the new gloss of sophistication, often hiding a shivering immaturity underneath, now adheres to the products of what seem to the adolescent the most sophisticated places on earth—New York, London. The contrast between real sophistication and assumed is greatest in the village, where the adolescent's idea of what the urban tough-guy looks like is almost laughably pathetic, knowing as one perhaps does the child underneath the play-acting. The fault, of course, is in our whole popular culture which accepts that New York or London, megalopolis with its bright unease, is the highest and most central form of life: in fact nothing could be more remote from the centre of English and European life as lived by the ordinary decent man and woman than Shaftesbury Avenue or inhuman Manhattan: they are dead and hollow: no-one *lives* there and their 'swing' is manic.

But the adolescent wants to *look* and *be* wise: mainly because of fears that he will not be able to maintain his identity as a worker or in social life, or as a lover. He knows, for instance, that he is afraid of being alone with a girl, because of the fierce surge of feeling such an intimacy evokes, with inadequate capacity understand or cope: so he 'plays it cool', or pretends to have been the lover of many women, or talks 'big' about love. Some people go through their lives behaving in much the same way—they can be found in any pub—and their braggadocio seems to be a compensation for weakness of identity.

At this crucial moment, then, the young person is fed with this:

> Ding-dong, ding-dong, ding-dong, ding-dong, boogie
> Ding-dong, ding-dong, ding-dong, ding-dong, woogie

or this:

> 'Till the end of the world' means forever,
> And forever you'll always be mine;
> For my darling, you know I could never
> Love anyone but you till the end of time.

Till the stars in the sky cease to shine,
Till the sand of the desert grows cold;
Till the last petals fall from the roses,
And the silver in your hair turns back to gold;

Till the sun and the moon hide in darkness,
And we wait for that great light to shine;
Oh, my darling, that's how long I will love you,
Till the end of the world you'll be mine.

Compared with *The Turtle Dove*, this song is at once seen to be entirely cliché, and rhythmically uninteresting, even merely incompetent (cf. line 4). More seriously, it is blurringly vague, in its emotion and in its poetic rendering of concepts of time—line 5 suggests a very long time; line 6 is about something that happens every night; line 7 happens every year; line 8 never happens except in an American mortician's works, or, perhaps, in Heaven—and thenceforward the attempt at an apocalyptic vision of the end of the world (with quotation from the Bible, line 9) collapses under the feebleness of the verse itself. Instead of the sincerity we feel in *The Turtle Dove* we have a collapse into the vaguest emotionalism. 'Rocks melt' is a precise visual, tactile and evocative image, defining an emotional experience: 'that great light' is the vague undefined tear-jerk of popular graveyard and funeral verses. The association of love with death, time and change here, because the terrors mentioned are not realised, seems morbid and unhealthy: 'run dry' is disturbingly beautiful. This mustiness in popular songs is particularly evident in those which can be sung either to God, or mother, or the beloved without altering a word. In the end, the only 'wisdom' a growing child gains from the popular song, or the popular press, is the knowing leer: the knowledge of the *voyeur*—for that is essentially what the film, the popular press, the popular song, the television, the cheesecake magazine tend to make us all into. They prompt us to hunger for a meretricious image which hides reality from us, often by arousing in us the anxious curiosities of infancy long since dormant.

The impact on actual living of our cultural deficiencies is not so much a matter of antisocial or wrong acts—such as are indicated by the rise of the incidence of violence and sexual disease among young people (though these may be taken as symbolic indications). It is rather a general deficiency in the sense of identity of us all. As D. H. Lawrence said, 'This ache for being is the ultimate hunger.' As with Mill, the typical modern predicament is to find inner resources inadequate to a real crisis in life—and this is surely linked with the paucity of sources of creative nourishment for the inward life. We all have a fund of unsolved problems of emotion and identity—but a world that attaches itself to outward solutions and acquisitiveness offers us too few opportunities to tackle them by creative effort. Meanwhile commercial 'promotion' devotes immense sums of money and effort to creating a spurious optimism and devotion to impossible ideals in advertisement copy and by the mass media which depend on advertisements. This image-spinning depreciates our more real values and ideals by indirectly or directly reducing the status of genuine creativity and first-hand living, or by implying that effort is futile and difficulties unnecessary: yet our satisfactions lie in overcoming these. That is, our culture too much disallows reparative effort. Since the middle of the nineteenth century the capacities of the ordinary people in England to celebrate by popular art and festival possible positive attitudes to life have been reduced almost to nil. The result is that life has become meaningless and ugly for many, and sadly deficient in those elements that make us feel alive and strong in the sense of discovering who we are by creative engagement with life. But here, too, even culture has abrogated its celebrative, constructive function: *avant-garde* art shudders if anyone suggests it should have something to say and to offer. It remains, then, the task of the school, and the secondary school at that, to begin to help re-establish a popular culture, to develop the popular activity of asking 'How to Live?', the shared organised experience of popular arts, and the 'very culture of the feelings'. If the reader is not yet convinced of our dilemma and the need for such work let me end by quoting from a collection of letters written by friends of a friend. Here is a generation, intelligent, largely grammar school educated, finding its way through adolescence in the war (when community life was perhaps more vigorous in England than it is now, however disrupted).

Many of these young people were training to be teachers. Here are fragments of an ugliness of spirit, a hopelessness, a deadly knowingness, for which our commercial popular culture, and quality culture too, can be seen to be directly responsible. It is, too, a terrible and saddening indictment of an education which has ignored 'the very culture of the feelings' as something without which we die, if not an actual death, a death of the spirit. This is our life: the terms by which we live it are those of popular language art:

(A). I went to the flicks the day after we came up. We saw *Twin Beds* and some equally antediluvian cowboy flick. Honestly this place is absolutely laughable in its selection of entertainment. It's pouring today so cannot follow up any dates for walks from the hop last night (these usually lead you to Harlech for some reason). The only thing to do on a wet Sunday in Aber is to go to the Milk Bar (in a hen party) and see what you can do in the way of picking up R.A.F. Not that we want them, in the least, but it gives you a certain satisfaction in seeing that your technique is still in working order. We invariably walk out on them when we get to the penultimate stage...

(B). I couldn't tell you on Sunday night but it is definitely mutual between Marjory and me. She's a great kid and I'm growing awfully fond of her. By now all the walks that were 'ours' have been revisited, but not yet 'our field'. We went up round by the 'Maen' in the dark and came back over the mountain.

You may remember when you first told me about—that you said it couldn't last very long—well, I don't say the same. We are both crazy and so far have had some lovely times together. We saw *I Married An Angel* in Newport and thought it was lousy. Wed. we visited the 'Castle' at Caerphilly and saw *Uncensored*—have you seen it yet? Unfortunately we had to leave it before the end to catch a bus as it was a lousy night...I'm not telling you I'm in love because I just won't say so until I'm perfectly sure. Actually I've a feeling that I don't really know what it is yet; but I must find out in time...That's one thing I must be definite about, perhaps you think I'm silly—but after all, it's my life.

The poignant impression one gets from such private letters is that the natural sincerity is there, and derives from our native traditional culture—but imposed on it is the disabling, limiting, sophistication of the commercial art-product: 'a great kid', 'crazy', contrast strikingly with the tender decency of the end in (B) above.

(C). Honestly speaking, I don't think you're his type, neither is he your type. Forget it girlie, take it in good heart and take a more proportionate outlook on life.

You ask me what I think of —; I'll tell you; sexually, I like her, I have always liked that type, plump and blond: mentally, I think she is very refreshing in small doses; she is different in her dumbness, and her idiotic flow of (almost) senseless talk is a welcome change. What she would be like to live with I cannot imagine...If only you were here with me to hear *Begin the Beguine* and *St. Louis Blues* on the electric guitar...it's a Henry Hall programme: Oh! Boy! Those blues...I am sensitive and hard in turns and am prone to fits and moods, during which I can be very nasty and damned cruel...concerning you: you're pretty; and attractive *only* because I know you so well and can be frank with you; I would very much desire an 'affaire' with you (that word is to be taken in it's fullest sense) and may sometime approach you about it (it sounds rather funny put that way)...

In the above extracts knowingness conceals under an ugly and cold explicitness the failure of sexual *mœurs*: the tenderness of folk-song and of seventeenth-century love-songs, in their very *double-entendre*, embody a code of love-making which is subtle and delicate, because inexplicit. We live, uncultured in our feelings, at a level of discourtesy which brings consequent shocks.

(D). ...I would be highly delighted to take away your virginity at one fell swoop; there is something strange about your sexual attraction for, quite often, when I've suddenly met you at —'s, or elsewhere, my mind has managed in imagination to strip you, piece by piece, of all your clothing; I have been able to imagine, surprisingly clearly, myself gently and slowly pulling your frock off and all your other garments until you stood naked before me; I have sometimes, again in great detail, been able to imagine you on a bed and myself having intercourse with you. With no other girl have I experienced that dazzling clearness. I hope I haven't embarrassed you, though I don't think I have. Anyway, enough, things are getting out of hand...Your flames never seem to strike a chord in my being...

The adolescent has such visions and the troubling and fierce passions which accompany them: yet without the encouragement of the popular press would he consider it appropriate to write them out in a letter to a girl who was little more than a chance acquaintance? She records:

(E). Had an amazing letter from — who was in a foul mood. For about half an hour I was filled with a passionate longing for him—he arouses my worst desires. Was actually v. worried, — (the writer of A.) antagonised me immediately and gave vivid accounts of her apparently unvirginal life in —.

(F). Well, sweetheart, in six days we'll be together again, and so heaven will have come to stay. Darling, your letter seems full of song titles, I can find about five...

Among the bundle of papers from which these extracts are taken are some examination papers: 'Show how Milton is indebted to the classics in *Paradise Lost*'; 'Discuss Goldsmith's power of characterisation and of handling a story in *The Vicar of Wakefield*'; 'Write a short essay on the influence of Scandinavian languages on the vocabulary of English'. Some of the young people passed their exams, some didn't: the literature they studied hardly seemed to offer from its sarcophagus a warm helping hand in their lives. Two of the above writers were shot down in aeroplanes; 'It is my life...' The father of another killed himself in the Mediterranean. Another has since been married in a foreign country and divorced.

But why particularise? This is our life—the turmoil, the horror and the beautiful are inevitable—they are, if you like, the *real*. But the real can be better borne, and lived through, by an imaginative awareness by which we may discover some significance in our experience and escape from isolation by discovering how much we share with others. By the symbolism at our disposal we can gain insight and come to terms with inner needs. In these excerpts we have a terrifying picture of a generation left with only the 'real'—and an empty idiom by which to explore their experience. Such a culture and the associated capacity for feelings it gives— or restricts—is utterly inadequate to the chaotic avalanche of turbulent experiences falling on young people in our world—indeed on all of us at times—from within and without. These are letters written by young people imprisoned by the modes of an uncreative education, and of an immature culture. Have things improved since? Surely the destructive immaturities of the ethos of

Lucky Jim have made things worse? Behind the poverty of idiom
are commercial pressures. What, by contrast, could we take as a
touchstone in the use of words in the personal life? We may end
with an example of a piece of writing which shows language at
one with the achieved harmony and balance of a man—a great
man—who, cultured in his feelings, faces death. Readers may
wish to turn to the whole of Sir Walter Raleigh's last letter to his
wife. Here I quote only part, to show what maturity, civilisation,
in the whole man, may be: 'dignity and grace', yes, but, more
fundamentally, the courage, the adequate attitude to life, which is
adequate even if (to refer to Albert Schweitzer's requirement for
an adequate philosophy) the world ends tomorrow:

As for me, I am no more yours, nor you mine, Death hath rent us
asunder; and God hath divided me from the world, and you from me.

Remember your poor Child, for his Father's sake, who chose you,
and loved you, in his happiest times.

Get those Letters (if it be possible) which I writ to the Lords,
wherein I sued for my life. God is my witness, it was for you and
yours I desired life. But it is true that I disdain myself for begging it,
for know it (dear wife) that your son is the son of a true man, and one,
who in his own respect, despiseth Death, and all his misshapen and
ugly shapes.

I cannot write much: God he knows, how hardly I steal this time,
while others sleep: and it is also high time, that I should separate my
thoughts from the world...

This is at the other extreme from the relaxed hold on life of the
American prisoners in Korea whose predicament must have been
that they found it difficult to be sure who they were and why they
were where they were. With the sensibility of a deeply civilised and
secure man intelligence and spirit are triumphant even to the block.
Here a magnificent sincerity is couched in the same language as
that which now, alas, abased and abused, leers and gestures at our
helplessness from the gutter press and the flip novel, and lies
jaded on our own tongues. Before we can begin to help restore
gravity, richness and vitality to our language, and creativity to our
life, we need as teachers to understand first what it is we are
trying to do: this long and complex chapter has been an attempt
to give some thought to that.

PART II

THE PRACTICE
OF TEACHING ENGLISH

CHAPTER 5

Poetry in the Classroom

If we know what we are doing when we teach poetry then we shall be secure: the rest of our work in English will follow by implication. Poetry is language used for its deepest and most fully exact purposes. That more people are writing poetry than reading it, that few pupils go on reading poetry when they leave school, that poetry matters little to the modern world—these arguments of today we must take into account, but reject if they are used to discourage us. If, that is, we care at all for our language or our civilisation—for 'England' as part of 'the mind of Europe', And if, and this is essential, we like poetry.

Teaching poetry is at the centre of English, and yet it is something you cannot do unless you enjoy poetry. A teacher can only teach the poems he or she likes: there is no joy or purpose in teaching a poem you loathe out of a sense of duty because you are told it is a 'classic'. Whatever those excellent people who believe in old-fashioned discipline say, you cannot teach a poem under such circumstances. You will be doing something, certainly, maybe something of value, such as giving the children the experience of how dull and exasperating adults can be at times. But you will not be giving them the disciplines of enjoying poetry. The vigorous joy of the writer's delight in his power is expressed perfectly in Psalm 45:

My heart is inditing a good matter: I speak of the things which I have made touching the King: my tongue is the pen of a ready writer.

It is that great delight we must seek to give our pupils.

To make sure we understand what we are doing, so that we are confident in the face of the gloomy situation in which we work, we must first be quite clear in our minds what value poetry has for us.

Let me take one or two simple pieces of poetry, and try to

show what the experience of poetry can give us, and how it gives it us. Poetry differs from other kinds of statement in language, and because it is a way of employing language to which we are not nowadays easily and commonly accustomed in our daily life, we have to train ourselves self-consciously to respond, to tune ourselves in to poetry, as it were.

Thaw

Over the land freckled with snow half-thawed
The speculating rooks at their nests cawed
And saw from elm-tops, delicate as flower of grass,
What we below could not see, Winter pass.

EDWARD THOMAS

This is an eminently suitable poem for use with our pupils. It is short and simple and makes an immediate impact in terms of things 'seen'. The puzzling points in it—the word 'speculating' for instance—can be profitably discussed. That is, trying to see the flavour and meaning of the word 'speculating' here helps us to deepen our relish for the English word.

We may begin, in asking what kind of statement this poem of Edward Thomas' is, by saying that it is a description of a scene. But having said so much we begin to feel how inadequate it is merely to call it a description. Of course we 'see' the 'elm-tops, delicate as flower of grass' in our mind's eye: but the words do more than merely describe or state—they give us a particular experience by the poem *doing what it says*. It is not enough to say, 'Edward Thomas saw and heard some rooks on the top of elm trees who seemed to be speculating about the end of winter which they could see, because they were high up, although the poet couldn't.' In reading the poem we hear the rooks, and share the poet's experience in, virtually, becoming a rook, and looking down on the earth as the season changes. The poem does this by various 'technical tricks', though in calling them that we must not suppose they can be done at will, as mere tricks. It takes a great deal of training for a poet to make use of his gifts in the handling of words and rhythm for adequate ends, and still the poem comes 'unwatched from the pen' (to use D. H. Lawrence's phrase).

Poetry cannot be manufactured and the technical devices are, as are technical devices in the composition of music, employed at the less conscious levels of the mind to put experience in order, and often come to the surface already formed.

Here there is, for instance, an internal partial rhyme or consonance—a rhyme or echo of certain vowels with certain consonants in the course of lines rather than at their ends, in 'freckled' and 'speculating'. This recurring 'eckle' sound actually makes the liquid soft guttural sound as of rooks cawing in high trees. The internal rhyme also links the 'speculation' with the 'freckled' appearance of the earth as the snow thaws, and suggests thereby a kind of awareness of the passage of the seasons from things seen by the birds: this is emphasised by the rhyme 'cawed'—'thawed'. When the word 'saw' echoes this rhyme in the third line we have become, with the poet, a rook. In this poem, slight as it is, Edward Thomas manifests the poet's extraordinary capacity to so identify with his symbols that he enters into the 'felt life' of them. We may perhaps associate this with Keats' remark that some things require a 'greeting of the spirit to make them wholly exist' for us; and also with his concept of 'negative capability', of being open to doubts and mysteries.

Because we are now, in the third line, a rook with the poet, we see the earth from above, from a great height. It is for this reason that we see the elm-*tops* delicate as flower of grass. Of course, the poet is really on the ground, and elm-tops do look delicate as flower of grass in winter from the ground. But the effect of the enactment in the words of this poem is to take us up to the *tops* to see them as we do from a hill or an aeroplane like flowering grasses, which we usually look down on.

'What we below could not see' takes us down, as it were, to the human being looking up, while the rooks are looking down: and in moving thus from the tops to below creates a slight feeling of *movement* in the poem. Caught by the comma after 'see', this movement pauses, and when we read or hear or say the words 'Winter pass', we experience the movement of the earth itself, of the season itself, which, from the rooks' height, can be seen to pass. In entering into the rooks' awareness the poet has come to gain a new perspective of the great cycles of the seasons, of nature, and conveys this fresh view to us in this short poem.

This is done by the use of all the elements of language—*imagery* ('freckled'), *association* ('speculating' which brings in many flavours of chance, preparedness, argument, hope, which, attributed by the pathetic fallacy to rooks, really give the human poet's feelings about the passage of winter), *rhyme* (thawed, cawed, saw; freckled, speculating), *texture* (the alliterative 'l's enhance the noise of the cawing rooks, the liquid tree-top noise) and *movement* (gently established by that 'saw from elm-tops'... 'What we below' and culminating in the pause on the comma and the rhythmic step forward, 'Winter pass'). All these elements of language enact in us the inward experience of the moment, of the delight of it, and of the wish that Winter should pass. For the last two words not only give the season's movement but also the human urge (Winter, pass!) that it should pass.

I read somewhere an apocryphal story about the composer Schumann who was asked the 'meaning' of one of his pieces of music. In answer he played it again. And when the questioner repeated his question he played it again. The piece of music *is* the meaning: the poem, as Gertrude Stein might say, is the poem is the poem is the poem.

However much we 'explain' Edward Thomas' lines, though we may help ourselves read it better, our explanation does not take their place, because the poem does what it says, enacts its meaning. From this we may make our first deduction for the classroom: *merely talking about a poem, particularly putting it into other words, is not teaching poetry.* To put an 'explanation' to stand in the poem's way is to weaken reading. Teaching poetry is reading poems, and helping others read them. Of course the kind of account I give here should not be inflicted on children. They may need to discuss the word 'speculating', but the brightest children will respond to imagery, rhythm, sound, and movement in poetry better than we can. Our task is to read the poem aloud well, and bring it to their attention in the simplest way. Much is best left inexplicit (like, say, the perspective I have dealt with, that moving up to the rooks and then down to the ground): and our second implication about classroom practice is: *try to know when to stop talking about a poem*.

What value has the the possession of the experience in Edward Thomas' poem? A deepened awareness of natural beauty, of the passage of the seasons, and the extension of sympathy, by awareness of how others besides ourselves long for such a change as that from winter to spring. Such deepening of our awareness can come from nature poetry: other poetry may convey an awareness of wisdom, embodied in similar ways in the enacting language, more obviously relevant to social living. When Crabbe, for instance, describes a scene, he is describing aspects of human nature:

> Rank weeds, that every art and care defy,
> Reign o'er the land, and rob the blighted rye:
> There thistles stretch their prickly arms afar,
> And to the ragged infant threaten war;
> There poppies nodding, mock the hope of toil;
> There the blue bugloss paints the sterile soil;
> Hardy and high, above the slender sheaf,
> The slimy mallow waves her silky leaf:
> O'er the young shoot the charlock throws a shade,
> And clasping tares cling round the sickly blade;
> With mingled tints the rocky coasts abound,
> And a sad splendour vainly shines around.

If we possess this experience by careful reading, we do not merely see the scene: we see it in the light of Crabbe's 'greeting of the spirit'. He sees these weeds growing in the poor people's land as symbolising the 'mingled' nature of life. The life of the weeds— and of the poor, by implication—is beautiful in a way: or at least it is 'painted' by 'nodding' poppies, 'blue bugloss', the 'silky' leaves of the 'hardy, high' mallow, and the 'mingled tints' of the coast. But while these weeds are vigorous ('clasping', 'clinging'), they also 'defy care', 'threaten', 'mock', are 'slimy', and 'throw a shade'. The crops are 'blighted', the soil is 'sterile', and the 'blade' of corn is 'sickly'. The activity of words such as 'blighted', 'ragged' and 'sickly' mingles with that of 'art and care', 'rob', 'stretch', 'threaten', 'nodding', 'mock', 'paints', 'waves', 'cling round' to evoke the whole desperate and ceaseless conflict between man and nature. And the whole affects us with a profound compassion for the poor: we enter into Crabbe's insight into human nature. So while Crabbe's description of the flora is botanically exact, the poem itself creates in us both the scene and the use made of it to explore human nature symbolically by this sensitive and humane clergyman. When he is excited, Crabbe's poetry, though written within the regular patterns of eighteenth-century verse, enacts its meaning in much the same way as Edward Thomas'. Here below, for instance, we not only see and smell the activity of boat-building, but also have in the repeated exclamation 'See!' the appeal to the eye of the symmetry of the boat's skeleton; and the movement of the cloudy wreaths of tar-smoke given in the two words that partially rhyme, 'far' and 'Bear', set across the line-break. This is another example of *movement* in poetry enacting the meaning:

> Near these a crew amphibious, in the docks,
> Rear, for the sea, those castles on the stocks:
> See! the long keel which soon the waves must hide;
> See! the strong ribs which form the roomy side;
> Bolts yielding slowly to the sturdiest stroke,
> And planks which curve and crackle in the smoke.
> Around the whole rise cloudy wreaths, and far
> Bear the warm pungence of o'er-boiling tar.

Such enactment in poetry, that gives great definition not only to a scene or experience, but to our attitude towards it, is perhaps found at its most urbane in Pope. The moral condemnation of, say, the wasted life of a rake may be given, as in Hogarth's engravings, in the one scene: in the lines below the very coarseness of the vowel and consonant sounds enacts the terrible end of Villiers, who disposed of £50,000 a year in vice, and died in misery:

> In the worst inn's worst room, with mat half hung,
> The floors of plaster and the walls of dung,
> On once a flock-bed, but repaired with straw,
> With tape-ty'd curtains, never meant to draw,
> The George and Garter dangling from that bed
> Where tawdry yellow strove with dirty red,
> Great Villiers lies...

In reading that we enter into the condemnation of the waste of riches, in a 'felt' way, and thus possess, with definition, the moral sensitivity and robustness of a great artist's wisdom.

Poetry has this great value as a civilising art-form because it is written in the language we use for everyday purposes. The reading of poetry can help restore life to our language habits, because it is language used at its richest and most accurate, in defining and enlarging experience. Poetry is not 'writing about', but exploring experience metaphorically, bringing aspects of experience with which we have not yet come to terms into our personal integration. In this sense poetry goes in advance of ordinary human consciousness.

For poetry is a development of metaphor. Metaphor is not, as we were taught at school, a figure of speech. In language it is the means by which we extend our awareness of experience into new realms. Poetry is part of this process of giving apparent order to the flux of experience by 'as if' symbolism, in the creation of structure and inner content.[1]

The movement is from the known to the unknown, and from the concrete to the abstract. The word *metaphor* comes from words meaning transfer: to carry across, as it were, the meaning of something known into experience which until that moment is unknown. Metaphor is the way in which our language is formed and developed. It makes language more accurate in describing and apprehending experience but it is not a process making for scientific exactness: the very accuracy itself depends on complexity and 'penumbras of uncertainty'. For one thing metaphor is inseparable from such components of meaning as *rhythm*, *texture* and *onomatopoeia*.

Words are perhaps originally formed by the mimicking of sounds, as by children (onomatopoeia, as in 'snap', 'clack', 'boom', 'tinkle'); by the imitation in the movements of the vocal

---

[1] I do not say communication: communication is no doubt implied in poetry but the poet is not at the moment of creation concerned with communication; rather, in communing with himself and his language, he is trying to walk alone into virgin country and to bring that under the human plough, as it were, in the act of organising it into words. Of course, in his search to put himself in order he is inevitably helping social order because others can share his achievement.

chords, tongue, teeth and lips of a movement or quality (as in 'snatch', 'clutch' 'open', 'craggy') or by the creation of a verbal pattern, involving both, to give order to experience. A pattern satisfies us because it is a piece of order imposed on the chaotic flux of sense-experience: at the simpler level, take the baby's 'dad-dad', or many simple primitive words: the rhythm and repetition reassure the user that 'this experience comes again and I recognise it'.

Languages belonging to young civilisations and to the people doing the work in them seem to embody the rhythms and textures of everyday living: if one looks at dialect words one can see this is certainly very true of Anglo-Saxon, and it gives our language a very expressive quality. The 'field-work' words contrast with the more elegant words of Norman and Roman origin, which often seem to belong to easier living: Chaucer, for instance, makes superb use of the contrast between Anglo-Saxon and Romance words in his *Nun's Priest's Tale*. An old widow lives in a *narwe cotage* with 'three *large sowes*', whereas her cock has 'in his *governaunce* sevene hennes for to doon all his *pleasaunce*':

> A povre wydwe, somdeel stape in age
> Was whilom dwellyng in a narwe cotage,
> Biside a grove, stondynge in a dale...
> Thre large sowes hadde she, and namo,
> Three keen, and eek a sheep that highte Malle...
>
> This gentil cok hadde in his governaunce
> Sevene hennes for to doon all his pleasaunce,
> Which were his sustres and his paramours...

In old East Anglian words for the soil and crops we have the texture of a hard working life: of the soil: 'claggy', clogged with moisture, 'gulsh', mud, 'quaggy', soft and quaking, 'socky', moist to a degree that it sucks the feet. Of crops: 'full of foison', succulent, full of natural moisture; 'fozy', bloated or unsound. But then—and here we have the metaphorical process—this kind of word-texture comes to be used of qualities not only of the soil, but of people. Metaphor is essentially a moral process in language —it endeavours to extend our experience over the abstract, the spiritual, the intractable, starting from the known. In East Anglia they used to speak of a person as 'pulky' or 'a lummox' (of physical qualities); 'yipper' or 'crawly-mawly' (of physical conditions) and of 'a muck-spout' or 'swacking', which are expressive of qualities of character. In rural sayings the process has come to embody a moral wisdom and such saws are essentially the poetic use of language:

He's getting a tongue sharp enough to shave a hedgehog...
It's bare work and poor pay, like licking honey off a thorn...

It is these qualities and habits in the common English language that made the Authorised Version such a great poetical book.

We may study the metaphorical development of words in Skeat's *Etymological Dictionary*; and see the relevance of the process to poetry; *wrong*, for instance, comes from the Dutch *wrang*—acid, sour, 'because acid wrings the mouth', and *wrong* implies a disapproving turning down of the mouth, and an unpleasant taste (cf. 'a bad egg', or even, 'he stinks'). 'Scraggy' comes from Danish *skrog*, a carcass (cf. 'you look like death'). 'Flimsy' comes from Danish *flims*, a skin on milk (cf. 'He couldn't pull the skin off a rice pudding'). 'Imply' means to fold or weave in. By studying Onions' *Shakespeare Glossary*, too, one can discover words which have been extended metaphorically from concrete to moral and abstract by one poet: they have sometimes remained to enrich the language (consider Shakespeare's coinages: 'It *beggar'd* all description', 'ensconce', 'margent', 'mind's eye'). As Shakespeare's poetry became richer it also drew more from the plain vigour of the common people's tongue. In the making of saws, sayings, songs and poetry which express wisdom about life, language is refined and enriched.

I hope no-one will inflict such a difficult account of metaphor on children: a lesson on language (from Owen Barfield, *History in English Words*, or Logan Pearsall Smith's *Words and Idioms* or Wright's *Rustic Speech and Folklore*) is a different matter and a series by a teacher who finds the subject exciting could be most valuable. But it seems to me that with our pupils, and perhaps even with most grammar school pupils, too, discussions of 'figures of speech' only confuse. Most people, because of their teaching, confuse a *simile*, which is a figure, with *metaphor*, which is a fundamental process of language. And in any case to discuss them as 'figures' suggests they can be pulled out of the language like cherries from a cake, which is misleading. Or even as if they can be put into one's writing like ingredients in cooking, which is worse. The way to improve our understanding of metaphor, of figures of speech, and to improve the metaphorical and figurative quality of our speech and writing is to read, talk, listen to and write a good deal of metaphorical English; and to read poetry, which is the great metaphorical form of language. I have heard teachers protesting at children's figurative and homely ways of putting things, at idiomatic phrases, and at words such as 'lummox' or even 'scraggy'. That is, of course, deadly: and if some supposed business man doesn't like idiomatic speech and dialect in school leavers, well he's a 'nasty brabagious creature' anyhow, as our country ancestors would have said, and beneath contempt: or rather he will pay for it in the end in terms of inarticulate employees. (This is not to excuse slovenliness about making oneself understood: but to defend the vitality of local idiomatic expression. The new linguistics, at best, urges us to study these.)

The other constituents of poetry over which perhaps we may try to correct common misunderstandings are *rhythm* and *movement*. These are important because by responding to them we can often judge the sincerity of a poem, and distinguish, in choosing poetry for children, the live from the dead. There is no better example of the difference between the rhythm of a poem as given in manuals of prosody (anapaestic, dactylic, etc.), and the live rhythm of the true voice which over-rides the rhythmic scheme, than the poem mentioned in chapter 4: Wordsworth's *Surpris'd by Joy*. This is a poem whose rhythm *is* the meaning—it gives the rhythm of an experience. This kind of rhythm, it will seen, is as different from the rhythmic scheme which prosody finds in a poem, the 'tum-ti-tum' scheme, as the phrased rhythm of a piece of music is from its time, the number of beats in a bar. The latter belongs to the metronome: the rhythm which springs alive in the music well played belongs to life, to the heart-beat and stirrings in the bowels and limbs, and patterns in the psyche.

This point may be taken in better if one looks through the opening lines of a number of sonnets by Hopkins, Donne or Shakespeare; the scheme is five iambic feet:

Ti-TUM, ti-TUM, ti-TUM, ti-TUM, ti-TUM.

But the rhythm which strives its way out of the scheme by the rhythms of the speaking voice in defiance, or sorrow, or humility, has the variety of life—the heart misses a beat, or moves more slowly, or quickens:

Devouring Time, blunt thou the lion's paw...
Wilt thou love God, as he thee? Then digest...
No worse, there is none. Pitched past pitch of grief...
No, Time, thou shalt not boast that I do change...

A study of a few such lines makes it obvious that there is little point at all in attempting to make diagrams of rhythmical patterns: true rhythm is too subtle and needs the sensitive interpreter's voice. Instead we can discuss with children 'how it goes': indeed it is most important to do so, for in doing so we are coming closer to the meaning. And we shall need to discuss the number of beats in a line and the number of syllables in a foot, and the place of the stress in the foot, when we come to write verse ourselves. But another deduction here for the classroom is *to use little prosody*— children know the different rhythms from their game rhymes and songs, and they probably have a better sense of rhythm than we have. Our TUM-TI-TUM business, if we go in for it, will only crudify.

Besides *rhythm*, poetry does what it says by *texture* and *movement*. Texture is the feeling in the mouth, as it were, and movement the feeling in the body's muscles stimulated by certain consonants and vowels and combinations of words. Here is an example of movement:

I dipped my oars into the silent lake
And, as I rose upon the stroke, my boat
Went heaving through the water like a swan...
                    WORDSWORTH, *The Prelude*

Here between the sound of 'stroke' and 'boat' one has the sound of the rowlock rattling as it is released from the thrust of the oar.

But besides the sound the words also give the physical movement of rowing. We have the enactment in the rhythm of the beginning of the stroke (oars entering the water and the arms pulling on 'And,') the boy lifting from his seat ('as I rose upon my stroke,') as he pulls, pause for breath after effort at the comma, then the rowlocks clonking ('-oke', 'boat') as the oars leave the water, and the pause over the line break ('boat/Went') as the oars are brought back again while the boat is heaving onward as if by itself ('like a swan'), surging with the imparted way. Such 'movement' as this can be discussed with a class—'Can't you hear the rowlocks? And feel the boat go forward?' But there is no need to call it 'movement' in poetry to them. What is worth saying to children is that it shows how Wordsworth in writing these lines was able to hear and feel in his imagination what it was like to row a boat on a lake many years before. And, of course, we should then read the rest of the passage, to show the poet's power of *realisation*, making the imagined real.

But the word 'realisation' is too difficult for us to use in the classroom, and so we are brought to consider how we should present poetry to secondary school children. We may know what a great store of wisdom there is in English poetry; we may draw on it ourselves: but to lead our children to draw on it requires subtle tactics.

Now in the practice of teaching poetry we are, or should be, greatly helped by the fact that children possess and maintain a body of poetic wisdom themselves—in their nursery rhymes and game-rhymes. These are anonymous and not individual in their feeling; they are products of an oral tradition, being meant to be spoken aloud—sung. They are rhymically strong, simple and sincere. These characteristic nursery and game-rhymes provide what James Reeves has called a 'third ground' on which children can, as it were, exercise their spirits in fantasy, in order to return better equipped to the real world.

We can learn two things from them. First, that their qualities, as noted above, are those which endear poetry to children. And second, that to the child the nursery and game-rhymes, the songs he learns have a natural accepted *function*. A child learning Cowper may say, 'Why do I have to learn this?': it would never enter his head to ask why he learns

> One-ery, two-ery, tickery, seven,
> Hallibo, crackibo, ten and eleven,
> Spin, span, muskidan,
> Twiddle-um, twaddle-um, twenty-one!

He learns such a rhyme because he wants to belong to a group and its culture: and because unconsciously he knows it is helping him live, by developing his sense of rhythm and number (despite its arithmetical inadequacy!). The clue to sound poetry reading would seem to lie in producing a situation which continues this natural and splendid state of affairs.

Tradition hands down to children the most beautiful body of poetry, profound and inimitable, in our nursery rhymes. These cater for all a child's needs: his awareness of his fingers, toes, nose, eyes and face:

> Toe, trip and go,
> Heel, tread a bank,
> Shin, shinny shank,
> Knee, knick a knack,
> Thigh, thick a thack,
> Tummy, trouble us
> Trouble us...

his growing sense of number and periodicity, so essential to the living thing whose heart beats and who sleeps every night:

> Go to bed first
> A golden purse;
> Go to bed second
> A golden pheasant;
> Go to bed third
> A golden bird;

his growing awareness of the untrustworthy nature of the world, its transience and people's madness:

> There was a man, he went mad
> He jumped into a paper bag;

his secret troubling fears of sexual love, pain, and death[1].

---

[1] See, on this subject, the present writer's *Children's Games* (Gordon Fraser).

> He loves me,
>   He don't;
> He'll have me,
>   He won't;
> He would
>   If he could—
> But he can't
>   So he don't...

> Who'll carry the coffin?
> I, said the kite,
> If it's not through the night,
> I'll carry the coffin.

And in the nursery rhymes (no school library should be without the wonderful *Oxford Nursery Rhyme Book* edited by Iona and Peter Opie) is embodied a traditional wisdom, very English poetic habits, and habits of making moral judgements, though these are often indistinguishable from the fantastic view of life in the rhymes which helps make reality bearable for the child:

> There was an old woman and what do you think?
> She lived upon nothing but vittals and drink!
> Vittals and drink were the whole of her diet,
> And yet this old woman would never be quiet!

I will not labour the point, but it becomes obvious if one looks through school books, that poetry in school for many children has no such function as their game rhymes, nor can it have, because it is too often bad poetry. A child may be forced to sing some atrociously bad hymn every morning, and at his speech day someone may recite Newbolt, or a play written by some dreary hack will be performed. Poetry must, if we are to give it to children, have some place in the life of the school—the wisdom of poetry should be celebrated in the school's celebrations. And, with three-quarters of the population to train in poetry, it may be as well to remember that from, say, the Middle Ages until, say, 1870 our children's ancestors followed oral, not written, patterns of culture: and that their own is an oral verse culture.

That is, let us first of all make our own acquaintance with English folk-song and carol. And then let us restore poetry to its companionship with music, and collaborate with the music teacher to teach the children folk-songs, good hymns, carols and good composed songs *as poetry*. We may take some from America—nineteenth-century railroad ballads such as *John Henry*, or Shaker hymns, such as Aaron Copland's version of *'Tis the Gift to be Simple*. We must not allow ourselves to be persuaded that the folk-song tradition such as belonged to the old rural England persists, however: it does not. The beautiful and gracious songs collected by Cecil Sharp belonged to a rural England which has passed. Yet even the cult of folk-ballad in recent years shows that our England is groping towards taking up the threads of a popular culture with vitality.

In a note below I give some sources of folk-songs and would urge them as a main instrument in crossing the gap from children's own poetry, as a kind of poetry which has an obvious function, to 'educated' poetry. And a large proportion of the poems in my anthology, *Iron, Honey, Gold*, came from folk and popular sources. Then there are passages from the Bible as suggested below.[1] With this material, and in collaboration with the music and art teachers, a school could produce a festival of song and poetry every day, with perhaps one longer occasion, on one morning of the week, for the whole school. To the above material may be added devotional poems by Herrick, Herbert, Donne, Christina Rossetti, Gerard Manley Hopkins; and excerpts from the mediaeval mystery plays in verse, which are great, simple master pieces of poetic drama, eminently suitable for children.

Most school morning assemblies would seem to me an inoculation against poetry and delight in the word: yet in this ceremony we have the opportunity to give poetry its rightful function: at times poetry and poetic drama have been the most popular art-form. And they must be done by live voices: the experience of a school listening to some second-rate Bible play on the radio is painful, when the expressive voices of children are available. Then there are occasional festivals—Speech Day, Open Day, Christmas parties, and so on. At such occasions, and at other times, it may

[1] In Appendix B, p. 91, for which I am grateful to an article by Miss Susie Tucker in *The Use of English* VIII (3 and 4), 1957.

be possible to produce a play: though the labour involved is enormous and only a comparatively few pupils, in our kind of school, benefit. It may be better, if you have the talent and an energetic music teacher, to produce a school opera, with a chorus, and instruments if you have them. Certainly the English teacher should appreciate that opera is a form of poetry: and work of value could be done by reading the libretto to, say, *Peter Grimes* or *Let's Make an Opera* (or *The Little Sweep*), or *Noyes Fludde* followed by a visit to the opera or listening to a gramophone record. But for the common small occasions I would suggest a kind of 'programme' rather more like the mediaeval mystery plays, or something between them and a poetry reading.

I have doubts about the poetry reading as such, for it has often seemed to me embarrassing and cold-blooded. It seems to lack those dramatic elements which take us away from the individual voice and the individual poem on to a 'third ground'. Music, drama, percussion and spectacle seem to help this. I am doubtful, too, about, choral speaking: I have never heard successful choral speaking, and I do not believe you can train a choir to speak verse together in anything but a way which kills the essential and subtle rhythms, though there are a few obviously suitable poems, such as W. H. Auden's *Night Mail* and those of Vachel Lindsay. Groups of individual speakers speaking single lines or stanzas each one after another is a different matter and I am told there is some considerable value in choral speaking for weak speakers, to whom it gives confidence. It might be worth experimenting in choral speaking to musical instruments or a drum (using, say, *Sweeney Agonistes* by T. S. Eliot), in *Sprechstimmung* or *parlando*.

But it is possible to devise programmes of poetry, song, music, choral singing and even choral speaking of verses in turn, or line by line, which have sufficient drama in them to become something of a celebration, not just a reading. And this, I think, should be a regular feature of school life. The programmes can be set, dressed and the parts learnt, or they can be merely read: they should always be rehearsed. And (this is a major point) the content of the programme should be understood by the speakers, and discussed in class with the audience. The need for timing and cues makes for careful listening: little time is wasted, and many can be involved. Such 'programmes' are easy enough to devise, and the music for them should be live whenever possible. I have included an example of such a 'programme' in my anthology of pieces of poetic drama for use in secondary schools, *Thieves and Angels*.

With such entertainments a regular feature of school life (we are out to make our education a 'civilising and humanising practice'), the status of poetry, its function, should become un-questionable. And, of course, if you can include some pupils' own poetry the effect will be more telling. A child should grow up supposing he has a duty of entertaining others in his own com-munity. This may be done by such a simple expedient in forms as asking a pupil each day to choose a poem to read to his class the next day: it is by such simple tricks of the trade that the successful teacher creates the live environment.

Such small celebrations or occasions towards which our work might be directed require some understanding by our pupils of the meaning of poetry, and the way the poetry goes. Nothing is more painful than listening to poetry read by someone who doesn't understand it, or who mutilates its rhythm. An excellent method is to get the class to discuss gramophone records of poetry, once they have gone over the poetry themselves, to see if they agree with the way it is read. Some records are models of bad reading.[1] So we must pause, on some poems, to read them 'in low gear'. We must, too, enlarge our experience of poetry, for bulk is the essential in all imaginative work in English, and so we must read to our pupils a large number of poems. We must, too, train them to read poetry silently to themselves. And we must help them to write their own poetry. We must, in fact, have poetry lessons.

We need good material on which to work, and so we require one or two of the very few good anthologies. There should be in every English room an adequate poetry bookshelf, including books of folk-songs and chanteys.[2]

Using this material we may do the following (eschewing

[1] See Appendix A for a list of gramophone records of spoken verse.
[2] See Appendix A, p. 88, for list.

nearly all text-books and their wretched questions on bad poems):

1. Read poems to the class ourselves.
2. Ask children to choose and read poems and discuss with them the choice, and their reading of the poems.
3. Direct children to read poetry books silently to themselves. It is of value if the teacher is seen to be able to read poetry silently, too.
4. Let children copy poems they particularly like. They may recite these in class or at an occasion later. Or they may answer questions in writing on the meanings of poems (see below).
5. Go over a poem with the children in 'low gear' (see below).
6. Illustrate a poem in an art lesson.
7. Using a poem as a starting point, a poem such as one of those sketches from the Chinese translated by Arthur Waley, write a story or 'free composition'.
8. Write poems on the models before us. (The teacher may try too. I do not believe in the class composition of verse—that is, the group making of a single poem together—which seems to me to encourage meaningless forms of association between objects, and insincerity of expression—a kind of seeking for 'effective' phrases, and posturing—both of which faults are all too common in contemporary poetry. Such composition can only be done, it seems to me, by really denying the metaphorical function and the symbolic function of poetry.) The individual writing of poems is discussed in my next chapter.
9. Lend children poetry books to read at home.
10. Use the library to find out about poets, and to handle collections of complete works, though this is a minor activity.
11. Have readings of verse plays, such as the mystery play of *Noah*, or *Abraham and Isaac*. Or parts of *Macbeth*; T. S. Eliot's *Murder in the Cathedral* or parts of *The Rock*, and some of Yeats' plays in the class-room.[1]
12. Listen to gramophone records of poetry, folk-song and opera.

There is not much more we can do that is of use. I have left out all discussion of prosody, of the way poetry works or of what it is. I have left out the acting of ballads, and I have left out all forms of elocution. I see little point in dealing much with poets' lives, backgrounds and topography, though something might no doubt be done in co-operation with history teachers, and a good

[1] See my chapter on *Drama*, p. 204, and also *Thieves and Angels*.

teacher could do exciting work by using, say, Dorothy Words-worth's *Journal* along with Wordsworth's poetry. The main effort with poetry is the poetry, and its meaning: and everything de-pends upon *what* we ask in lessons on the meaning of poetry.

The way to discover what to ask children about poems, in order to help them with the meaning, is to read the poem our-selves and notice what we ourselves do not know, cannot easily explain. There are no right answers here, and we must not give in to the children's urge to have something which can be ticked as 'correct'. Nor must we give in to fears that we may look foolish if we don't know an answer. Walter de la Mare's poem *Song of the Mad Prince* is beautiful and profound: it also appeals to children. Let us ask how we might deal with it.

> Who said, 'Peacock Pie'?
>   The old King to the sparrow:
> Who said, 'Crops are ripe'?
>   Rust to the harrow:
> Who said, 'Where sleeps she now?
>   Where rests she now her head,
> Bathed in eve's loveliness'?—
>   That's what I said.
>
> Who said, 'Ay, mum's the word';
>   Sexton to willow:
> Who said, 'Green dusk for dreams,
>   Moss for a pillow'?
> Who said, 'All Time's delight
>   Hath she for narrow bed;
> Life's troubled bubble broken'?
>   That's what I said.

First of all we may read it aloud: poems should always be read aloud more than once, and in this poem we should notice first that the balance, of feeling, between faery and real life, between grief and acceptance of the death, is done in the *sounds* of 'troubled bubble broken' (assonance and alliteration, but let that pass: the point is the sound of the words, so integral to the meaning). So we must read these words with great care, as though (with the *b*'s) we were on the verge of tears, but actually expressing in the plosive '*b*' an acceptance of the transience of life: 'That's what I

4   81   H E F

said' is the final placing, refusal to give way. This gives us the clue for dry and fully-articulated speaking of the consonants, whose strength, as it were, holds off the power of grief, e.g.:

> Rust to the harrow...
> Sexton to willow...

These are 'dry', as against the wail of 'Where sleeps she now?'—

> That's what I said

is consonantal firmness against tears. The dry firmness is exerted against what the poet's 'terrifying honesty' has seen about time ('rust to the harrow') and death (cf. the ambiguity of 'All Time's delight hath she for narrow bed'—she is in the grave, and that is 'all Time's delight': the grave brings us out of time and into 'all Time' or eternity). There is an undercurrent of bitterness that must never be allowed to break through in the voice. But, of course, the teacher will ignore my reading and do his own!

Now we may ask ourselves: we do not expect to be able fully to see an explicit meaning in this poem, yet what must we understand before we begin to respond to it? And then, what do our children need to understand, before they can take the full strange flavour of this poem? Here are some possible questions to put to children:

1. What kind of bird is a peacock? *Answer*: A peacock is a richly coloured proud bird kept by rich people and kings.
2. What is a harrow? When is it used?
3. When are crops ripe?
4. 'Eve's' means 'evening's': What loveliness of the evening might someone's head be bathed in? *Answer*: The light of the setting sun, or twilight.
5. What does 'mum's the word' mean?
6. What is a sexton?

That is, we must be clear about the mundane, and then let the non-mundane take care of itself: to ask, 'What do you think the poet meant by "life's troubled bubble"?' seems to me asking for the wrong activity—that of turning good poetry back into the cliché from which it fought its way. (This is not to say you can't dwell on 'troubled'—'the water's surface was troubled': the thing is to know where to stop.) De la Mare's poem, because it is like a nursery rhyme, can be 'taken in' by children without any conscious puzzling being necessary—the sound, imagery, rhythm provide the satisfaction.

With a line such as this from *The Ancient Mariner*:

> All in a hot and copper sky,

you can ask, 'Why "copper"?', and discuss relevant associations of the word: colour, metallic sheen, the unnatural sound of the word and its echo of 'hot'. With lines such as Tennyson's

> He clasps the crag with hooked hands,

children may be asked, 'The poet in one version wrote "crooked" —which do you prefer?'

> Ring'd with the azure world, he stands.
> The wrinkled sea beneath him crawls...

What does 'ring'd' mean? (*Answer*. Ringed by the round horizon.) How is the sea 'wrinkled'? (*Answer*. Because the eagle is so high up that waves look like wrinkles: this makes you feel the height of the eagle's eyrie, because you are looking down from it.) And at times you may compare prose passages with passages of poetry to show the difference between the two different ways of approaching subjects.

Here, to show what can be done, are some pupils' answers (given in writing) to questions on Edmund Blunden's *The Molecatcher*. Here is the poem, or rather, the first half of it, with which the questions below deal:

> With coat like any mole's, as soft and black,
> And hazel bows bundled beneath his arm,
> With long-helved spade and rush bag on his back,
> The trapper plods alone about the farm:
> And spies new mounds in the ripe pasture-land,
> And where the lob-worms writhe up in alarm
> And easy sinks the spade, he takes his stand
> Knowing the moles' dark highroad runs below:
> Then sharp and square he chops the turf, and day
> Gloats on the opened turnpike through the clay.

Out from his wallet hurry pin and prong,
And trap, and noose to tie it to the bow;
And then his grand arcanum, oily and strong,
Found out by his forefather years ago
To scent the peg and witch the moles along.
The bow is earthed and arched ready to shoot
And snatch the death-knot fast round the first mole
Who comes and snuffs well pleased and tries to root
Past the sly nose peg; back again is put
The mould, and death left smirking in the hole.
The old man goes and tallies all his snares
And finds the prisoners there and takes his toll.

This is by no means a great poem, but it has the merits of decent careful writing, and stimulates a sense of other lives (such as that of the mole-catcher) and other possible experience (that which we share with moles and other animals; and the experience, which a child will ponder over a dead mole, of death). Here are the questions I consider suitable, and answers (from children in a second year A stream) which I consider good. (Of course the children were allowed dictionaries.)

1. What are the 'hazel bows' the catcher carries under his arm?
   Answer. The 'hazel bow' that the mole-catcher uses is a hazel switch cut from a hedge and a string tied round one end and looped. It is bent, and the string is tied in the hole with the loop ready to catch the mole in the lasso.
2. What do you think the rush bag is for? What is a rush bag?
   Answer. The rush bag is to put the dead moles in. A rush bag is a bag made of plaited rushes.
3. How can pasture land be called 'ripe'?
   Answer. The pasture land is called 'ripe' when the pastures are ready for reaping, or eating by cattle. The pasture land is 'ripe' because of the green grass which is sweet, and looks ripe like fruit, and is fresh.

   The pasture land can be called 'ripe' because the grass is green and juicy.
4. Why does the spade 'sink easy'?
   Answer. Because the ground is soft and has just been turned over by the mole. There is also a hole where the mole has his hole.
5. What is 'the mole's dark highroad'? What other word in the poem fits into the metaphor?

Answer. The mole's dark highroad is the mole's main tunnel, and it is dark because the tunnel is underground and no light enters the highroad. The word that fits in with the comparison is 'turnpike'.

6. Why does the poet use the phrase 'day *gloats*'?

Answer. The day seems to 'gloat' over the hole waiting for the mole.

7. Do you like the choice of words for verbs in the first stanza? Whether you do or not, quote three and explain carefully what sort of actions they indicate. (This question is intended to draw attention to the aptness of 'chops', 'plods', 'sinks', 'writhes', 'spies').

   Yes I do like the verbs. 'Plods' means clomps, lumps along as if his feet were too heavy. 'Writhes' means wriggles and squirms about. 'Chops' means to cut off in lumps.

8. Can you work out from the second stanza how the trap works? What 'arcanum' means? Why does the poet use such an old-fashioned word? Why does he say 'witch the moles along'?

   Answer. You get a pin and prong and tray and tie the noose to the bow. With the 'arcanum oily and strong' scent the peg, put the bow in the earth ready to shoot and snatch the death-knot round the mole. (Some accounts accompanied by drawings.) The poet uses the word 'arcanum' as it shows that it is a mysterious mixture or elixir.

9. What does 'tallies' mean?

   Answer. 'Tallies' means that he goes and gets the dead moles from the traps. The number of moles that he catches.

10. When you have read the whole poem, how do you feel towards the mole-catcher? Towards moles?

    Answer. I feel that it is cruel on the mole, but on farms I expect it is necessary as the mole may be destructive to the vegetation. I feel that in a way the trapper is spoiling the mole's life, but it is a terrible job for the trapper I should think.

This work could be followed up by class discussion of some of the answers, good and bad; asking them, does this help? The teacher can add any explanations be thinks fit, and clear up anything which has baffled the children. He could point out one or two more points, how, for instance the plodding, careful movement of the first stanza goes with the steady movements of the old man. Finally an attempt should be made to get the best possible reading aloud of the poem by one of the children.

Such work, it will be seen, is a real discipline: the real discipline of developing our response to language. And how satisfying it can be! How well the children do respond to poetry—those beautiful answers on the word 'ripe', for instance, and the comments on the verbs. (By the way, to anticipate our consideration of grammar—here was an opportunity, not in cold blood but in excitement, to deal with what a *verb* is.) And in such work the relation between the word and life (see question 10) is never lost sight of. Of course, the success of such work will vary, between boys and girls at different stages of their growth and their related interest in poetry; with the teacher's interests; and with different levels of ability. But this work should be done with only a few of the large number of poems we read with our pupils, not more than perhaps once a fortnight.

It seems to me that very little of use can be achieved in the modern school by way of exercises in discrimination, choosing good poetry from bad. At times the teacher may perhaps need to say, 'I don't think that poet is being very sincere or honest—it's too jolly in its rhythm for such a sad subject. I don't think he can really mean it, do you?' Or, 'I think that's bad/obvious/careless rhyme.' It should become clear to children that adults prefer some authors to others, and some poems to others and that they will sometimes say, 'I know a better poem than that.' Children will be making their own choices all the time, for reading: and they are bound to choose flowery, candy-floss and sentimental poems as they go through various stages of emotional experiments in life. They may fall for what we regard as the most dangerous false heroics (Newbolt) or a hysterical devotion (Isaac Watts) or sadistic sensationalism (*The Highwayman*, Alfred Noyes): but then many adults go on liking some bad poetry all their lives, and cling to their immaturity in defence against accepting the conditions of life, and we must expect children's taste to go through all kinds of bizarre forms. To ask the modern school child to develop the abstracting capacity to judge superior from inferior poetry seems to me using a method appropriate to the higher forms in the grammar school on children incapable of benefiting from it. With the majority the same ends must be achieved by other means, namely, by giving them access to a great deal of good poetry in enjoyable ways: and by encouraging them to write poetry themselves, so that they become aware of how much superior in every way their own poetry is to popular songs and such written by commercial hacks. ⋊ We need not suppose that poetry, however well taught, will make all our pupils, or even the best, into mature and balanced 'whole' men and women. It is rather that without access to English poetry they are deprived of one form of sustenance, one positive aid to living. The great need of the child is for love: in the light of object-relations psychology our primary needs are believed to be relationship, at first with the mother, later in adult love, and with all outward things. These developments towards maturity are harder to achieve than anything else in the world. They may be obscured in individuals by what society does to them, or their parents' failings. Our pupils will experience sorrow, trouble and death: they may need aid from the divine or the physician rather than from poetry, yet even these—priest or psychiatrist—are impotent without the aid of the inward creative effort in each individual to find wholeness and the capacity to love. All our wrestling with life, if it is to have any substance and courage, needs to draw on the power of the word, the metaphorical power which makes the flux of inner and outer experience that much more tractable.

Whether our pupils undertake the disciplines of seeking God, or harmony in love, or personal maturity and order, or social order, they are unlikely to succeed more than partially if they cannot draw more than a pathetic insufficiency from the poetry of their own tongue. Poetry can help give 'the very culture of the feelings' and a grasp on life in terms of the whole sensibility: poetry is a civilisation's positive hold on life. If these things sound rare we can perhaps remember they are there in children's own traditional game-rhymes as well as in our libraries.

BOOKS AND RECORDS OF POETRY

BOOKS

I know of no anthology pre-eminently suitable for secondary modern school use. The best in existence is *The Poet's Tongue*, in two volumes, edited by W. H. Auden and John Garrett. This contains a good deal of folk and other anonymous material, but it also contains a prodigious amount of nonsense, and on the whole would seem to be devised for the upper forms of the grammar school. James Reeves' anthologies are all good if a little whimsical.

In order to try to remedy the lack of a suitable anthology I put together four volumes which were published with the present work, *Iron, Honey, Gold*.

The following books may be purchased for use on the 'poetry shelf' of the classroom:

Auden, W. H., & Garrett, John, *The Poet's Tongue* (Dent).

Britton, J. N. *Oxford Books of Verse for Juniors*, Books 1–4 (Oxford University Press).

Brown, Douglas, *Selected Poems of George Herbert* (Hutchinson).

De la Mare, Walter, *Come Hither* (Constable); *Collected Poems* (Faber). *The Faber Book of Children's Verse* (Faber).

Green, M., *Stars and Primroses* and *Magic Lanterns* (John Lane).

Hughes, Ted, *Here Today* (Hutchinson).

Lewis, C. Day, *The Echoing Green*, Parts I, II and III (Blackwell).

O'Malley, Raymond, and Thompson, Denys, *Rhyme and Reason* (Queen's Classics).

Opie, I. and P., *Oxford Nursery Rhyme Book* (Oxford University Press). *The Oxford Book of Ballads* (Oxford University Press).

The Puffin Book of Children's Verse (Penguin).

Oxford Book of English Verse (Oxford University Press).

Read, Herbert, *This Way Delight* (Faber).

Reeves, James, *Heinemann Poetry Books* I–IV (Heinemann); *The Blackbird in the Lilac* (Heinemann); *The Merry-go-round* (Heinemann); *Orpheus I and II* (Heinemann), *Selected Poems of John Clare* (Heinemann).

Scott, A. F., *Poetry for Pleasure* (Cambridge University Press).

Poetry in the Classroom

Stevenson, R. L., *A Child's Garden of Verses* (Oxford University Press and Penguin).

Graves, Robert, *Ballads* (Heinemann).

Waley, Arthur and others, *Plucking the Rushes*, an anthology of Chinese poems in translation, edited by David Holbrook (Heinemann).

RECORDS

The following recommendations are from an article in *The Use of English* by James Gibson (Summer 1966):

ARGO. 12 in. *The English Poets from Chaucer to Yeats.* This is a collection of more than sixty records with accompanying books by O.U.P. Each of our major poets has at least one record. Especially recommended of those already published: RG 401, Chaucer, 'The Prologue' read in Middle English; RG 403, Donne; RG 404 and 427, Metaphysical Poets; RG 343, Pope; RG 345 and 7, Wordsworth; RG 341, Keats; RG 342, Tennyson.

ARGO RG 10. 12 in. *Poems of T. S. Eliot.* Read by Robert Speaight. Includes 'The Waste Land', 'Alfred Prufrock', 'The Hollow Men' and 'Ash Wednesday'.

ARGO RG 11. 12 in. *Four Quartets.* Read by Robert Speaight and thought by many critics to be better than Eliot's own reading.

ARGO RG 360. 12 in. *The Barrow Poets.* A lively and varied programme by the 'Poetry in Pubs' group.

ARGO RG 192. 12 in. *Favourite Poems at Home.* A fine and moving series of readings by Robert Donat, published after his death.

ARGO RG 385. 12 in. *What Passing Bell.* Poetry and prose of the First World War. Owen, Rosenberg and Sassoon juxtaposed with Brooke.

ARGO DA 26 and 27. 12 in. *Poetry and Jazz.* The poets are Adrian Mitchell, Dannie Abse, Jeremy Robson and Laurie Lee.

ARGO DA 55. *Poetry and Song*, edited James Gibson.

CAEDMON TC 1015. 12 in. *Ogden Nash Reads Ogden Nash.*

CAEDMON TC 1046. 12 in. *Walter de la Mare Speaking and Reading.* This and the Ogden Nash record show that there is a case for *some* poets reading their own work. De la Mare's opening remark to the recording engineer, recorded unknown by him at the time, is very moving.

CAEDMON TC 1081. 12 in. *The Poetry of Yeats.* A well-chosen selection read by Cyril Cusack and Siobhan Mackenna.

CAEDMON TC 1140. 12 in. *The Poetry of Thomas Hardy.* Read by Richard Burton with a sensitive understanding of Hardy's subtle and personal rhythms.

CAEDMON TCE 107. 7 in. *Dylan Thomas, No. 3.* The poet reading three of his own poems and Auden's 'As I walked out one evening'.

CAEDMON SRS M241. 12 in. *Shakespeare's Sonnets*. Supremely well read by John Gielgud.

JUPITER JUR OOA1 and 2. 12 in. *The Jupiter Anthology of 20th Century English Poetry, Parts 1 and 2*. A very interesting collection of fairly modern poetry with many of the poems read by the poets themselves.

JUPITER JUR OOA3. 12 in. *The Jupiter Book of Ballads*. A mixed bag of ballads ranging from the genuine to the ersatz (McGonagall). Well worth studying in some detail in class.

JUPITER JUR OOB4. 10 in. *An Anthology of Christian Poetry and Prose*. An unusual anthology very well read by Alec Guinness.

JUPITER JUR OOA9. 12 in. *The London Library of Recorded English*. A new issue of the outstanding 78 records of the 1940s.

JUPITER JEP OC37. 7 in. *Poets Set in Jazz*. Jazz settings of poems by Hood, Byron, Rossetti and Sidney. Most children like this, some dislike it, all want to talk about it.

FONTANA TL5206. 12 in. *Shakespeare and All That Jazz*. Cleo Laine sings some interesting Shakespearian settings by Arthur Young and John Dankworth. This, too, will get them talking and should lead to a very valuable lesson.

TOPIC 12T103. 12 in. *English and Scottish Folk Ballads*. A selection of ten of the finest English and Scottish ballads sung with authority by A. L. Lloyd and Ewan MacColl.

DECCA LXT2941. 12 in. *Serenade for Tenor, Horn and Strings*. Sublime settings by Britten of six poems. Ideal for discussing the relationship of words and music.

DECCA LXT2977. 12 in. *Facade*. 'Patterns of sound' by Edith Sitwell set to music by Walton. Here again the relationship of sounds, words and music is well worth discussing, and it is a most attractive record in its own right.

The following addresses of gramophone companies may be found useful. The British Council, 65 Davies Street, London W. 1, supply a catalogue of all speech records free of charge. Teachers should write for the latest lists as records quickly go out of production.

ARGO RECORD CO. LTD, 113 Fulham Road, London S.W. 3.

E.M.I. Records, E.M.I. House, 20 Manchester Square, London W. 1.

BRUNSWICK RECORD CO., 1–3 Brixton Road, London S.W. 9.

LINGUAPHONE INSTITUTE, 205–9 Regent St, London W. 1.

SCOTTISH RECORDS, 230 Union Street, Aberdeen.

JUPITER RECORDINGS LIMITED, 22B Ebury Street, London S.W. 1.

READING IN THE AUTHORISED VERSION
OF THE BIBLE

The following suggestions are taken from two most helpful articles in *The Use of English* (Spring and Summer, 1957) by Miss Susie I. Tucker of the University of Bristol. I am most grateful to Miss Tucker for allowing me to reprint them, for she is far better qualified to make this selection than I am.

Miss Tucker points out that the Greek, Latin and Hebrew classics are in danger of being studied less and less in our time, with a consequent decline in the common stock of knowledge, and in the possibilities of allusion. The Old Testament and Apocrypha, she points out, are a complete national literature, representing men at differing stages of growth and understanding, through history and legend, folk-tale, battle-song, elegy and lyric, legal document and priestly code, by allegory and apocalypse, by proverb, and meditation, both in verse and prose. The qualities of this Hebrew literature have become inseparable from the habits of the English language. Miss Tucker quotes the *Spectator* of 1712:

There is a certain Coldness and Indifference in the Phrases of our European Languages, when they are compared with the oriental forms of Speech; and it happens very luckily, that the Hebrew Idioms run into the English Tongue with a peculiar Grace and Beauty...They give a Force and Energy to our Expression, warm and animate our Language, and convey our Thoughts in more ardent and intense Phrases, than any that are to be met with in our own Tongue.

The New Testament writers were saturated with Old Testament literature, and often they use references from the Old Testament for their poetic rather than their strict theological or doctrinal significance. Miss Tucker suggests we should remove from our minds the comments on allegory and personification provided by chapter summaries in the Vulgate, the Geneva Bible and the

Authorised Version alike, and see such writings as the story of Jonah and the fate of Nineveh as an allegorical plea for tolerance of other nations, and the Song of Songs as a collection of sheer secular love lyrics.

Miss Tucker suggests that the New Testament is probably accepted by most Christians as doctrinally superior to all the Old Testament put together: but that apart from virtues of clarity and cogency it has much less claim to literary qualities. The finest piece of writing in the New Testament, she says, is the Book of the Revelation, perhaps due to the fact that the Authorised Version translators rendered it into the highest style they knew, regardless of the quality of the writing they had before them.

Miss Tucker ends her articles (which repay reading) by quoting Coleridge's words, 'Sublimity is Hebrew by birth', and goes on to say, 'From the first book of the Bible to the last, it is a quality which is never lost and is often enhanced in the translation produced by learned divines to whom the Hampton Court Conference entrusted the making of the Authorised Version of the Bible.'

Of course there is no end to the work that may be done round reading from the Bible in collaboration with teachers of history, geography and religious instruction. But in this book I am not concerned with the latter subject: rather with the need for young people, if they are to make the best possible access to their culture and civilisation, to know the Bible as a very great work of literature.

SUGGESTIONS FOR READING

Narrative

The Wooing of Rebekka (Genesis xxiv).

The Life of Joseph (Genesis xxxvii, xxxix–l).

The Death of Sisera (Judges iv).

Jephthah's Daughter (Judges xi).

The Adventures of Samson (Judges xiii–xvi).

The Books of Ruth, Esther, Judith, Tobit.

The Saga of David (i Samuel xvi to end of Book; ii Samuel–i Kings ii).

The Death of Saul (i Chronicles x).

Solomon (ii Chronicles ix).

Daniel (Daniel I–VI).
The Nativity (St. Luke II).
Paul at Ephesus (Acts XIX, 21–41).
His Sea-voyage (Acts XXVII–XXVIII, 14).

Wisdom

The Book of Job.
Passages in praise of Wisdom (Proverbs III, 13–19; Proverbs VIII).
The wisdom of Solomon (VII, 22–VIII, 9).
The virtuous woman (Proverbs XXXI, 10 to end).
Her opposite (Proverbs VII).
The virtuous woman and her opposite (Ecclesiasticus XXV).
'Vanity of Vanities' (Ecclesiastes, end of last chapter).
The occupations of men (Ecclesiasticus XXXVIII, 24, 59).
Human misery (Ecclesiasticus XI, 1–10).
Natural Beauty (Ecclesiasticus XLIII).
'Let us now praise famous men' (Ecclesiasticus XLIV, 1–15).
'Let us crown ourselves with rosebuds' (The Wisdom of Solomon II).
The Souls of the righteous. (The Wisdom of Solomon III, 1–9).

Selected Psalms

XVIII, XXII, XLV, L, LXV, LXXXVIII, XCI, CVII, CIX, CXXXVII, CXLVIII.

Satire and Invective

Against Idols (Jeremiah X, 1–16; Isaisah XLIV, 9–20).
The Fall of Tyre (Ezekiel XXVII).
False Shepherds (Ezekiel XXXIX, 1–10).

Elegy

David's lament over Saul and Jonathan (II Samuel; I, 17–27).

Love Lyrics

The Song of Songs (Solomon's Song, Canticles).

Poetry from Isaiah

Chapters I, XI, and dramatic dialogue in LXIII 1–14.

Pauline Prose

Hymn to Love (I Corinthians XIII).
The Whole Armour of God (Ephesians VI, 10–20).
'What shall we then say . . . ?' (Romans VIII, 31–37).
Letter to Philemon.

Visionary Writing

The Valley of Dry Bones (Ezekiel XXXVII).
Dies Irae (Joel II, 1–11).
Revelation I and XXII.

To which excellent list I would add the poetic story (associated with ritual dramas enacting it) of the Creation, Genesis I–IV 15. And the stories of Noah, Genesis VI–IX, 17; and of Abraham and Isaac, Genesis XXII 1–19.

The above list will suggest a kind of use of material from the Authorised Version in English work: we can, alas, no longer count on our children even knowing the principal stories of the Bible.

Another point is that our pupils may even come to be married or buried without having considered the words of the Church of England liturgy being said over them. The wedding festival, sacred and secular, has gone: we no longer celebrate marriage in poetry and music: the few gabbled words in an ugly office, the risqué and even brutal jokes at the reception or in the telegrams —these are all that remain to us of ceremony. The English teacher would do well to take parts of the English Book of Common Prayer, particularly the ceremonies for marriage and burial, and make his pupils acquainted with the rituals which have brought together many generations to hear simple and beautiful prose, in these moments of contemplation of the meaning of life.

It comes as a surprise to some people to be asked to consider such common features of life as part of our language culture. They are not entirely to be blamed: many clergymen gabble the exquisite words of church services as though they were meaningless mumbo-jumbo. And most of the hymns we are asked to sing do not even begin to be good prose, let alone verse.

A NOTE ON HYMNS

It has always seemed to me foolish in school to subject pupils, at their impressionable first moments in each day, to bad music and atrocious verse in assembly, and then send them off to study poetry and music. Of the hundreds of hymns in our hymnals most are bad. They are dull, or meaningless, or without rhythmic interest. Some are thumpy; some are emotionally cloying, brash, or wallowing. Many are so encumbered with 'dost's' and 'hath's' that they defy interpretation. Most are impossible to sing with even assumed conviction. And many are simply plain bad, such as *Our God is marching on* ('Mine eyes have seen the glory...') by Mrs Julia Ward Howe, *God who created me* by Beeching, and *We are the music makers* by O'Shaughnessy. Yet many devout teachers flinch when they are told that the singing of bad hymns does more than any other single influence to corrupt musical and poetic taste in England. If music is for the glory of God, then surely the conversation of rubbishy hymns is an offence to the Deity?

The situation is particularly to be deplored when there are so many very beautiful hymns mixed with the dross: hymns which as poetry and music should be given to their pupils by every teacher of poetry and music. Such are George Herbert's *Sweet day, so cool, so calm, so bright*, Bunyan's *He that is down*, and Donne's *Wilt thou forgive that sin*, Milton's *Let us with a gladsome mind*, Wesley's *Rejoice, the Lord is King* (to a magnificent tune from Handel), and some of the hymns from the *Scottish Psalter* of 1650 such as *Pray that Jerusalem may have*.

It is a great national disgrace to have such songs surrounded with meaningless dullness in our many hymn-books, and mixed with rubbish in the offices of the various churches. If the organisation of the churches, or their conservative observances and habits do not allow hymns to be purged, then Christian worship is due for another reformation. The schools, however, can hardly wait for such a ponderous happening, and it seems unlikely that the churches themselves will ever be able to part with some of their favourite horrors. I write, of course, of the hymns normally found in school hymn-books, not the more extraordinary songs found in Mission Books such as *Don't forget the promise made to mother, Jehovah Tsidkenu,* or *My all is on the altar.*

Teachers may care to try to make their own lists of unobjectionable hymns for use in assembly. To the great hymns by Wesley, Nahum Tate, Herbert, Bunyan, John Byrom, Bishop Ken, J. H. Newman, Richard Baxter, Isaac Watts, may be added many carols, and also some divine songs in other modes. The latter could include the Chorale from the *St Matthew Passion,* 'O wondrous Love'; *Come all you worthy Christian men,* a folk-song from Somerset; *Hold on,* a sacred folk-song from Kentucky, *No-e in the Ark* from the Appalachian Mountains; *Were you there when they crucified my Lord?,* a negro spiritual; *'Tis the Gift to be Simple,* a Shaker song set by Aaron Copland; and some carols from mediaeval issues of *Musica Britannica.* The purpose of hymns, as poetry and music, surely is to provide for the celebration in schools of the human experience of God, and to make sincere and fine poetry and music the vehicle of this celebration.

There seems a need for a short book of good hymns which could be taught in poetry and music lessons, without exception, and without confusing standards, in the spirit of the *Cambridgeshire Syllabus of Religious Teaching for Schools* (1939), pp. 16–17, '...the words...should be studied...'—But how many hymns bear study?[1]

---

[1] *The Cambridge Hymnal* by Elizabeth Poston and the present author was published in 1967. In this the editors have attempted to provide a collection of words and music which really will bear study, so that the preparation of hymns for morning assembly can be rewarding or even exciting instead of dreary.

CHAPTER 6

Folksong as Poetry

What do our children sing when they leave school? A few hymns, *Nelly Dean* and *Bless 'em All* in the Army, *We'll live in a World of Our Own* or *I am a King Bee* in the street, and *Abide with Me* at a cup final. Nothing is more indicative of the failure of music teaching in the schools, of our hopes for the educational effects of broadcasting ('creating a nation of music lovers'), and the loss of traditions in our standardised urban life than the Englishman's inability to sing. Christmas Eve in the pub *is* agony: the inhuman noise in the cinema only a development from the inhuman noises in the old school tradition:

Standard Five girls were having a singing lesson, just finishing the la-me-doh-la exercises and beginning a 'sweet children's song'. Anything more unlike song, spontaneous song, would be impossible to imagine: a strange bawling yell followed by the outlines of a tune. It was not like savages: savages have subtle rhythms. It was not like animals: animals *mean* something when they yell. It was like nothing on earth, and it was called singing.   D. H. LAWRENCE, *Lady Chatterley's Lover*

Yet Cecil Sharp could say in 1907:

I have talked with scores of old country people on this subject of folk-singing. They all repeat the same tale. Everyone sang in their young days, they will tell you; they went to work in the mornings singing; they sang in the fields, and they trudged home in the evening to the accompaniment of song...the evidence is overwhelming that, as recently as 30 or 40 years ago, every country village in England was a nest of singing birds.   *English Folksong—Some Conclusions*

In her *Guide to English Folksong Collections*, Miss Margaret Dean Smith lists some 2,000 titles of songs with many variants of each, collected by 86 collectors since the middle of the last century. As late as 1919 Sharp could say the typical English folksong, *The Seeds of Love*, was 'known to the peasant folk all over England'; since then the folksongs as 'a purifying and refining influence' have been finally 'withdrawn from the nation'. Now our young people have re-discovered folksongs which have gone from England to the Appalachians, thence to industrial America, and back to England, and there is much keen discrimination—but much corruption too (see p. 244 below) for when folk becomes 'pop' it enters a world where the words aren't really heard. Commercialism, seeing in the increasing popularity of folk material a threat in terms of spontaneity and simplicity, has taken over the skiffle and folky movement. Commercial entertainment cannot exploit a mass market using the true melodic and verbal beauty of folksong, and so to take it over, promoters seek to drown, vulgarise and sentimentalise it. Valuable work might be done in modern schools in comparing sentimental versions of folksongs— easily to be found on commercial records—with the genuinely traditional versions (such as most of those published by authentic firms such as Topic Records).

We need to know, before we can tackle the problem, what a folk-song is: *Take me out to the Ball Game* is listed under 'folksong' in one catalogue, and the term is loosely used everywhere to mean 'popular song of which no-one knows the author' or 'folksy-song', and so on. The folksongs I talk about in this book are those made up and sung in England from the Middle Ages until the middle of the nineteenth century, from which time they began to die out. These songs are those which were 'created by the common people, in contra-distinction to the song, popular or otherwise, composed by the educated.' The folksongs were not, then, composed by educated musicians or poets, they were not an 'escape' from formal music, and so they are always anonymous.

As Cecil Sharp shows, in his remarkable book, the folksongs are 'constructed on certain well-defined and intelligible principles'. It is difficult for us to believe it possible for uneducated people to produce such fine songs and to hand them down over the centuries accurately, even without writing them down: yet the facts are incontrovertible. A song like *Evening Prayer*, for instance, which was taken down in 1890 from an old woman in the workhouse at Tavistock, contains mediaeval phrases, and its music, in a rare mode, is like mediaeval plainsong: it is the White

Paternoster, magical prayer of the Middle Ages, and had lived in the oral tradition for centuries. Obviously, as Cecil Sharp says, someone once made up each song, it was sung by others, and people *changed what they did not like*: thus a song was formed which reflected the taste and outlook of the whole community. The folksong shows what the people want: and it is something very fine, whatever those, following Northcliffe, who deliberately lower taste in order to exploit sensibility, may say.

Before we look at a typical folksong it may be as well to say what the special characteristics of folksongs are, and how they are to be distinguished from other kinds of song. As I have said, they are anonymous: they are not to be confused with the popular composed song, like *Rule Britannia* or *Two Lovely Black Eyes*; nor with the popular song with a folk-tune to which words written by an educated verse-writer have been put, such as the songs in *The Beggar's Opera*, or *The Vicar of Bray*. Then, there are many folksongs which have been edited out of all recognition by editors like Chappell, who did not understand the peculiar nature of the music of folksong: in Cecil Sharp's book readers will find useful comparisons between versions of *Polly Oliver*, and *The Miller of Dee*. This latter point is a most important one, because most school song-books seem to contain these insensitively edited versions of folksongs, and they are not as good as the originals.

Folksongs should be sung unaccompanied: certainly they suffer from intrusive accompaniments, or those which force inappropriate harmonies on them. That folksong melodies are unharmonic is one of their characteristics.

Many folksongs are not in major and minor keys: they are modal and they do not modulate. They seem to belong to the kind of music which the human voice most naturally sings—to that music one finds in children's own game-songs, which is why they are so valuable for school use. In editing the songs for schools, Cecil Sharp, recognising the conditions under which teachers worked, set the songs to piano accompaniments: based on Sharp's understanding of the nature of folk-music, and his own gifts, these accompaniments are very fine, if an accompaniment is felt to be necessary. A guitar is perhaps preferable.

Other musical features of folksong as an art *sui generis* are the prevalence of 5 and 7 time in the music; irregular bars; the use of non-harmonic passing notes; a vagueness of tonality, especially in the opening phrases of modal tunes, and the use of the flattened seventh, after the manner of a leading note in the final cadences of modal airs. The features of the poetry are that it is impersonal and objective; the *dramatis personae* speak in the first person and often unannounced; the language is simple, direct, and un-laboured; there are numerous choruses, and conventional openings or developments in the stories:

> Come saddle, saddle my milk white steed
> The black one's not so speedy...

or

> Some put on the gay green robes,
> And some put on the brown...

The story, if there is one, is sketched in a few bold strokes. Some folksongs belong, obviously, to certain occasions: wassailing, May Day, cumulative songs for harvest suppers, chanteys and work songs. All these qualities, as Cecil Sharp discusses them, distinguish a traditional body of poetry and music, separate from our inheritance of English 'educated' poetry and music, but not inferior, and going with peculiarly English habits of looking at life. The words and music live together in subtle ways as the symbolism of subtle and sensitive explorations of inner aspects of our experience as deep as love and death.

For all these reasons folksongs seem to me most appropriate for children, because of their naturalness and simplicity, and especially for the unacademic, because these songs were unself-consciously on the lips of every English villager for hundreds of years before our civilisation decided it could do without them: they represent fine popular taste—and it is that we must try to restore.

We may see the quality of the songs better by examining them more closely: here is one song Cecil Sharp said was 'known to the peasant folk all over England':

The Seeds of Love

and gain'd the willow

I sowed the seeds of love,
I sowed them in the spring:
I gathered them up in the morning so soon,
While the small birds did sweetly sing.

My garden was planted well,
With flowers everywhere,
But I had not the liberty to choose for myself
The flower that I lov'd so dear.

The gardener standing by,
I asked to choose for me:
He chose for me the Violet, the Lily, and the Pink
But these I refused all three.

The Violet I did not like
Because it fades so soon;
The Lily and the Pink I then did overthink,
And vowed I'd stay till June.

In June is the red, red Rose,
And that is the flower for me:
I often times have plucked that red rose-bud
And gained the willow-tree.

The willow tree will twist,
And the willow tree will twine:
I wish I were in that young man's arms,
That once had this heart of mine.[1]

Consider the advantages—remembering that there were many hundreds of such songs known by everybody—of a teacher who

[1] For a slightly different version see No. 17: *English Folk Songs for Schools*, collected and arranged by S. Baring Gould and Cecil O. Sharp (Curwen).

might have pupils with such a song as *The Seeds of Love* in their veins rather than *Let's Spend A Night Together*. The language of the song is simple and direct, clear, alive. There is no levelling down, as there is, say, in todays comic strips ('Jane' in the *Daily Mirror* used to run for a month on a vocabulary of 750 words); the word 'overthink' is a unique preservation from local idiom, being analogous with 'oversight', and reminds one of some of Shakespeare's original employments of language. The phrase 'I had not the liberty' is an example of the occasional graciousness of phrase one finds in local idiom too, the fondness for the longer word such as one finds in Norfolk in 'discomfrontle', or 'imitate' (for 'try': 'I can leave the door open but that old dog won't imitate to come in'). Taking these examples alone one can see that a child used to this language would have little difficulty with Hopkins'

> What heart heard of, ghost guessed:

or King Lear's

> But I am bound
> Upon a wheel of fire, that mine own tears
> Do scald like molten lead!

which brings one to consider the language habits manifest in the poetic imagery of the song. They belong to the English folk tradition of symbolising inner life, exploring its patterns and significance, in terms of common objects, metaphorically.

The Seeds of Love deals with a universal danger in experience—betrayal by passion. The imagery of the lyric is common enough to folk poetry, but it is preserved from cliché by the simplicity of the language and the uniqueness of its phrasing. This is simplicity which conveys a kind of anonymous sincerity:

> The violet I did not like
> Because it fades so soon:

'overthink' and 'plucked' give a fresh force to the lily, the pink, (symbols, according to James Reeves in his *Idiom of the People*, of purity and courtesy) and the 'red, red rose'. 'Twist' and 'twine' enact, in the texture they give the lines, the remorse of which the willow tree is a conventional symbol. And in that these poetic symbols are given this freshness, so that they belong to this song rather than to any of the dozens of others in which they appear, they also become emblems of an individual experience within the universal and anonymous statement of the song.

'The seeds of love' are the beginnings of human love, in childhood or early youth, and the seeds of love sown in others by the first bloom of early maturity. There is no direct simple analogy, but the first stanzas convey the rapture of the first awareness of love and the young girl faced with the profusion of objects of relationship. The ' gardener' is, to me, rather circumstance than God: parents, time, conditions of life and the force of convention—the other-than-self. The self chooses the passion of independent vitality.

> I often times have plucked that red rose-bud

has a potent sexual suggestion, as has Blake's

> Hath found out thy bed
> Of crimson joy.

But this passion is a consuming one, just as the rose is 'red, red' and of the hot June of manhood, and it is less fragile, evanescent, than the 'violet' and less cultivated than the 'lily' and the 'pink'. The gardener's advice is rejected in the spirit of

> Let Rome in Tiber melt,
> Here is my space,

but it betrays the anonymous 'I' of the song 'to the very heart of loss' as his passion did Antony: the young man who is her choice in independent maturity, in her June passion, has betrayed her. The theme of betrayal, of the dangers of hate in love, is a favourite one in folksong, and recurs, as in *O Waly, Waly*.

The lyric poetry is organically bound to the melody: it does violence to both to separate them. The melody is modal, and at one point contains a common feature of folk melody, the leap of an octave. And here, at 'refused all ⟋ three', 'stay till ⟋ June', 'willow ⟋ tree', 'heart of ⟋ mine', it underlines the meaning, and strengthens the structure of the stanza by being a leap from the lower note of the fall of a fourth at the end of the second line,

on 'spring', 'every*where*', 'for *me*', 'so *soon*', 'twine'. The rhymes
in the verse, that is, seem to suggest a musical echo with a shape:

expressive of the way out of the depth of the suffering of the
experience, which is given by this:

This structure gives us the strength of the coming-to-terms with
that suffering and it is that coming-to-terms which *is* the song.
Words and music together enact the movement of a universal
experience, and the impulse of the song is triumphant, affirmative,
rather than an indulgence in gloomy nostalgia. However foreign
it is to our society, whose culture is so full of sentimentality
and hate, a song like *The Seeds of Love* is of a permanent, if minor,
value as a work of art.

Folksongs were maintained by a body of singers within the
community who had amazing loyalty to their material (they
would not sing a song unless they could sing it properly), amazing
memories, and extraordinary stamina. ('Mr Henry Burstow knew
400 songs...he once sang them all to a gentleman, and it took
him a month to do it.') Yet while they could preserve the essential
song (so that one Robin Hood ballad collected by Sharp had in
fact remained, word for word, almost identical with a black-letter
copy in the Bodleian Library recording the song as it was sung
some 200 years previously), they were also capable of most subtle
and lively variations to relate music to words. And they sang the
songs, as artists, within the 'shelter of convention'—'during the
performance the eyes are closed, the head upraised, and a rigid
expression of countenance maintained until the song is finished'.

Nowadays, out of school, our children whistle and sing songs
like this:

You'll always be my all in all,
And by your side I'll stand or fall.
With love that's true, your bidding I'll do,
I place my trust in you for ever.

I am a King Bee buzzin' around your hive;
I can make honey, baby: let me come inside…

There is little need to dwell on these, either as verse or as music. The words are nonsensical or obscene; rhythm is non-existent; a sufficient number of words are roughly drilled like an awkward squad into the line of feet, fitting and rhyming by the skin of their toes. As for the quality of the music, one could take the melodic structure of any one of these songs and see that it has the simplicity of banality rather than of innocence. No-one listens anyway.

Whatever the folksongs deal with, they do so with delicacy and grace: the natural instinct of people is towards these things. Those who made and sang the folksongs helped themselves to develop a real popular civilisation, with a deep energy of creative symbolism of inner experience, whether about illegitimacy (*The Foggy Dew*), or murder (*Edward*; *Lord Randal*), the declaration of love (*Through Bushes and Briars*), or death (*Lady Maisry*), or birth and generation (*The Trees they do Grow High*, *Queen Jane*) or belief in God (*Evening Prayer*), or attitudes to children (*Dance to your Daddy*). By comparison with the tenderness and stoical recognition of reality in the folksong, the toughest product of Tin Pan Alley reveals that, being manufactured to play on emotions, it lacks creative symbolism, and so contributes nothing to our capacities to deal with life.

Folksongs may be handled in class in much the same way as poetry, though they should be sung or heard sung well rather than read. In my experience children like singing folksongs very much, particularly such songs as *The Cuckoo*, *The Two Magicians*, and the *Nursery Songs from the Appalachian Mountains*. Much, of course, depends upon the willingness of the music teacher to co-operate. Folksongs and ballads certainly seem to me nowadays an important means for us to cross the gap between children and young people's own interests and tastes, and the best intentions of education.

BOOKS AND RECORDS OF FOLKSONG

BOOKS

Auden, W. H. (ed)., *The Poet's Tongue* (Dent).

Beckett, Mrs Clifford, *Shanties and Faebitters* (Curwen).

Butterworth, George, *Folk Songs from Sussex* (Augener).

Carey, Clive, *Ten English Folksongs* (Curwen).

Folksongs of English Origin (Novello).

Gould, S. Baring, and Fleetwood-Sheppard, N., ed. Sharp, Cecil, *Songs of the West* (Methuen).

Hammond, H. E. D., *Folk Songs for Schools* Set 8 (Novello).

Holbrook, David, *Children's Games* (Gordon Fraser); *Iron, Honey, Gold* an anthology in four volumes (Cambridge University Press).

Journal of the English Folk Dance and Song Society. Cecil Sharp House.

Karpeles, M., *English Folk Songs from the Southern Appalachian Mountains* (Oxford University Press).

Kidson, Frank, and Moffat, Alfred, *A Garland of English Folksongs* (Ascherberg, Hopwood and Crew).

Leach, MacEdward (ed.), *The Ballad Book* (Harper & Brothers, New York, 1955).

Lloyd, A. L., and R. Vaughan Williams, *The Penguin Book of English Folksongs*.

Moeran, E. J., *Six Folk Songs from Norfolk* (Augener).

Nettel, Reginald, *Sing a Song of England* (Phoenix),

Oxford Book of Carols (Oxford University Press).

Reeves, James, *The Idiom of the People*, *The Everlasting Circle* (Heinemann).

Sampson, J., *The Seven Seas Shanty Book* (Boosey).

Sharp, Cecil J., *English Folksong—Some Conclusions* (Methuen); *Folk Songs for Schools*, 9 parts (Novello); *English Folk Carols* (Novello); *Folksongs from Various Counties* (Novello); *English Folk Chanteys* (Schott).

Sharp, C. J., and Gould, S. Baring, *English Folk-Songs for Schools* (Curwen).

Smith, C. Fox, *A Book of Shanties* (Methuen).

Terry, R. R., *The Shanty Book* (Curwen).

Vaughan Williams, R. (ed.), *Folk Songs for Schools*, Set 6 (Novello).

Wells, Evelyn Kendrick, *The Ballad Tree* (Methuen).

RECORDS

English teachers should take care to listen to records before buying them or using them in class. In America there would seem to be a more genuine and more perceptive interest in the wit, poetry and melody of the true folksong. In England the preoccupation with folksongs seems to lapse at times into a loose cult of the 'folksy' and an odd obsession with the bawdy. The folksong movement, too, seems to be endeavouring to pretend that the tradition persists, and that what persists reveals more accurately the tastes of 'the people' than what is in published collections such as those of Cecil Sharp. Inevitably this leads to the publication, side by side with the great folksongs, of a good deal of rubbish by way of working men's songs, and the resurrection of a good deal of bawdy stuff of poor quality (as in James Reeves' *The Idiom of the People*). The confusion does not help the threads of a popular poetic and musical culture to be picked up again, because it fails to cherish the best in popular taste. It is surprising, for instance, to hear the talent of skilled singers such as Isla Cameron and Ewan MacColl wasted on the comparatively crude journalism of a wireless programme such as *The Ballad of John Axon*. But this kind of error is based on idealism: elsewhere there is a deliberate corruption of folksong, as by the commercial exploitation of 'protest' and 'amorality'. This unfortunate trend is discussed in Appendix G, p. 244.

Here I give details of what seem to be the most valuable gramophone recordings available for the teaching of folksong in school. These notes, and the further ones in Appendix G, were kindly prepared for me by Mr Maurice Howarth.

There is one very useful series of ten L.P.s of British field recordings under various headings. Although these records contain songs by some inferior performers they will prove invaluable for illustrating the scope and strength of folksong:

1. *Songs of Courtship*: Green Grow the Laurels; The False Bride; Our Wedding Day; When a Man's in Love; Ailein Duinn; Bonnie Katie; Old Grey Beard Newly Shaven; Sweet Primeroses; The Coolin; Shule Aroon; The Mountain Streams; The Brown Thorn; As I

Roved Out; The Magpie's Nest; Dame Burden; Casadh an tSugain; Twisting the Hay-Rope; My Darling Ploughman Boy; The False Young Man; I'm a Bonnie Young Lassie; Oh No John No; Cois Abhainn na Sead; Sogies Bonnie Bell.

2. *Songs of Seduction*: The Nutting Girl; The Bonnie Wee Lassie who never said no; Bundle and Go; Blow the Candle Out; The Foggy Dew; Toorna ma Goon; The Jolly Tinker; Long Peggin Awl; The Thrashing Machine; The Rigs of London Town; The Wind Blew the Bonnie Lassie's Plaid Awa; The Cunning Cobbler; Dublin City; The Light Dragoon; The Orkney Style of Courtship; The Cuckoo's Nest; The Soldier and the Lady; Never Wed an Old Man; The Maid of Australia; The Merchant's Son and the Beggar's Daughter; The Bold English Navvy; Cruising Round Yarmouth.

3. *Jack of All Trades*: The Jovial Tradesman; The Roving Journeyman; Candlelight Fisherman; The Cannie Shepherd Laddie; The Dairy Maid; Green Brooms; Gruel; Jug of Punch; The Gresford Disaster; The Jolly Miller; The Irish Washerwoman; Farewell to Whisky; The Roving Ploughboy; The Buchan Miller; Fagan the Cobbler; The Ould Piper; Sweep Chimney Sweep; The Mason's Apron; The Taylor by Trade; The Wee Weaver; Jim the Carter Lad; Drumdelgie; The Merry Haymakers; I'll Mend Your Pots and Kettles.

4. *The Child Ballads I*: The Elfin Knight; The False Knight on the Road; Lady Isabel and the Elfin Knight; The Twa Sisters; Lord Randal; Edward; King Orfeo; The Cruel Mother; The Broomfield Wager; Captain Wedderburn's Courtship; The Twa Brothers; Lord Bateman; Lord Thomas and Fair Ellen; Lord Lovell; Lord Gregory; Barbary Allen; George Collins; Cruel Lincon; The Prickelly Bush.

5. *The Child Ballads II*: The Royal Forester; The Baffled Knight; Johhnie Cock; Robin Hood and Little John; The Jew's Garden; The Battle of Harlaw; The Four Maries; The Gypsy Laddie; Geordie; The Dowie Dens of Yarrow; Glenlogie; The Grey Cock; Henry Martin; Lang Johnny More; Willie's Fate; Our Goodman; The Farmer's Curst Wife; The Jolly Beggar; The Keach in the Kreel; The Golden Vanity; The Trooper Lad.

6. *Sea-songs and Quayside Ballads*: The Liverpool Packet; The Green Banks of Yarrow; Our Gallant Ship; Paddy West; The Alehouse; Rosemary Lane; Ratcliffe Highway; The Lowlands of Holland; The Quaker; Kishuml's Galley; The Whale Fishery; The Grey Silkie; Warlike Seamen; The Boat that First brought Me Over; The Hand-

some Cabin Boy; The Uist Boat Song; The Smacksman; Sweet Willie; The Campanero; Andrew Ross; The Bold Princess Royal; The Boatie Rows; Our Ship is Ready; Nancy from Yarmouth.

7. *Soldiers' Songs and Recruitment Ballads*: List Bonnie Laddie; Swansea Barracks; The Dying Soldier; Willie O'Reilly; The Banks of the Nile; The Bonnet of Blue; Recruiting Song; William Taylor; Johnny Harte; The Soldier and the Sailor; Bold General Wolfe; Muddley Barracks; Handsome Polly; The Deadly Wars; McCaffery; Drink Old England Dry; Prince Charlie Stewart; My Son Tim; Napoleon Buon-ie-parte; The Bonnie Bunch of Roses-o; Napoleon's Dream; The Forfar Soldier.

8. *Sporting Songs and Conviction Ballads*: The Northamptonshire Poacher; Jimmy Raeburn; Drumhollogan Bottom; Sweet Fanny Adams; Sylvia; Young Willie; The Lakes of Shallin; Brennam on the Moor; The Butcher Boy; Three Jolly Sportsmen; The Standing Stones; Polly Vaughan; The Lion's Den; Van Diemen's Land; The Blind Man He Can See; Jack Hall; Oxford City; Erin Go-Bragh; Derry Gaol; Newlyn Town.

9. *Songs of Various Seasons.*

10. *Children's Songs.*

The singers on this series include Jeannie Robertson, Cyril Poacher, Seamus Ennie, Harry Cox, Bob and Ron Copper, Jimmy MacBeath, Phil Hammond and a number of others. The recording company is Caedmon (America). See below on *The Purchase of Records*. Notes on traditional singers are given in Appendix G. More obviously useful for teaching purposes are records by singers of the revival. There, however, there are difficulties of presentation.

Contrary to fashionable opinion, it is *not* easy to sing folk songs and ballads well. It takes years of practice and experience; of allowing the song to move its own course through the body; of learning that the song is greater than the singer, and performing accordingly. The trouble with the present revival of folksong has been that many singers have been unable to resist the temptation of financial gain and social advance in return for destroying by their performances much of the delicacy of folk song, either from sheer contempt for the art, or inadequate experience and sensibility.

We have, therefore, been careful to limit our choice of singers (as in the previous section, though for different reasons) to those whom we believe to have the necessary quality of performance and respect for the material; for only by choosing such performances can teachers hope to pass on what is true and worth-while in folk song.

A. L. Lloyd and Ewan MacColl are certainly the best singers of the British revival. Both have extensive knowledge of folksong, and their delicately balanced delivery is indicative of many years' work in the field. MacColl, especially, has made very many recordings and I list here only his most important (with full notes) and a number of other which may prove useful (titles and numbers only):

Ewan MacColl

Bothy Ballads of Scotland: The Keach in the Creel; I'm a Rover; The Skranky Black Farmer; The Band o Shearers; Jock Hawk's Adventures in Glasgow; The Brewer Laddie; The Wind Blew the Bonnie Lassie's Plaid Awa; The Monymusk Lads; The Muckin o Geordie's Byre; Bogie's Bonnie Bell; Lamachree and Megrum; The Road and the Miles to Dundee; The Lothian Haist; It Happened on a Day; I'm a Workin Chap; Johnny Snagster; Drumdelgie; She was a Rum One.

Folkways L.P.   FW 8759

Scottish Popular Songs: Accompanied by Peggy Seeger.

Folkways L.P.   FW 757

The Jacobite Rebellions: Accompanied by Peegy Seeger.

Topic L.P.   12T79

The Best of Ewan MacColl: Accompanied on banjo, guitar and concertina by Peggy Seeger and Alf Edwards. The Card Song; The Shepherd Lad; The Gallant Colliers; General Wolfe; The Girls Around Cape Horn; Henry Martin; Come all Ye Tramps and Hawkers; The Foggy Dew; The Diamond; The Cruel Mother; The Black Velvet Band; The Deserter; Farewell to Tarwathie; Tatties an Herrin.

Prestige/International L.P.   13004

Still I Love Him: With Isla Cameron and banjo and guitar accompaniment: Whistle Daughter Whistle; Once I had a True Love; The American Stranger; My Bonny Miner Lad; Let No Man Steal Your Thyme; Geordie; Buy Broom Besoms; The Maid on the Shore; Are Ye Sleeping Maggie; Still I Love Him; The Waters of Tyne; The Bleacher Lassie o Kelvinhaugh; Bobby Shaftoe.

Topic L.P.   10T50

Folksong as Poetry

Ewan MacColl and A. L. Lloyd

English and Scottish Folk Ballads: With Alf Edwards on concertina. Specially produced for schools. Henry Martin; The Baron of Brackley; The Cruel Mother; Lord Randal; The Bitter Withy; The Sweet Kumadee; The Demon Lover; Hughie the Graeme; The Prickly Bush; The Beggar Man.

Topic L.P.   12T103

English and Scottish Popular Ballads: a series of 82 ballads in nine albums. Seventy-two of these ballads are versions of pieces included in Child's compilation, on eight L.P. records (Riverside RLP 12–621–628). Ten others are in a separate album, 'Great British Ballads not Included in the Child Collection' (Riverside RLP 12–629). This series—recently re-issued—was specially designed for schools and universities, and has full valuable Notes. The Ballads are:

1. Lord Randal; The Devil and the Ploughman; The Laird o' Drum; Herod and the Cock; Thomas Rhymer; Our Goodman; The Unquiet Grave; Minnorie; Hind Horn.

2. Eppie Morrie; Sir Hugh; The Shepherd Lad; Robin Hood and the Tanner; Richie Story; Get up and Bar the Door; The Outlandish Knight; The Bonnie Hoose o' Airlie; The Rantin Laddie.

3. Barbara Allen; The Broom o' Cowdenknowes; The Broomfield Hill; The Cooper o' Fife; My Son David (Edward); Fair Margaret and Sweet William; Geordie; George Collins.

4. Glasgow Peggie; Johnnie Cock; The Jolly Beggar; The Keach in the Creel; The Knight and the Shepherd's Daughter; Lord Bateman; Maid Freed From the Gallows; Sir Patrick Spens; The Trooper and the Maid.

5. The Battle of Harlaw; The Brown Girl; Willie's Lyke-Wake; The Golden Vanity; Earl Brand; The Dowie Dens o' Yarrow; Robin Hood and the Bishop of Hereford; The Gairdner Child.

6. Gil Morice; The Crafty Farmer; The Gipsy Laddie; Lang Johnnie More; Lamkin; The Beggar Laddie; Rob Roy; The Cherry Tree; The Heir o' Lynne; Hughie Graeme.

7. Jock the Leg; The Daemon Lover; The Earl of Aboyne; The Elfin Knight (Scarborough Fair); Lord Gregory; The Bonnie Earl o' Murray; Henry Martin; Clyde's Water; The Grey Cock.

8. The Burning o'Auchendoun; Bonnie Annie; Bessie Bell and Mary Grey; Bold Sir Rylas; Captain Wedderburn's Courtship; Captain Ward and the Rainbow; Dives and Lazarus; The Cruel Mother; Lord Thomas and Fair Eleanor.

9. The Bitter Withy; Lang a-Growing; The Bramble Briar; The Seven Virgins; Down in yon Forest; The Bold Fisherman; The Blind Beggar's Daughter of Bethnal Green; Six Dukes Went a-Fishing; The Holy Well; The shooting of his Dear.

Three E.P.s of sailors' songs and shanties with Alf Edwards on concertina and chorus:

Blow the Man Down: The Blackball Line; Do Me Ama; Reuben Ranzo; Blow the Man Down.

Topic E.P. TOP 98

A Hundred Years Ago: Blood Red Roses; The Handsome Cabin Boy: A Hundred Years Ago; Johnny Todd.

Topic E.P. TOP 99

The Coast of Peru: Santy Anna; The Gauger; The Dreadnought; The Coast of Peru.

Topic E.P. TOP 100

Bold Sportsmen All: With guitar accompaniment.

Topic L.P. 10T36

Gamblers and Sporting Blades: With Guitar accompaniment.

Topic E.P. TOP 71

A. L. Lloyd

A Selection from The Penguin Book of English Folk Songs: With Alf Edwards on concertina. The Devil and the Ploughman; The False Bride; A Sailor's Life; Rounding the Horn; Salisbury Plain; One Night as I Lay on My Bed; George Collins; The Gaol Song; The Whale-catchers; The Trees They Grow So High; Ye Mariners All; Six Dukes Went a-Fishing; The Grey Cock; The Sailor from Dover; Lovely Joan; The Gentleman Soldier.

Collector L.P. JGB 5001

CHAPTER 7

Making Things Up

One of the most effective ways of developing a sense of the connection between the written and spoken word and life is by
stimulating children to invent their own imaginative literature—
their own stories and poems. Our aim is maturity: to be controlled
towards that aim the imagination must be active, strongly and
freely, in the first place. This work can be in mime or drama, by
word of mouth, or in writing.

In imaginative composition work one perhaps needs to start
with an interest similar to that of Sir Herbert Read's in children's
painting and writing, and then something more—something
more in the nature of an aim. Sir Herbert Read, as those who have
read his *Education through Art* will know, seems to be primarily
interested in the psychological tendencies which a child's free
painting will reveal. But he seems to have made this revelation
something of an end in itself, the philosophy behind it being 'the
secret of our collective ill is to be traced to the suppression of the
spontaneous creative ability in the individual'. In his note on the
Children's Own Writing Literary Competition organised by the
Daily Mirror, Sir Herbert says: 'What matters is: (1) the freshness of the vision, expressed in clear images; (2) the depth of
feeling evident in the choice of words and the rhythm of the
sentences...; (3) ...an ability to organise expression into effective form.' The concern is that indicated by the repetition of the
word 'expression'. Apart from the fact that there is something
spurious and unfortunate about a national competition (with
money prizes) in freshness and spontaneity (organised by the
Daily Mirror of all things!), the judges will willy-nilly be making
assumptions and judgements about the cultural context of the
child today—which context, of course, besides the work of the
schools, includes the *Daily Mirror* and national competitions.

Creation cannot, I think, be as spontaneous as Sir Herbert

suggests; the creation can only be made through technical conventions which, because they are involved in a tradition 'outside' the individual, provide a kind of control. This 'control' is not 'suppression': it may be a means to creation that seems 'spontaneous'. There always is control in the school, and our object should be to make the control adequate in its aims and in its sensitiveness. Sir Herbert Read has no doubt read D. H. Lawrence on self-expression: 'A child was to be given a lump of soft clay and told to express himself, presumably in the pious hope that he might model a Tanagra figure or a Donatello plaque, all on his lonely-o ...Now it is obvious that every boy's first act of self-expression would be to throw the lump of soft clay at something: preferably the teacher. This impulse is to be suppressed. On what grounds, metaphysically? since the soft clay was given for self-expression.' The child being coached to write some 'freshness of vision, expressed in clear images' for a money prize in a competition run by a national newspaper (devoted to unfreshness of the limited view of the lowest common denominator) is in fact taking part in a most unspontaneous activity. What in fact such a competition does is to make a stalking ground for teachers and writers out of the child's natural capacity for imaginative exploration of life, with the best tools his cultural context gives him: children should not be treated as singing mice, perhaps.

I would like to give here a personal account of some work in children's writing. My own aims in stimulating children's imaginative compositions, and in discussing them with the children, were as follows (and I will offer what I consider to be satisfactory results):

First, I wanted to encourage the expression of feelings, in an atmosphere in which such expression was regarded as seriously as the expression of facts. I wanted to make the child explore his own feelings, whether he realised he was doing so or not, and to have between him and me—in a public world, outside ourselves —a statement of them, revealing, maybe, the kind of psychological traits Sir Herbert Read might be interested in. As soon as I had some clue thereby to his emotional growth and needs, I could help to develop his technique in relation to them.

Secondly, and complementary to the first point, I felt the only way to achieve this expression was by using as stimulants poems, passages, and themes which the child already recognised as means to the depersonalising of his individual emotion—a way to that 'third ground' which is a meeting-place between the 'mind' of a community and his own. Such a depersonalised world, I have tried to suggest, exists in the sea-shanty, the folksong and the game-rhyme. It also exists in such poetry as the Chinese poems translated by Arthur Waley. The fairy tale provides it, and so too, I think, do certain other conventional types of child's story—the story of exploration, for instance. And, it seems to me, that even the Wild Western may provide a 'half-serious, half-irresponsible world' where self-identification may be indulged in, and painful feelings tolerated in an unfamiliar setting.

Thirdly, I was concerned to maintain attention on the poem or tale *as poem or tale*: it was assumed between us that the content, the emotions and thought expressed, were to be respected. And if they are to be respected, they must not be taken outside the pattern whereby the child has realised them. This is the reason for the need for emotional sparseness in the poetry lesson—and in the teaching of imaginative composition: to be 'emotional' is to betray the child into having to consider explicitly something he could only grasp implicitly.

Few, if any, of our pupils will go on writing poetry when they leave school: few will even go on reading it. But a taste of the craft will give them a respect for the written and spoken word, if we respect their work. The children were gratified to find that I never *ridiculed* (I've heard others do it) any expression of feeling, any venture into fantasy, any improbability of situation. I did point out occasions when the terms of the fanciful situation were not accepted—when the child had self-consciously shrunk, imagining the fantasy wouldn't be acceptable, and I often asked, 'Would a person in such-and-such a situation really behave like that, do you think?' But I tried to keep myself to failures of expression, and to related points of grammar, spelling, and punctuation. The quality of each piece of writing as a contemplation of experience was examined well enough, not by me so much as by being read aloud to the class, whose excitement or boredom, and whose occasional comments, made it plain enough how much 'universality' the imaginative composition had.

And finally, I was concerned with getting quantities of work produced. In the novel and in the total of a poet's work there are dull patches and failures—our reading and discussion of works of literature depend on the relatively scarce moments when the control and inspiration show themselves at their highest. Unless he produces a quantity of work a child can never allow his best ability in expression to come 'unwatched out of his pen'. Some of the best work—paragraphs where the spelling and punctuation are better, and where the language takes on a life of its own— came (one can tell by the writing—it's hurried but not slap-dash) on comparatively rare occasions when the story itself 'took hold'. The only way to achieve this is to maintain the stimulation (by reading the 'stories' aloud often, and by collaborating with the art-teacher in their illustration) and to allow period after period when the injunction is simply, 'Get on with your stories'. It requires patience, and confidence in one's aims (and co-operation from 'authority'). The dullest boy in one of my classes sat for four weeks in front of a page on which he had written, 'This story is about'. I had heard him in other classes being brow-beaten. I left him alone, praying that 'authority' wouldn't come into the room and bluster at him. I didn't even notice him beginning, but he did and by the end of term he had produced eight pages, compared with an average of about twelve. It is pedestrian stuff, but for someone who had never written more than half a page off his own bat, it shows some ability to put a series of events in order:

they saw an old door and they found it a bit stiff to open so they all gave a hand and the three men shouted, one, two, three, heave and the door was soon open it was very dark inside they had some torches and took their shovels they were tripping over rocks and they kept going through the ruins and they found a big tunnel the five boys went first and the three men followed it was very dark they shined their torches to see ahead...

The attempt to stimulate imaginative composition I am describing here was made by reading with the children two poems (they had read similar poems in poetry lessons in various ways—dramatised or spoken in parts, and, an 'A' stream, they had been asked questions on them)—the sea shanty *A Yankee Ship*, and Arthur Waley's translation of the Chinese poem *At Fifteen I went with the Army*. I concentrated most on the verse-form of *A Yankee Ship*, but threw in the other as a makeweight for those who might produce poetry without a regular form, or in a form they chose themselves.

> A Yankee ship came down the river;
> *Blow, boys, blow.*
> Her masts and yards they shone like silver,
> *Blow, my bully boys, blow.*

I described the shape of this—two chorus lines with their beats, which could be as nonsensical as one wished, and the two changing narrative lines which needed to have four 'beats' and to rhyme. Some of the poems they wrote were conscious or unconscious reminiscences, but in so far as they are departures, they represent individual explorations of experience within the same objective mode:

> Once there was a girl called Mary,
>   Oh la, oh la,
> She milked the cows in the farmer's dairy,
>   Oh Mary, la.
>
> Oh she was tall and slim and fair,
>   Oh la, oh la,
> She combed her golden hair with care,
>   Oh Mary, la.
>
> But she is there no longer now,
>   Oh la, oh la,
> For she looks after the one-eyed sow,
>   Oh Mary, la.
>
> She hopes that she will wed one day,
>   Oh la, oh la,
> The handsome farmer's son, in May,
>   Oh Mary, la.

Girl, 2nd year, 'A' stream.

There was an old woman,
    That old woman,
A very old woman was she,
    That old woman.

She was as merry as she could be,
    That old woman:
She danced and sang a riddle-de-de,
    That old woman.

When she was tired,
    That old woman,
She got in a bed that she had hired,
    That old woman.

She was dead that next morning,
    That old woman,
She died at the dawning,
    That old woman.

Girl, 1st year, 'B' stream.

Themes of love and death—intolerable and embarrassing to the child outside fantasy—are here dealt with directly, and have taken on at their own simple level the timelessness and resignation of the folk-legend. The boys, on the whole, were technically more able, concerned less with the 'human situation' perhaps, and expressed their experience of life in technical virtuosity. This is a competent version:

A pirate ship once sailed the sea,
    Heave, boys, heave,
She sailed into the pirates' quay,
    Heave, lazy boys, heave,

She came in loaded up with gold,
    Heave, boys, heave,
And also slaves to be sold,
    Heave, lazy boys, heave.

Her terror filled the Spanish Main,
    Heave, boys, heave,
And all that struggled, they were slain,
    Heave, lazy boys, heave.

A lazy boy, 2nd year, 'A' stream.

but these show interesting technical explorations in onomatopoeia:

> The Bawdsey 'bus came down the Strand,
>   Honk! Honk! Honk!
> Inside there was an army band,
>   Clang! Clang! Clang!
>
> The conductor was a tall old man,
>   Click! Click! Click!
> He was so hot he had a fan,
>   Swoosh! Swoosh! Swoosh!
>
> The driver had a big moustache,
>   Twirl! Twirl! Twirl!
> To look at him you'd think him posh,
>   La de da de da!
>
> The 'bus looked like an old tin can,
>   Rattle! Rattle! Rattle!
> Each seat was like a frying pan,
>   Frizzle! Frizzle! Frizzle!
>
> The old 'bus reached its destination,
>   Screech! Screech! Screech!
> They all got out and caused creation,
>   Clatter! Clatter! Clatter!

Boy, 2nd year, 'A' stream.

and in end-rhymes:

> A silly dog went to the dog show,
>   Ha, de, ha,
> Although his owner did not know so,
>   Ha, de, ha, de, ha!
>
> But all the neighbour's dogs did know it,
>   Ha, de, ha,
> And all the owner said was, 'Blow it!'
>   Ha, de, ha, de, ha!
>
> And when that doggie made way homeward,
>   Ha, de, ha,
> His owner said 'That dog's gone boneward',
>   Ha, de, ha, de ha!

Boy, 2nd year, 'A' stream.

Both use their technical interest to explore a kind of nonsense-fantasy which has the slightly ironic commentary on life of the nursery rhyme.[1]

But some of the poems not written to the formal pattern turned out to be more personal in feeling, though maybe it was possible for them to be so written simply because their classmates were writing the more stylised poetry—the 'third ground' was assured, as it were, by the whole context of work. And, I think, the poetry written to different verse forms echoes other poems they had learnt. This, for example, by an orphan (that she was so I only discovered later):

> Jimmy Hast went out to play,
> On a bright and sunny day:
> Mary went out with him too,
> Lost her doll's shoe that was new.
>
> Mary was a naughty girl
> To get the scissors and cut a curl:
> Jimmy was a naughty boy,
> Broke his car and brand new toy.
>
> No one loves them, not at all.
> Won't even let them play at ball:
> So you see they're very sad,
> Much the opposite to glad.
>
> *1st year, 'B' stream.*

And some of the 'free' poems turned out to be in the folksong mode, too:

> Spring is a season,
> All happy and gay;
> Flowers have a reason
> For blooming in May.
>
> Flowers grow up
> And buds come out,
> Animals wake up,
> For the world wakes up.
>
> *Boy, 2nd year, 'A' stream.*

[1] 'But all the neighbour's dogs did know it' reminds one of Pope's

> I am his highness' dog at Kew:
> Pray tell me, sir, whose dog are you?

Making Things Up

An owl flew into a barn;
   The barn belonged to a dairy farm.
The farm was big,
   As big as a pig.
The pig was fat.
   As fat as a vat.
The vat was round,
   As round as a mound.
The mound was ground.

Boy, 2nd year, 'A' stream.

These poems weren't the result of any spontaneous expressive urge of the children: they were produced by the stimulus of my emphasis on a mode and a technique—that of the nursery rhyme and folksong. Their creative activity was thus twofold—controlling their own experience in terms of mastering a technique. How successful they were appears at times when the speaking voice breaks through the scheme of the poem in its excitement:

> No one loves them, not at all,
> Won't even let them play at ball...
>
> Flowers grow up
> And buds come out...

And it seemed to me that the achievement of the 'know it'–'Blow it' and 'homeward'–'boneward' poem, and that 'barn–pig–vat' piece of nonsense, which has such an air of completeness, made a great difference to the two authors—neither very bright—in their attitude to language.

For one technical success which satisfies the child can provide a foothold for some advance in expression: but the teacher must know where he wishes to lead the pupil. I was discussing recently with some teachers a passage of strained film advertisement-copy. While most condemned it, many said it represented a form of accomplishment ('If I could write stuff like that I shouldn't be teaching'). It is not commonly recognised how easy it is to 'write stuff like that'. Some children acquire sophisticated conventional styles easily—and I was able to read my group of teachers this, by a boy in IB, asked simply to 'write a short story':

Suddenly a man came from behind a tree with two guns. He was not quick enough. Jesse's hand dropped to his holsters and in a flash his twin colts roared, and the Sheriff of Sante Fe, his chest riddled with hot lead, collapsed in a heap on the trail.

He has the idiom and cadence of the Wild West perfectly, and to master a style like that suggests an interest in language which one might well use to show a child how much better he writes than most writers of westerns. Such pastiche might even bring dissatisfaction with the base idiom. A more accomplished pastiche of the style is this—however alien to those little boys the idiom seems, the rhythm shows a real excitement in imagined incident (that the writer is aware that this is a pastiche is shown by 'Wild Woolly West'):

About seven years ago on the plains of the Wild Woolly West there was a wagon train travelling through Indian territory. The leader of the train was a scout named Rod Cameron. Rod, who had been scouting ahead of the train, suddenly came galloping back, shouting 'Indians on the warpath! Circle those wagons! Bill, you ride on to the fort and try and get some help!'

'Sure thing, Rod,' shouted Bill.

'What about the women and kids, Rod?' asked an old cowpuncher.

'Better get them under the wagon,' said Rod.

'Here they come', shouted Jim Blake.

The battle started. Men on both sides were killed. Twice the Indians retreated, but came on again bringing even more men each time. There were pitiful yells from each side, 'Ai! Ei! Ugh! They got me!'

The cowpunchers were rapidly getting less while they were still about a thousand Redskins left. The cowpunchers had hardly any ammunition left. Suddenly a wagon caught fire, then another, until there were only seven wagons left out of the twenty-three. Suddenly Mike, a cowpuncher of about sixteen years of age, who had never taken part in a battle before, went outside the circle of wagons and was caught by some Indians who scalped him.

The Indians retreated again. While the Indians were away the cowpunchers were attending to the wounded people. The results were plumb bad. There were fifteen people dead and twenty-seven wounded leaving only twelve men to carry on the battle.

'Well, fellows, I guess this is the end', said Rod.

'Hey, Joe! How many cartridges have you got left?' asked Rod.
'Fourteen,' answered Joe.

'Well, with my six cartridges that leaves us twenty altogether,' said Rod.

Suddenly the peace was shattered by a war cry. 'Here they come!' shouted Joe. The fight started again and after about fifteen minutes there were twenty more Indians dead. Then above the sound of battle came the sound of a bugle. The soldiers from Fort Worth had arrived. The Indians turned to face the soldiers and the fight commenced. The soldiers won and so ended the battle of Bitter Creek.

> *Written and published by the one and only Ian Laidlaw, I B.*

The writing is indeed superior to many stories in comics which I have read: it does not strain, the detail of the to-and-fro of events is rendered with great clarity (a numerical accuracy suggestive of Defoe's), and some of the rhythm is appropriate—'Suddenly a wagon caught fire, then another, then another.' The reader who has my anthology may like to compare this child's story with the contemporary account of such a battle, *Lovewell's Fight*. It has several similarities.

For this reason it seems to me that the teacher who 'takes himself down' to what he considers to be the child's level (or the kind of text-book which condescends to children by using words like 'smashing') or who tries to teach by using comics in the classroom is betraying the child. The child has more interest in language than the writer of the comic, and knows it; the teacher need only wait for an opportunity to show this to him explicitly, and offer standards by which the advance can be made, away from the stultifying habits of language which the comic and comic strips aim to give him.

Take these passages from two very dull boys in a first year 'B' stream. They combine an aggressive sophistication with a naïve childishness. But what there is in the way of observation and excitement gives a clue to the teacher where to lead:

Once upon a time there was a boy and he had a little pup called Toby. They went rabbitting and a gamekeeper said, 'Hi you, get off this land or I'll kick you up the behind.' Toby and me never went rabbitting in his field. I only caught one little bunny that day.

It was on a Saturday afternoon when I was standing on the slope watching the speedway. There goes Denis Day, here comes Arthur Pilgrim, thundering round the track. Yes! and he's catching up on him, a-a-oh...and he's past him. 'One, two three, four, what did we come for? W, I, T, C, H, E, S, Witches!' And here is the score; Arthur Pilgrim 3, Denis Day 2, Ray Wright 1, and if I count right Ipswich is the winner. The scratch race follows. Titch Read won nearly every race. Denis Day is only eighteen with no kids.

Even this latter disjointed Joycean piece has a rhythm in places which betrays an excitement, and his reproduction of the chanting of the word and the manner of the loud-speaker commentator shows some observation. If the English teacher can direct that excitement and observation on to other themes he may take the writer's attention beyond the dirt-track.

These prose passages all come from an exercise with the one form, at which, after several periods of making up stories orally, they were asked simply to 'write a short story'. The only 'control' here was in the previous discussion by me of their oral stories, which were in the nature of 'serials'—i.e. an episode was told by one child and continued by the next—though they had previously written poetry as above (see the two poems from IB). Some of the children revealed an astonishing ability to tell stories, particularly in the rendering of brisk conversations:

They went up and up the tree to the very top. When they got there they found they were both on the same branch. When they tried to get down they could not. They cried and they cried.
    'It was all your fault,' said Pepper to Salt.
    'It is not,' said Salt.
    'It is,' said Pepper.
    'It is not,' said Salt.
    'Don't argue,' said Pepper.

Another piece of composition work I will describe here was with a second year 'A' stream, each pupil writing a story 'of exploration'. On occasions I suggested they should write as part of this story an extract from a diary, a letter from one of the characters home, and so on, though I found this often detracted from the child's absorption. The stories were read out by me at various times—about once every three weeks, I suppose, each child could expect his story to be read aloud, and they had roughly two periods a week given to writing it. I marked errors regularly in light coloured pencil (simply using symbols: 'S' for spelling and ⊙ meaning 'you need to start a new sentence here') and they corrected them in the test. The adventure story of exploration was a conventional medium for their own dealings with experience. Many of the stories began with legacies which made the expeditions possible, but the stories on the whole weren't thin improbabilities—the children either used the unfamiliar scene to write about their own experience, or did realise their inventions vividly. Again, the emphasis being on the finished product, on the technique whereby something was realised, and because feelings and fantasies were respected, nearly all the books contained what I sought after—the page or paragraph where the desire to express had overridden the labour of spelling, punctuation and 'construction'.

I spoke above of the gift some children have for rendering conversation. One boy's story revealed very early a desire to explore argumentative conversation (perhaps his mother was always 'on' at him) for which his grammar and punctuation did not equip him. But a technical lesson, using his work with the whole class on the setting-out of conversation, enabled him to go on with a story whose realism came from its exchanges of conversation:

> So Pete went down the hole.
> 'Have you got a match?' asked Dick.
> 'Why should I have a match?'
> 'Well, I thought you might have one because you are cook in camp.'
> 'I'll have a look.'
> Pete felt in all his pockets and after a while he said, 'Yes, I've got one.'

Such care over a small matter (he forces the argumentative exchange on himself, despite the labour of extra punctuation marks involved by that 'Why should I have a match?') is the product of the excitement of fantasy.

This writer's need to explore argument wasn't severe: one or two children revealed the need to grapple with a severe personal problem. One girl, in a story of a trip to Switzerland, explored for many pages the idea of death:

The matron replied, saying that Mr and Mrs Crain could have no visitors because they were nearly dead. Joan said that they were their father and mother and it was very important that they should see them before they died...so they tip-toed along the corridor up the stairs and in the first door on the right...Sheila went and looked at her mother and whispered to the nurse, 'Doesn't she look ill.' 'Yes', said the nurse, 'but the doctor said that they would give her two hours to survive and if she didn't survive she was sure to die...'

What exact value this may have been 'therapeutically' I've no idea: the theme brought us to a standstill—the next chapter, 'Waiting for Survival', was never finished, and I was so affected by the Kafka-like frustration of the corridors in the writer's hospital that I dared neither urge nor criticise the detail of the rendering. The writing to the above point was adequate enough, but obviously no idiom or technique of hers could carry her further: she had come too much out of that 'third ground'— half-serious, half-irresponsible, and was trying to grapple with a theme demanding more maturity. Maybe (I didn't, of course, enquire) she had to face the theme in real life while immature: the situation reveals at least that to teach English 'for the living' it won't do to be cynical, or to expect a young child to show a 'terrifying honesty'.

The last writer might have had more success if she had turned to the realisation of a remoter fantasy, as others did. (That the reading aloud was in the children's minds when they wrote is shown by the fact that the writer of the following devised this for me to say: 'It was believed to be Pharoah Gilgusmustutugilgernustonusmen'!):

They drew their gurkhas and charged but Jim produced something he had kept quiet all the trip: it was a machine-gun. He placed it on a hill of sand and small rocks. The arabs came nearer. Jim fired. The Arabs fall like flies. The rest took cover behind their dead. The tommy guns had been taken by some villainous thief. The Arabs crouched as still as the rocks themselves. They stayed there until nightfall...

A psychologist on Sir Herbert Read's principles might have seen in this an undertone of feeling about death if he had known, as I did, that the boy's brother had died shortly before he wrote it ('hill of sand and small rocks...fall like flies...dead (which he spelt 'died')...taken by some villainous thief...crouched as still as the rocks themselves'). But, whatever the emotion, it is depersonalised to such an extent in the tale that we have a description whose details and rhythm produce an effect remarkable for a not-very-literate boy. And such qualities can be pointed out to him and others.

Finally, I would like to try to indicate by quotations both from the same story what kind of development there was, once interest developed in the writing, and the communication the child needed to make to the 'audience' was seen to depend on technical improvement. This is near the beginning of the story of the bottom boy in the form:

The cliff we came to was so high we had to use ropes and pick axes. Halfway I saw Mickey disappear over a ledge, next Pete went over. But when I went over I heard a voice; say 'keep walking.' And there (at least) in front of me were 8 or 9 black men. They (took) me to a mud hut were Mick and Pete were pushed on in and put a guard.

This a few pages later:

John after going to sleep in the trees with the others, woke up in the night after being disturbed [by] a monkey, which ran right accrossed him, felt very thirsty and he set out to find a stream which he could hear. He soon found it and had a good drink. Suddenly when he stood up he had a shock and felt the ground falling from under him. 'Bump.' Suddenly he stopped falling and found himself in a kind of tunnel.

The mistakes in the first spring from a lack of interest: the second flows more easily and the mistakes are those which come from the expression outstripping his acquaintance with 'the rules'. In the second the story has taken hold—teacher and pupil meet on that 'third ground' and we can endeavour to improve the English for the sake of the story.

This imaginative composition work is, of course, complementary to the reading of poetry and stories, and the practical training in English as a skill. That none can do without the others I feel sure—the teaching of grammar and spelling cannot be successful without much reading and imaginative writing. Imaginative writing is often avoided because it is difficult to mark, and the returns are difficult to justify to authority. It depends, too, on the teacher having a delight in literature and being well-read in it; only a teacher who has exposed himself to the discomfort of increased awareness which a reading of, say, Blake's *Songs* or Shakespeare's *King Lear* must bring, will be able to respect a child's fantasy. (This is a problem for the training colleges and departments; for all the 'psychology' lectures, many teachers begin their work with insufficient training of the sensibility, and confess to it openly. How can they maintain their ground when they meet hostile authority?)[1]

By reading works of literature a child may be brought on to that traditional meeting place of minds where he can measure his own experience against the experience of 'the race' and its values. This relevance of literature can be much deepened by his being encouraged to use the modes whereby others reached their 'organisation of expression' and develop from them his own symbolism. Such imaginative writing, in sensitive hands, makes the habit of employing the word meaningfully part and parcel of each pupil, and therefore more possessed, more permanent.

[1] See *The Exploring Word* and *Children's Writing* by the present author.

CHAPTER 8

Practice in Writing

Teaching practical English apart from practice is far more difficult than teaching imaginative composition. Ideally 'practical' English should be left to teachers of practical subjects, but can't be. Fluency in 'making things up' is the first aim—it gives the delight and the consequent linguistic power. And in fact it is impossible to teach clarity and fluency if we try to begin with 'practical writing' before we have done the real work. Many of the forms of inarticulateness in our time may be attributed to an education in English by text-book exercises and pointless 'Essays'. The common faults may be summarised thus:

1. 'Education' being shown by elaborate writing, the educated person will write in the most complicated way, and consider plain words distasteful. He will say 'stertorous inspiration' rather than 'breathing hard', and so on.
2. Conversely, the educated man (it is commonly believed) avoids common words such as 'rat-catcher'; to be called a dustman or to live in Back Street is an indignity: so we must be called sanitation operatives and live in Anterior Grove.
3. Some of such avoidances of plain words are deliberately or unconsciously used to deceive ourselves or others for propaganda purposes, or about the nature of things. Cf.—the word 'recession' for slump, 'incident' for bomb explosion, riot or lynching, 'desirable period residence' for 'old house' and so forth.
4. The avoiding of directly emotional words by the educated: the word 'love', for instance, is often avoided, because it has been weakened by misuse in the popular song. But 'educated' people often have a sterile way of saying, for instance, 'I accompanied her to her domicile' instead of 'I took her home', as if they want to shrink from things real. Conversations of this kind can be heard in undergraduate cafés: 'I have an intolerable addiction to the female species' and so on.
5. Genteelisms: 'repast' for 'meal', 'powder saloon' for 'lavatory'. These go with the lifeless world of clean kitchens, and the tooth-

paste smiles of the ad-men and the magazines by which they operate. 'The smallest room in the house' is a good example of a genteel phrase. Such flinching from what human life *is* is created by the emergence in our society of a huge industry, huge out of all proportion, devoted to the lucrative business of selling products for cleaning ourselves and our houses. Its danger is that it goes with the sterilisation of language and of attitudes to life and death (see *The Loved One* by Evelyn Waugh on morticians in the U.S.A.).

6. Civil Service and committee language. See Sir Ernest Gowers, *The Complete Plain English*.
7. Sheer illiteracy, as in 'The applicant should be a man with experience and who have already done work of a similar character'.

The rules for writing English are simple, but no-one may suppose that writing plain good English can be learnt by exercises: *le style c'est l'homme*—and the man is made what he is by his whole culture, including his reading. The rules are:

1. Be lucid.
2. Be sincere.
3. Use the fewest possible words to say what you want to say.
4. Be natural—try to write as you speak (it will not, in fact, be anything like the way you speak) and do not imitate other styles, except for fun. Swift said, 'Proper words in proper places makes the true definition of a style.'
5. Choose words for their exactness—the best possible word—and shortness.
6. Don't set much store by failure in writing about something about which you care very little. Of course we all have to do this in life, and we must try to do it graciously. But if it doesn't come easily, then it can't be helped. 'To write without purpose or feeling is degrading', is an ideal rule, but impossible to hold to in practice.
7. Read your writing aloud as often as you can, or try to hear it over in your head.

The following books should be in every English classroom:

Roget's Thesaurus of English Words and Phrases. (Longmans).
The Concise Oxford Dictionary (O.U.P.), or a larger dictionary. The larger the better.
The King's English, Fowler, H.W. and F.G. (O.U.P.).
The Complete Plain English, Sir Ernest Gowers (HMSO).
Mind the Stop, Carey (C.U.P.).

Practice in Writing

With these rules and warnings in mind the following stimuli may be used for practical composition work:

A. ORAL WORK

(*With lower streams especially*)

1. One child with his back to another gives verbal instructions for threading a needle, tying a tie, drilling a hole in a piece of wood, while the rest of the class watch and criticise failures. (This can become a written exercise later.)
2. A class watches an operation performed by the teacher (e.g. connecting a flex to an electric plug), and then one or two pupils describe what was done (or write it down).
3. Blindfold and concealed children are asked to *describe* an object placed in their hands without saying what it is or giving obvious clues—the rest of the class guess what the object is (e.g. a pineapple, a fur glove, a castor, a wooden spoon).
4. A child draws on the board something as it is described by another child who has his back to the drawing. The class guess the object.
5. The children write down descriptions of sounds made behind a small screen of books. (Or this may be used to start a free composition.)
6. The children describe what there is in a photograph or picture orally, or in writing (or this again may be used to start off a free composition).
7. The children describe tools and processes involved in a piece of carpentry or metalwork. The work itself should be in front of the class.
8. In upper forms debates may be organised by three or four children, or by the whole class, on the significance of local or national incidents, or some paintings, hung in front of them, or on the design of furniture, clocks, fountain pens, clothes or cars.

B. WRITTEN WORK

1. *Collaboration with other subjects*

The English teacher might undertake written work on projects carried out in other classes. Other teachers may limit their concern with words to note-taking—the English teacher could organise into prose the knowledge acquired in the other class. This, however, might be a dangerous practice if it were to lower the feeling of responsibility of the teachers of other subjects for good English.

The steps in such work, if done, might be to:

(a) examine the notes taken in the domestic science lesson;
(b) write a rough draft of instructions;
(c) discuss, if possible with equipment (why not have an English lesson occasionally in the laboratory or workshop?), what happens when the draft instructions are followed (faults can now be demonstrated);
(d) write on a board the final instructions as agreed by the class;
(e) erase this, and the children then write the instructions from their grasp of the processes and their notes.

2. *Visits and other such projects*

Suppose a class is to visit a farm with the geography or biology teacher; the English periods might be used for:

(a) writing a letter to the farmer asking for his collaboration;
(b) reading the farmer's reply and writing a letter making the final arrangements with him;
(c) consulting timetables and making arrangements with bus companies (this would need to be supervised carefully, of course, and confirmed by the teacher);
(d) preparing questions for the farmer and his men;
(e) taking notes at the farm;
(f) looking up information in the library before the visit;
(g) writing a letter of thanks;
(h) writing a letter to a friend, or an article for a magazine or the local paper about the visit;
(i) writing an essay for the geography and English teachers on aspects of farming to do with social life (e.g. on toxic sprays).

3. *Practice in letter writing*

(a) actual advertisements can be answered;
(b) letters to advertisers may be written in class;
(c) a group of children are appointed 'employers' and have 'interviews' with 'applicants';
(d) these 'employers' discuss each 'candidate' before the class.

Such work is bound to lead to self-conscious banter at first, but with persistence self-possession and clarity of speech can be given by such training for behaviour in life in the same way as we can train children for the stage.

Other pupils could give oral summaries of pamphlets giving vocational guidance: or the class could invite a factory-worker, shopworker, pilot or farmer in and prepare questions to ask him.

4. *Work with newspapers, comics and other reading matter*
   - (a) What are the main news items of today?
   - (b) Which paper gives the best summary of them?
   - (c) Rewrite those you consider the main news item in your own words.
   - (d) The pupils read these out to the class.

   Upper forms may write news items in contrasting styles of, say, (*a*) *Daily Mirror*, (*b*) *Daily Mail*, (*c*) *Morning Star* and (*d*) *The Guardian*.
5. Pupils rewrite public notices or official letters to make them plainer. Or the teacher may construct a public notice for this purpose.
6. Collect examples of misuse of language and (with upper forms) of bad argument. Put together your own rogues' gallery.
7. Use as much as possible the actual elementary techniques which are involved in daily life:
   - (a) Order, verbally or by letter, certain articles—e.g. fertiliser for garden, clothes for a child, kitchen tools.
   - (b) Have telephone conversations with different purposes: discuss telephone manners.
   - (c) Write descriptions of people for the police.
   - (d) Give an account of an accident or incident perhaps seen on a film or film-strip.
   - (e) Write a post-card for a specific purpose.
   - (f) Give instructions to someone else by telephone, by letter or in person.
   - (g) Practise making sense out of a telegram or a message. (There seems little point nowadays in practice in making up telegrams as no-one can afford them!).
   - (h) Practise filling in common forms (e.g. applying for a driving licence).
   - (i) Keep a diary, for instance of the school smallholding.
   - (j) Make practical research into some small item: e.g. people's reading habits or television viewing habits.
8. Stage proper debates, using parliamentary procedure.

This all presupposes a great deal of work on the part of the teacher—finding post-office forms, exploring the school environment, and seeking points of collaboration. But it is impossible to do really useful work of this kind using a text-book, though some contain useful help.[1]

[1] Use Denys Thompson, *Practice in Reading* (Chatto and Windus).

C. THE CONTEXT

It is bad for young people to see their efforts during ten years of education going to fill waste-paper baskets. All use of words in school should be given as much audience as possible:

1. Oral work should be between one pupil and another, with the class participating in the game.
2. Letters should have a real recipient in view, wherever possible, even if only one letter is posted. There are plenty of lonely people in the world to write to, after all.
3. Other ways of providing an audience are the form magazine, the school wall newspaper and the school magazine, or pupils may bring in difficult personal letters offered for the form to compete at answering.
4. A stage in dramatic work will come when oral spontaneous drama needs to be written down as dialogue so that it may be repeated—as drama which is no longer spontaneous.
5. With upper forms matters of public communication may be practised—writing up news from ticker-tape, the examination of film-scripts, and attempts at writing 'programmes', film-strip scripts, film-scripts, or plays.
6. Some methods of marking involve the class as audience and encourage critical thinking:
   (a) The teacher reads the essays or letters: marks out of 20 are read aloud and the children put their hands up at the mark they choose. A rough average is found by general impression of the number of hands.
   (b) With longer essays—a few, say five, can be chosen, read aloud, discussed and marked thus.
   (c) The teacher gets other members of class (upper streams) to mark each other's work, giving a general comment, indicating errors and awarding a mark. The teacher then marks both the essay and the pupil's marking. The teacher must make clear the *principles* of marking and draw names out of a hat. He reads the 5 best, in the order chosen by the class—and then reveals his own order of choice and reads the one he considers best.
   (d) The teacher may use the pupils' work for taking up grammatical and other points. 'X has failed here to get across what he wanted to say. Why?' He may then go on to show that when subject or verb is imperfect or missing, communication may break down.

CHAPTER 9

Marking, Encouragement, and Criteria

What are we doing when we 'mark' children's work? As investigations have shown, there can be little that could be called 'objective' about marking such work as composition—one person will put a piece of work at the top of his scale when another will put it at the bottom of his. And in practice we often give good marks for a poor piece of work because we know the child has tried and needs to be encouraged, while if his neighbour had turned it in we would have given him the minimum reward: every child carries his own scale, as it were, or a formula by which we modify the general abstract measuring rod.

Much of our marking, then, in English at any rate (and one suspects this is true of many other subjects where teachers assume that attainment can be objectively measured), does not indicate anything in the nature of tangible results. Analogies with the baking of jam tarts or the manufacture of brass nipples are misleading: the proof of an English lesson, or an English course throughout a school, is not in the number of α + marks, or G.C.E. 'O' level passes, but intangibly in the capacities for living of our pupils. It is possible in fact, more so than with jam tarts or brass nipples, to obtain complete success i.e. *no* failures in terms of living; but even this cannot be measured, and it bears no relation to whatever it is that is measured by the intelligence tests, or to the capacity to get sums right. This whole book is written with the assumption that all members of that three-quarters of the population which goes to the secondary modern school have needs as beings which English must supply to each equally: obviously it would be nonsense to say that a pupil was top of the form in being a human being, however great are our differences in sensibility and intelligence.

So, as far as our pupils are concerned, let us cease to strive to believe we can measure what we teach them, or that it is worth trying to measure it. Let us forget examinations for the moment.

Examinations are a sign of weakness: they keep the mill working in the absence of adequate aims. Significantly the president of the Incorporated Association of Headmasters recently said 'Working schoolmasters have always been sceptical about the benefit of freeing the syllabus from the *pressure* of external examinations.' Note his terms! If the outside world, through governors or parents, demands measurement, then let us measure by giving an honest account of the child's regular work in his school report. Of course we can measure the ability to read aloud and to spell fairly mechanically, and these, with measurements of other subjects such as arithmetic, will help us with 'setting'. But if we set mechanical English tests and mark them for examination purposes we are not really doing what we suppose we are doing—we are not measuring those qualities it is our duty to try to give. Our marking is primarily not a matter of measurement, real measurement, but for giving satisfaction, a complex for the work, and a a sense of security. Whatever any of us does, we need the satisfaction of accomplishment.

The teacher must, then, accept his role as being as important to the child emotionally, as my last paragraph implies. To deride or insult a child's work is to do his spirit, his being, an injury: and it is still done, in my experience. To avoid such evils, we must, above all, recognise what the child's work means to him.

Children needing the equivalent in school of mothers' praise, need to feel a function for their work—and this marking gives. Marking gives, too, a sense of security. Children's games are full of strict rules and taboos—tops played outside March and April may be 'smugged' or confiscated by others, for instance; in the game *Trades* those who must guess the meaning of a mime must not show their teeth, or they are punished; at parties we have forfeits. And we all know the self-imposed restriction of not stepping on the lines of the pavement. These rules make the child feel regulated: if he can keep these rules he can keep the strange ones imposed on him by inexplicable turns in the circumstances of life. But the keeping of these rules seems to reassure him that he can endure fears and troublings crowding in from his relationships with his parents, brothers and sisters.

Marking, Encouragement, and Criteria

So marking children's work is firstly a matter of giving them a feeling of their being approved of or disapproved of in relation to the satisfaction of doing a task. Secondly it provides at least the audience of one, and shows that both teacher and pupil feel this work is *worth doing.* Children sometimes press for exercises which have 'proper answers' and are measurable, and they like spelling tests for this reason. Such exercises provide, too, apparent answers to 'How am I getting on?', 'How do I stand among the others?' and so on. I needn't discuss here the effects of some children always being 'top' and others always being 'bottom'—obviously we should aim at giving each child the experience at some time of being the most important person in the room. Thirdly, a child who does not experience a code of values, of approval and disapproval, of the sense of his work being received and valued, will feel unhappy through insecurity—he will feel, perhaps, that no-one cares much whether he exists or not.

Marking, then, has a positive function—it is not merely a tedous grind such as stocktaking. If what I have said is true, then all children's work must be marked—that is, read by the teacher, and some indication given that he has taken in every word. The most important physical mark is that which shows that the teacher has responded to the content of what is written: both to its explicit meaning—and (more subtly) to *what it means to the child* implicitly.

But marking everything, to the extent of showing that it has been read, does not mean correcting every fault. Of course one must pounce now and then, correct a page in detail, and ask for it to be completely re-written correctly. But this should be done in rough books or loose-leaf books—the satisfaction to be aimed at is that of a child possessing a well-laid-out exercise book containing a good deal of his own writing, in which he continues to be interested enough to re-read it, and containing, too, a few helpful annotations on the content by his teacher. Here and there, perhaps, there could be an (S) for spelling error, (P) for punctuation error, or a question mark in the margin where the sense was not clear because a slip had been made. And every school should agree on a code of correction marks, including that great time-saving mark ⊙, meaning: 'At this point you have ended one sentence and begun another and you must indicate this by putting a full stop and capital letter to begin in the next sentence.' Another sign we may usefully borrow from the proof-reader is ⋀, indicating an omission. But to cover every page of every book with red or green ink will have a depressing and destructive effect, depreciating the value of the work—suggesting that the teacher regards it only as a means of looking for trouble and exerting his sense of superiority of *knowing*. It is depressing to look through children's marked books and see nothing anywhere but negative comments. This is a bad habit, an occupational disease of teachers. The work is 'a piece of him' to the child and the object of our inspection, as in the army, is to make for neatness and positive virtues, not to provide subjects for a punishment parade.

Let me quote a piece of work—by a child of eight, in fact—and discuss what might be a teacher's reaction. It is a story.

One day Oliver Owl flew across the sea and he said to himself what shall I do. Then he said I know I shall see if there are any mice in the sea isn't Oliver silly? Oliver was so sad when an old man said to him there are no mice in the sea I'm afraid. Oh dear he said I will have to fly back to England again Suddenly an idea came into his head I know he said I will fly to the isl of White so away he flew soon he came to the isl of White he flew round and round. Trying to find a mouse suddenly he saw something grey it was a mouse hurray Hurray said Oliver Owl he flew down and Picked the mouse up by his tail. The mouse made a horible noise shut up said oliver very cross indeed still the mouse made a noise it went on and on for hours when he had eaten it he went to find another he saw one but strait into a hole it dashed oliver waited to see what happened Suddenly he saw a bettle he ate that so still he was hungary then he thought I will see if ants are good to eat so he tasted one it was nice he ate more and more till at last he ate one that stung him and he did not eat anything else that day he flew home again he flew all through the night he got home just in time for when he got back it was six oclock in the morning then he caught a terible cold...

This continues for another eight pages and ends:

That night a wind blew strong. Meny trees were blow over but Mrs and Mr Owl were lucky that tree was thick it could not be blown down the wind tryed to but it could not do it after all that troble the tree was the fatest of all with beutefull green leves.

Let us ask first of all, What are the qualities of this; and then, What might we usefully say to the child about it? First then, it is fragmentary and episodic, as, perhaps, a young child's experience is —she moves from one thing to another, and the story wanders to whatever interests her at one particular moment. We cannot, obviously, expect her yet to make an organised whole of a story —neither should we expect this of stories developed orally round the class, or of invented drama, or mime, or free composition. Discuss the incompleteness, yes: but leave the movement towards completeness to the next effort: the writer should never be forced to re-mould his story into a frame which does not emerge with the story (moulding experience into the frame of a verse is something different). Here it might be pointed out that Oliver does not start from home, although he returns to it: might it not have been a good thing to say at the beginning that Oliver Owl lived in a tree in a certain place? But this is likely to appear pointless to a young child: in this particular story Oliver dies, 'but soon was alive again', worked for 8 years on a railway station, flies away (because someone said that he 'must be turned out that moment'), his skull is found and put in a museum for 'people to see they said to themselves gosh and golly and koo', and the story ends with another pair of owls and their family, Mr and Mrs Martin Owl.

To us the story may be inconsequential nonsense: but if we look at it closely we see that the child is drawing on literary experience ('Suddenly an idea came into his head', 'with beutefull green leves') to explore her own experience and say things which trouble her deeply. The whole story is about home—being away from home, returning to it ('just in time'), home being threatened (by the wind), about time and space, and about cruelty and death: all these belong to growing up, becoming aware of one's mortality, of time and age, and the perplexity of one's relationships with other people. The mouse which makes a 'horrible' noise may be a little sister, and Oliver Owl who says 'shut up' and eats it may be father: but they are also animals feeding on one another and dying, and Oliver's skull has a function like that of Yorick's, in this little story, followed as it is by the public's 'goshes' and 'koos', a comic accompaniment to the preoccupation with death.

That these preoccupations are triumphed over by the making of the story will appear in certain livelinesses of rhythm: here, of course, restraint is indicated—an order to re-write is an order to destroy the rhythm which is an essential part of the meaning. For this reason, here, the teacher would not fuss about the child's inability to write out direct speech properly, making a mental note to take a lesson on it later. Being a matter of punctuation it, may be done as drill: and at about 12 or 13 a child needs to learn it. Indeed, the teacher who knows his job is one who knows when a child needs to learn a particular skill like this. (And the corollary is that the larger the class the less able the teacher is to be a good teacher.) On the other hand a useful point ought to be made, taking up the interjection, 'isn't oliver silly'—this, as it is the writer addressing her audience about the character—who oughtn't to hear, really—should be in parentheses, surely? The sentences could be written out properly on the board, thus:

Then he said, 'I know—I shall see if there are any mice in the sea.' (Isn't Oliver silly?)

The writing is unpretentious and pleasantly free—as a child would speak. For this reason it outstrips the child's ability to use a full stop and a capital letter to indicate a new sentence. But here this would only matter where the absence of the full stop leaves the meaning vague. The child has *written* sentences—it is simply that she hasn't shown where they end and begin (*and we should distinguish this from the lack of ability to write a sentence*). For instance the sense demands 'flew round and round trying to find a mouse. Suddenly he saw something'—it goes better like that. Again sense demands 'it went on and on for hours. When he had eaten it'— here the new sentence ought to begin a new paragraph, as the mouse story is now ended. (But no-one should suggest putting in a sentence—'Oliver ate the mouse'—the very avoidance of dealing directly with this shows the incident is something the child shrinks from, and has, in a sense, conquered by passing it by...'When he had eaten the mouse'.) Then at 'got home just in time for', and 'but it could not do it after all', the reader might be confused unless we use a comma after 'time, and a full stop after 'do it'.

But these corrections should either be done with the class, as examples of how to make things plainer, or merely marked in the pupil's story—just a few of them. Laborious re-writing will have no useful effect, though obviously, if a fair copy of the best of a child's work is being put in a special book, all mistakes should be corrected. I would not correct the punctuation of speech in this story if written by a child under 12 and would not indicate all the missing full stops. She can *write*: I should know that she will one day take punctuation in her stride, and will draw it from her reading when the time comes, or she will ask me.

Spelling is a different matter: children learn to spell by reading, but mis-rememberings can be cured by drill and rote. From this story we could collect *Isle of Wight, horrible, straight, hungry, terrible, tried, trouble, fattest, many, beautiful* and *leaves* for the next spelling test, and ask the child to copy them out in a drill book or on paper from the board, or the teacher's notes in her book, ONCE. But had she spelt, say, more than ten words wrongly a teacher should make a judicious selection—otherwise to write more and more fluently only brings the penalty of laborious correction. Sometimes it will be enough for the teacher to write the word correctly and for the child to *look* at it: nothing is worse than seeing a child copying out a word ten or even twenty times which he has copied down wrongly from a good copy on the board, because he has not looked at it sufficiently well. Laborious correcting which is punishment-implicit defeats its intention. This is not to say that the really slovenly or sly mess is to be taken without a showdown.

The liveliness of the language in this child's story depends on a few departures from the norm. If such departures enliven, a sensible teacher will cherish them. 'a wind blew strong' is here much better than 'a wind blew strongly'; 'fattest' for the tree is Biblical. Nor should any exception be taken to such direct use of speech from everyday life as 'shut up'. (Obscenities of course, would only be put in by an unbalanced child to see how far he could go.) The end of this story has some of the qualities of the simple vernacular of the mediaeval sermon:

blowe the wynde never so blist, haild it never so harde, thrundre it never so oribliche, wel a stont stille, nothyng grevid nor disesid with them. But an this be a vair tre vul of fruit, bewtewus of bowes, love-lich al abowte and lusti of leves, the sowthrenwynd schaketh hym o the ton side, the northwnwynd blasteth hym on the tother; ye, he is so vor-puffid and so vorblowyn, that unnethe a may kepe his bowes hole to-gedder...but yit, thei it be so that a lest overwhile a bow or a tweye, yit for the most parte, and a be wel rotid, the rotis abide ever-mor stedvastliche in the grownde but yif the wynde be the greter.

G. R. Owst, *Literature and Pulpit in Mediaeval Life.*

And it would seem to me that such simplicity and directness and honesty should always be the aim (of course they are more easily found at the earlier years)—and credit given for those marks in the rhythm and use of words which show the child is caught up in, interested in, his writing. 'What to look for' is something one can never tell anyone—the ability to encourage plainness and honesty, and to discourage insincerity, will depend upon the teacher's own character and taste, and on his or her training. But here are some examples:

A Walk in the Country in Spring

One fine Saturday morning, I left behind the busy thoroughfare of the City, and proceeded on a walk in the country.

I soon arrived among sunflecked meadows, and on scaling a stile, was very surprised on being confronted by my friend. We at once united, and made our way past a babbling brook towards a quaint little village. One garden was enriched by the lovely aroma of flowers. After a tour of the village, we climbed a steep hill, and visited an ivy-clad church, set in its own little Garden of Gethsemane. Here we partook of a scanty lunch and after a while, we descended the hill. The whispering trees which environed us seemed to be sending out mes-sages, and the birds seemed to (be) chirping replies. On inquiring the time we found it was four o'clock, so we decided to return home, as it would take us more than one hour.

We were delayed for some time, though, and our last glimpse of the countryside was the trees silhouetted against the skyline, with the rosy hues of sunset departing in the solemn west—a perfect picture of the work of the Creator.

Marking, Encouragement, and Criteria

To this the reader's reaction is, 'this is insincere': but we must take care to distinguish between what we recognise in the piece of work, and *what we say to the child*. With the Primary School child, such as the author of Oliver Owl above, it will be enough to say, 'I like your story very much' (a much more encouraging thing to say than merely 'Good' or—the faint, damning—'Quite good'). But with our pupils we need to be more careful— sophistication is setting in, and the child needs to go through stages which we, as mature adults, have behind us. One of these stages is the bizarre or flowery use of language: significantly our greatest poet moves from the early floweriness of 'the morn in russet mantle clad' to the simplicity of 'the blanket of the dark' in his later works.

In this example we notice some words which might belong to a passing taste for the extravagant—'sunflecked', for instance. But some words are more literary—'enriched by'. Others are down-right cliché: 'babbling brook', 'quaint little village'. More show the portentous choice of a long awkward word for a simple one— 'proceeded' for 'went', 'scaling' for 'getting over' or 'climbing'. And other phrases are borrowed from the calculated exploitation of religious feelings by hack writers—'its own little Garden of Gethsemane', 'the work of the Creator'. The latter might seem to us nauseous in their insincerity: while we must allow for powerful devotional feelings in a child, and for the appearance of strong immature feelings, we should hope that unaffected devotion would almost certainly not be expressed in such conventional borrowed terms.

But it would be brutal to express these reactions outright to a child (unless the passage was obviously written with his tongue in his cheek by, say, a tough fifteen-year-old boy). Condemnation should be reserved for the teacher who taught the child to write like that: the child's own impulse may have been the *sincere* desire to please the teacher. And to this desire he may have sacrificed his own interests—for, in fact, the worst thing about the passage is the almost complete absence of any originality of phrase or rhythm to show that the child was 'caught up', or even really interested in what he was writing about—the progress of the account is dull in the extreme.

The first thing one could say to the child (how much one says depends upon what one knows of his resilience) is that he uses long words when short ones would do, just because they are longer. But what do we say of those phrases which belong to 'fine writing'—and come from a habit mechanically inculcated by bad teaching: 'enriched by the lovely aroma of flowers' and so on? One answer is probably, with a neutral expression, to ask for class criticism of the passage, which is read out by the writer. For such a live complex for the work will reveal the mechanical quality of the writing: 'we at once united'. The irony of his classmates will be more savage than that of the teacher. The teacher can help undo the harm caused by his fine-writing colleague by defending the writer against ridicule: 'silhouetted', though cliché, is not a word to be despised—the writer has some talent. 'Departing in the solemn west', well, apart from the pomposity of it, it is not very precise. Other imprecisions are 'more than one hour' (why not merely 'an hour'?) How can one be 'surprised at' being 'confronted...*on*...scaling a stile'—a stile gives one a vantage point from which it is very difficult to be surprised or confronted: wasn't it perhaps the other way about? Did the brook really babble? Do brooks babble in this part of the world? Why do they? The garden 'enriched by an aroma of flowers'—did it have flowers in it itself? The writer doesn't say so: it might have been a vegetable garden enriched by the aroma of the one next door. The Garden of Gethsemane was where Jesus was 'exceeding sorrowful, even unto death' and prayed 'O my Father...let this cup pass from me'—is that the feeling the writer wished to convey, of suffering and the wish to be released from the agony of life? Is the picture of the work of the Creator meant to be a picture of 'hues ...departing in the solemn west'—of a disappearing sad illusion? Is that what is meant?

Without grosser ridicule the writer could come to see that, apart from the insincerity, this piece of writing is *imprecise* in both description of events and in the evocation of feeling. That is primarily why it is so bad. The points are best made here, obviously, not so much by marking as by discussion in class, and comparison with examples. For instance the teacher could urge simplicity, and read simple and moving passages: 'Jesus wept' is one of the most moving sentences in English; Bunyan's account of Christiana being shown the room, the muck-rake and the robin is utterly simple and yet profound. The teacher should have at hand his touchstones—and the Authorised Version and Bunyan are among the best.

Of course such a thorough examination of a piece of work is often impossible with classes of thirty or forty children: and we must recognise that sound education is really impossible with classes over twenty: what we do is always makeshift and below standard, inevitably. But if class time is not available the teacher could (*a*) rewrite part of the passage in simple English; or (*b*) write, simply, 'You can use long words, often well, but I don't find this interesting because it isn't about you. How do you 'unite' with a friend—wouldn't you say 'joined up' or 'went off together'? Take all the phrases I have underlined and re-write them as you would say them in telling one of your class mates about this walk'; or (*c*) write, when a child has resilience: 'This is sloppy: it's like Patience Strong. I don't think you really feel like this about the countryside. Read *Bevis* by Richard Jefferies, or some of it: or Edward Thomas' poem *Nettles*. Write simply, as you speak—choose the short word rather than the long, the plain word rather than the fancy'; or (*d*) write, 'Jackson, this is drip. See me.' Such personal comments are more valuable than any striving after scales or grades: except that we must satisfy that 'how am I doing?' competitive urge of the child. But let's not pretend, with those who believe in Education as a subject, that children or their attainment in development of powers of being can be measured.

But, of course, the passage invites the condemnation of aims and methods rather than of a child. We cannot, obviously, always keep to the rule that 'to write without purpose or feeling is degrading'—school conditions in a highly organised society are bound to be artificial. But we can give the child as much as we can, by way of feeling that he has an audience—the wall-magazine, the class anthology, marking by his neighbour, reading his story to the class, the one-man audience of a teacher who will sometimes 'publish' a piece of work by reading it aloud or having it put in a magazine or on a notice board. These contexts can be a guarantee of sincerity (the *school* magazine often has the opposite effect of stimulating precociousness): and the development of 'free writing' and imaginative composition to literary models should give writing a meaning, in that it is the largely unconscious symbolisation of the inward experience of a child.

Thus mere descriptive writing has value as it becomes the use of 'objective correlatives' to put in order something in the soul. This may sound outlandish—the phrase in quotation marks is Mr Eliot's—but what it means is that different people looking at the same cornstack will see the cornstack in the light of the associations it arouses in their fantasy. These would include every reaction from the farmer's (how much corn and straw?) and the labourer's (how much work?), to the town motorist's (a shelter for a meal or a place to relieve himself), the tramp's (a place to sleep), the lovers' (a place to lie together), or the child's (a place to jump and slide). And there are many complex associations in each of us with cornstacks—the writer has slept in one, nearly fallen off the roof of one, helped to make and unmake one, watched the cutting of one, helped to test one for heat, seen one burn, another fall because it was ill-made, and so forth. And so, if we paint a picture of a cornstack, or describe one, we select those aspects of it which go with our inward feelings about cornstacks—and more: many of these will be unconscious, springing from infant associations, or literary ones (e.g., 'Borne on the bier with white and bristly beard'). Cornstacks may look to us like heads of hair, or loaves of bread, or our mother's pies; some deeper symbolism from unconscious phantasy will be there, unrecognisable by us.

Now we often hear of photographic or descriptive writing, or of 'reportage'. But writing by human beings can never be really photographic or merely descriptive: we are not cameras. The shadows and light of a cornstack will go through a lens and mark a piece of flat paper with an imprint which we conventionally accept as meaning 'cornstack'. By altering the light and shadow, or by putting someone on the stack we can alter the photograph to mean 'old cornstack' or 'rich cornstack' or 'farmer's cornstack' or 'child's cornstack': but the meaning will always be general (as titles to pictures in a Photograph Exhibition will show). But if a painter paints a cornstack the picture he produces will not come from his retina, but through the whole complexity of inner symbolism and the act of choosing, turning into conventional patterns by brushstrokes, which the retina image starts off. He cannot paint a cornstack without being affected by unconscious and conscious phantasy as well as knowledge about cornstacks—and life—and by his urge to use the cornstack as an 'objective correlative' for aspects of his experience, his being, which he is always trying to put in order. He paints not to give the representation of a cornstack, but to develop an inner structure and content of being, from which to deal with the world as real.

So, if he is a good painter, for great skill is required in the technique of art, his picture will have a meaning which is *precise*—it will not be general, and we will not be able to put it in words—the picture is the picture, and it is its own meaning.

The same applies to 'descriptive writing': to ask a child merely to describe a scene is to some extent a forced exercise in writing without inner purpose, unless it is simply an exercise in writing for geographical purposes. And we must be clear, I think, between these different aims: (*a*) to enable a child to look at things and record them, (*b*) to enable a child to select things seen relevant to a practical subject (for instance, geography); and (*c*) to enable a child to use things seen as a means of developing its grasp on experience with all that is involved subjectively.

This is a preamble to the discussion of some excerpts from an exercise in descriptive writing. A teacher who writes about a scene in this way as an example to his pupils may perhaps be confusing the above categories:

We are at a height of more than five hundred feet above sea level and we have an unimpeded view of a vast stretch of country...

(geographical)

Woods march up gently swelling hills, their trees blushing brown with October glory...

Now the clouds are greater, and it is only the light that travels up the hill: a huge spotlight picks out the lonely farm, and passes on leaving it almost in darkness. I feel cold as the colours die. Come this way, sweet spotlight, marching like an army between the hills!

(poetic)

A train, in toy-like fussiness, trundles past the woods, waving a white pennant... ('philosophical')

Work by pupils will carry the confusion further: they will look not at what interests them but at what they feel should interest them. Some will make the kind of observations demanded of them by (*a*) and (*b*) well:

We are at what I should say was the highest part round here... Between us and the houses there are fields which at one time contained wheat or barley... A little way behind the car is a big water tower... The fields are divided by small hedges about one foot high...

Others will choose what is meaningful to them:

All the grass bends to one side, the branches lean over and creak, and the leaves rattle... on the horizon I can see church spires sticking up all over the countryside... A flock of birds rise up, and drop again like stones... Up in the sky clusters of birds are flying, trying to fight the wind... The dark clouds come together like a black mass of soot in the sky, blocking the sun up so that it won't shine on the fields again.

All these seem to me to be excellent writing—simple, plain, sincere. But the overstrain in the teacher's own writing (it is a very splendid thing, of course, for a teacher to do the exercise with his pupils, and to show how he recognises its difficulty) produces in the pupil's work some strainings after effect which seem insincere: this is criticism, I think, of a method again—it would seem as though the children have been encouraged to look at this or that, to hunt out the beautiful and 'philosophy'-provoking, rather than left to themselves. This produces some bored reactions:

I am looking down on a beautiful piece of scenery... there is a very lovely view...

The colour of the fields is making the view more interesting... A single haystack is beside the road and it looks like a house. I can see quite a distance away.

And there are overstrainings to please teacher, some seeming to come from direct suggestion, which must surely be avoided:

The hedges are bowing their heads in the wind...a train goes puffing merrily. I can hear some larks singing for all they're worth...giant shadows cross the earth...God couldn't have made the world more beautiful.

A lonely tree is happily swinging from side to side. There is a forest of brown trees in the sunlight...the hedges on the side of the road are waving just like a drunken man.

This latter phrase shows how difficult it is to decide on whether a phrase is original, literary, or suggested by the teacher: and indeed, how difficult it is to know what to look for, and how to mark.

What we must recognise is that our task is to guide the child's own development of his powers: that we shall only be able to mark and judge correctly if we know what our aims are, and what it is we are doing in marking and judging: and that more reading of the best possible literature is the best and most positive way of eliminating mistakes, dishonesty and inarticulateness.

Here, finally, are two pairs of examples of children's writing: in each case the first seems to me the result of bad teaching—competent but forced by the wrong sort of 'marking' into a mould not the child's but that of some inadequate notion of what education should produce. The second in each case seems to me the more essentially articulate, though the children who wrote each of these were probably less gifted than the authors of the two (*a*) passages. I would welcome the passages (*b*), and rejoice with the children over them. Spelling, punctuation, grammar I know could be worked at later—not to worry—the thing I sought was already there—delight in the word and its power. It is the writers of the passages (*a*) who seem to me disabled, and who will need me to help undo the work bad teaching has done to hamper their sincerity. Examples I were discussed by Mr W. Worthy in *The Use of English* Volume 4 No. 1 and are reproduced with his permission. Both are by children of ten. Examples II were discussed in an editorial of *The Use of English* Volume 3 No. 1 and are reproduced by permission of the Editor. (*a*) is a grammar school child, (*b*) a child of nine.

Other examples may be found on the following *Use of English*

Reading Sheets, obtainable from Messrs Chatto and Windus; and they might be used, with care, in discussions with children on what is the best way to write: VB, XIVB, XVB, XVIB, XVIIB. The book *Young Writers, Young Readers*, edited by Boris Ford, contains many examples of good children's writing.

I

(a) *A Visit to the Zoo*

On my return from school on Wednesday afternoon, my father invited me to accompany him on a visit to the Zoological Gardens. I answered in the affirmative, and we at once boarded a tramcar bound for the city. Here we caught the omnibus, and soon arrived at our destination.

We had heard such a lot of talk about the new polar bear pit, we decided to visit this modern structure first of all. After a good discussion on this piece of workmanship, we made our way to the Monkey Temple. Here we had a gay half-hour watching the peculiar antics of the monkeys, who seemed almost human in some respects. We then partook of a frugal tea, and continued our tour by a visit to the noisy parrot house. This was very interesting despite the deafening shrieks of the brightly coloured birds. Next came the most exciting time of our excursion—a call at the Ape House. Alfred, an ape, and Adam, a baby chimpanzee, were the chief entertainers. On looking at the clock we saw that it was twenty minutes past seven, so we concluded our journey by viewing the humming birds.

We soon arrived back at our abode, and I retired to bed, feeling that I had gleaned much knowledge during the evening.

(b) *What I Hope To Do when I leave School*

When I leave school I am going to be a comosole traveler, I would go to all sorts of shops and see what goods they want. I would go to the sweet shops espeshly. Why I would like to be a comosole traveler is because you get good money and on Sunday you can keep the car and go out to the seaside free. I have a long time to go before I leave school yet because I am only ten. My mother wants me to be a comosole traveler as well. At first my mother wanted me to be a macanicle engineer. She said you can pay up for a car weekly the boss would take it out of your wages but I would rather get a car free. If I would get the sack which I most probably will I would like to be a coal miner and dig coal from the pit. Theres one thing I would not like to happen to me or eney miner in the mine is the coal to fall in. What my mother thinks of it is too dangerous but I like using my muscles of caurse you have to have only a vest and trouses on. You get good mony on it because it is a dangrous job of course.

II

(*a*)

A fleecy cloud, a right ploughed field, the chatter of birds— they are still with us. We have been moved by the beauty of spinning, dancing toes, we have touched St. Paul's with reverence, and laughed at the audacity of the wind. Perhaps we have added to this loveliness some of our own. We have seen the silver planes swimming through the air with the grace of ageless birds, and bridges swaying pendulum-like over Lilliputian rivers. We have cried at the beauty of flowers, glowing red, violet, rust and palest blue up the aisle of a roofless church. We are not ashamed of wondering.

(*b*)

Once I went on a visit to a dairy farm. I saw the cows being milked, they were milked by machine. There was a bucket under their tummies. Then the farmer took it to another machine to be cleaned. Then it had to be put into big milk churns. The cow has to be milked twice a day. It is useful when it is dead as well. We get beef from it and its skin is used for leather, and its horns are used for knife handles. It feeds on grass, it has four stomachs. He gets a lot down him, I will tell you why he does it. Because a long time ago, while animals came and ate him up, that's why he still does it. He has still got a habit of that. The food goes down one stomach that is called a paunch. Then when he gets into his barn he brings up a little at a time. He does not bring it up in a great pile. After he has had a lot to eat, he has to be milked. After, as I told you, it is cleaned and brought to the market place and sold to the dairy shops and some is delivered by milk-men and comes to houses. My mother has one pint a day. A good cow gives 600 gallons a year.

Other passages for discussion along these lines may be found in *Criticism in Practice*, edited by Marie Peel (Chatto and Windus, 1964), e.g. on p. 112 ff. I have also included many such passages in my 'sampler' for student teachers and for in-service courses, *Children's Writing* (Cambridge, 1967).

Reading

Reading in the secondary modern school is an uncertain and perplexing subject. A great deal of English in the secondary modern school is taken up with a comparatively recent and special literary form—the novel. At times the lack of usefulness of this preoccupation seems frighteningly evident. After learning to grasp the sense of words and sentences from a series of dull exercises children are dragged through *Lorna Doone* (everyone supposed to read at the same pace, though their reading ages range from 8 to 18), and, having thus cut their eye-teeth, they pass out into adult life, where they read the *Daily Mirror* and *Reveille* perhaps exclusively. While we are obliged to teach reading, 'reading' is divided from 'literature' in the syllabus (it is even in Mr A. E. Smith's most useful book on *English in the Secondary Modern School*). Reading is a required habit, and certain books are given the dreary title 'reader', with its echo of 'feeder'. Now that the modern school begins to emerge as a kind of school *sui generis*, the publishers' lists fill with 'readers' for them. These are often a mixture of novels with a 'second-class' air, by journalists rather than creative writers, and out-of-date 'classics' which belong to the Victorian middle-class nursery. What are we doing under the heading 'reading'?

We must in an industrial age accept a literate population: but while we are obliged to create literacy, we are all too aware of the abuses of it, and the exploitation of it. We know our children become prey, at an early age, to the distractions of the comic paper, the lewdness of the week-end paper, the more brutal or unreal paper-backs and cheap novels. We fear their susceptibility to the blandishments of the advertiser, and the political or religious charlatan. Yet we feel that reading in this age of 'gape and gloat, clatter and buzz' (as Sir Winston Churchill once called it) has a value in itself as an important part of the life of a 'civilised' being.

Reading

In their endeavours to protect children against the worst habits
the schools tend to counter the weak language habits of children
either by boring them with 'classics' and 'educational novels'
about careers, South America, Hereward the Wake, and so
on: or, when this fails, by non-fiction with an educational slant
(the sea, Antarctica) written by pedestrian or hack writers. We
give them either a watered-down selection from the library of a
learned person of the nineteenth century, or non-fictional matter
which gives them, instead of symbolic material for work on inner
problems of identity and relationship, mere information about the
outside world.

The publishers' modern school catalogues suggest that 'joy'
and 'fun and adventure', 'joyous hours', are the aims of educating.
And books on English in school often talk about 'beauty'. Yet in
the end both give anything but such an impression—before long
one is confronted with a list of the dreariest books under an
'educational' heading.

The schools seem to uphold a long-standing tradition that the
end of learning, where words are concerned, is the capacity to
read very difficult and long books, preferably about the past, or
the Constitution, or morality, or theology. If a novel is read, it
must be something strait-laced and not, if possible, a book of
'amusement'. There is a half-hearted recognition that a certain
amount of 'fun' is necessary to train the basic skill of reading,
hence the awful titles like 'Happy Readers'. But, judging from the
dozens of publishers' catalogues I have looked through in writing
this chapter, most schools are obsessed with the practical value of
reading to the extent of linking it as much as possible to possible
careers and a utilitarian 'sense of purpose'—encouragement to
invent steam-engines and spinning jennies and live a life like that
of George Stephenson. This is all educational and *you are not supposed to enjoy it*; outside school the child reads *Eagle*, the teacher
happily relaxes with *The Bloody Spanner Mystery*, and in between the
two worlds of the English language lies the limbo of the library,
where Dickens and Mark Twain are ignored by both teacher and
pupil if they have not been ignored by the librarian. When the
library is open the teacher will take out the latest book to be

described as 'brilliantly dirty' by his weekly; the child Enid Blyton or Fleming. Both find, perhaps, a meeting place in the work of the latter, indeed: and both secretly despise the conservative snobbery which forces them to grapple with 'the classics'. Ask almost any child from a secondary modern school what books they read at school and the same names will be produced: *Lorna Doone*, *Jane Eyre*, *Ivanhoe*, spoken of in the same dull, unenthusiastic voice.

The schools often seem to have a blind faith in the habit of reading for the sake of reading. Certainly there seems to be some magical faith in the virtues of what are called 'the classics' or 'children's classics', even when they are reduced to the level of the comic strip and made into 'illustrated classics'; or even when they are cut to such an extent as to destroy much of the local quality of the writing. Douglas Brown, examining some abridged editions in an article in *The Use of English* (Vol. 8, No. 4) found, for instance, an edition of *Wuthering Heights* in which the following changes were made in those very passages which are the finest moments of the work and clinch its whole meaning: Cathy is speaking:

'If all else perished and *he* remained, I should still continue to be; and if all else remained, and *he* were annihilated, the universe would turn to a mighty stranger: I should not seem a part of it.'

The reader may care to read that over aloud, and then try this as it appears in the abridged edition:

'If all else perished, and *he* remained, I should still continue to be; and if all else remained, and he were annihilated, I should not seem a part of the universe.'

In the preface to this edition (*The Sheldon Library*, *Clarendon Press*) the publishers say, 'We have not altered the author's words'! They leave out altogether Cathy's great sentences:

'I cannot express it; but surely you and everybody have a notion that there is, or should be an existence of yours beyond you. What were the use of my creation if I were entirely contained here?'

And, as Douglas Brown says, the story is virtually reduced to the *Woman and Home* level. Why not, then, read *Woman and Home*?

Without the triumphant rhythm, the careful movement of Emily Brontë's qualifying antitheses and phrases, the deeply felt meaning in the words, what is *Wuthering Heights*? The answer, perhaps, is in the phrases from the advertisement copy to *Famous Authors Illustrated*, published at first in America, 'quote the famous stories

From an 'illustrated classic' first published in America. Lady Macbeth's words may be compared with the original text· a 'classic' of literature lives, surely, only in its words?

and impress your friends'—a child must leave school knowing the words 'Dickens', '*Wuthering Heights*', 'Milton', so that if he is asked he may appear to have *heard* of 'the classics' at least. And heartening as it is to read in the W. H. Smith and George Harrap survey of children's reading that John Buchan (2·53%) and Charles Dickens (2·43%) are among the first twelve favourite authors of grammar and public school boys, one still has to consider whether they got there because the questionnaire itself suggested 'prestige' names. What standards may these be said to represent, in any case, among the other authors?

Here are the figures:

Favourite Author	Public & Grammar School Boys	Modern School Boys	Public & Grammar School Girls	Modern School Girls
	percentage which says this is their favourite author:			
W. E. Johns	8·63	10·00	—	—
A. Conan Doyle	4·10	—	—	—
Paul Brickhill	3·30	3·70	—	—
Agatha Christie	2·53	—	4·63	5·00
John Buchan	2·53	1·60	2·70	—
Charles Dickens	2·43	4·80	4·33	4·80
C. S. Forester	2·23	—	—	—
Percy Westerman	1·86	2·00	—	—
Arthur Ransome	1·80	—	—	2·30
Nevil Shute	1·53	—	—	2·30
Leslie Charteris	1·46	—	—	—
P. G. Wodehouse	1·16	—	—	—
Enid Blyton	—	8·40	11·00	15·90
R. L. Stevenson	—	4·10	—	—
Richmal Crompton	—	2·60	—	—
H. Rider Haggard	—	1·40	—	—
Eric Leyland	—	1·30	—	—
Nicholas Monsarrat	—	1·00	—	—
Mark Twain	—	1·00	—	—
Charlotte Brontë	—	—	3·76	3·70
Louisa M. Alcott	—	—	2·70	4·40
Helen D. Boyston	—	—	2·56	2·80
Lorna Hill	—	—	2·33	—
Angela Brazil	—	—	1·60	—
Mazo de la Roche	—	—	1·26	1·10
Monica Dickens	—	—	—	2·40
Noel Streatfeild	—	—	—	2·10
Malcolm Saville	—	—	—	1·60
Jane Austen	—	—	—	1·10

The whole survey is worth examination, to show the state of reading, even at its best. One point of interest is that apart, from great weaknesses for W. E. Johns and Enid Blyton, the reading habits of modern school children include on the whole some better material than those of the grammar and public schools—it is modern school children who mention Jane Austen and Mark Twain, and give Dickens such a high rating. The reason becomes clearer if we examine the other figures: it is a class difference. The middle class, which dominates the public and grammar schools, has been literate for some time, and, as George Orwell might have said, has been more half-educated than the others; it has its own brand of middle-class rubbish which is read when the exams on 'the classics' are over:—Agatha Christie, Forester, Nevil Shute, Charteris, P. G. Wodehouse. The working class person tends, so far, either to read rubbish (at the *Lady Don't Turn Over* level) or, looking for what someone (talking of his schooling in a village) called 'the thick books', to expect 'good solid stuff'. Thus the middle-class child, if he comes from a home that reads, will tend to read middlebrow fiction, which may obstruct his response to good novels. The child outside the traditional middle-class influence quite rightly regards much middle-brow reading as soft stuff; significantly, Wodehouse, Lorna Hill, Angela Brazil don't appear among modern school children's first twelve choices, and there are other differences in the table which would seem to confirm this. The modern school child, as yet, is not catered for by the pretentious catchpennies, only the mass ones: his literacy is less developed and he can thus go to Mark Twain or R. L. Stevenson with less prejudice, unless caught by the drug of Johns or Blyton. But their secondary modern school is to blame for the girls mentioning Charlotte rather than Emily Brontë.

Another obvious deduction from the figures given above is that it is the home which influences the grammar and public school child (they read the books father and mother read or suggest, or those they inherit from older schoolmates); whereas it is obviously the *school* which makes the reading habits of modern school children. They find some of the authors 'by themselves', maybe, —but the presence of Jane Austen, Charlotte Brontë, Louisa M.

Alcott, Mark Twain, Rider Haggard, Stevenson, Dickens, Buchan and probably Arthur Ransome shows the influence of the schools. Why, then, should Nicholas Monsarrat and Percy Westerman appear where they do, unless also by the influence of the schools?

We are often urged to keep our feet on the ground. Indeed I was urged to do so by a correspondent in *The Journal of Education* once, after I had urged that the great novels of the English language ought to be put in a new country branch library *first*, and had complained that for the library at the Village College where I worked the authorities had bought yards of rubbish to fill the fiction shelves (at least half a yard of Dornford Yates, for instance), thus imposing a second-rate standard taste on an area which had previously had nothing much, and could, at least, have been spared being converted to middlebrow authors at the expense of better ones. The exchange is perhaps worth quoting. Mr Michael Argles wrote:

...I happen to have worked with some of those who equipped the branch library with 'yards of second-rate novels'. Curiously enough, one or two of them are quite cultured, even by Mr Holbrook's standards: one has, to my certain knowledge, read E. M. Forster; and another even confesses to a sneaking regard for the novels of Ivy Compton Burnett. While I was with them they bought several books by George Eliot; and they were even considering getting one or two by D. H. Lawrence. However, despite this aura of probably spurious culture they do not believe that they would be satisfying a legitimate public demand if they equipped every village branch library in Cambridgeshire with yards and yards of Mr Holbrook's eighty Great English Novels, much as they might like to on purely selfish cultural grounds. Perhaps they have learnt to keep their feet on the ground in the time which Mr Holbrook apparently devotes to intellectual snobbery.

Here is the text of my reply:

When I first looked through the fiction of the new branch library which Mr Argles's colleagues helped to provide for our village college, I found no works by Arnold Bennett, Emily Brontë, Bunyan, Samuel Butler, Fenimore Cooper, Defoe, Dostoevsky, Forster, Hardy, W. H. Hudson, Henry James, Richard Jefferies, James Joyce, Thomas Mann, Melville, Peacock, T. F. Powys, Mark Rutherford, Smollett, Stendhal, Sterne, Tolstoy, Mark Twain or Virginia Woolf. *Pride and*

Prejudice, *Emma* and *Northanger Abbey* were lacking from Jane Austen's works, and anyone who decided to read *The Secret Agent*, or *Oliver Twist*, or *Washington Square*, or *A Passage to India*, or *Moby Dick* after the recent film and broadcast versions, could not have found them at Bassingbourn. The classics are obtainable cheaply enough: I recently bought for the library the whole of George Eliot second-hand for a pound. Yet there were yards, even complete sets, of such writers as Dornford Yates, Angela Thirkell and Nigel Balchin, among which, I found on cursory inspection recently, are volumes which have not been taken out in two years. So why give them priority?

Any library worthy of the name should contain, *first*, irrespective of quantitative considerations about how often they will be read, good editions of the writings of those minds to which we need to submit ourselves in order to develop adequate attitudes to life and an adequate ethic. The presence of such novels on the shelves implies that standards do exist. Most of the public money spent on fiction for our library was spent on books which can only limit people's abilities to think and feel: on ephemeral and fundamentally immoral books. Yet the children's and the non-fiction sections were admirable for a small library.

I don't know what kind of ground Mr Argles keeps his feet on, but I believe that my adult students deserve the best; their experience of life and their moral awareness are more often than not superior to that of the 'educated' person such as myself. It is when the 'intellectual' fails to put the best before his students (though no doubt retaining it for himself) that he betrays his training and reveals his fundamental snobbery.

The attitude of the public librarian, obviously, differs considerably from that of the teacher: both struggle in the abeyance of standards, when there is little agreement about the function of reading.

So the same Education Authority pays both for the yards of popular fiction, and for dozens of teachers who are attempting to convert children to 'the classics', while those who concern themselves with the relationship between literature and life, and Matthew Arnold's pronouncement that 'the quality of a man's life during each day depends largely on what he reads during it,' may be regarded by both as intellectual snobs. Meanwhile the meetings of governing bodies and library committees ludicrously applaud the reading of non-fiction (including poor biography) as against that of fiction!

So one approaches the problem of reading, its aims and methods, with the greatest misgiving: for over this subject we are in the thick of the conflict and uncertainty of present-day values. Yet we must keep a clear head—no-one else is trying to do so—and try to decide, as carefully as we can, what it is that we are, or should be, doing.

Except for the more studious minority, people, particularly those inheriting the traditions of both the industrial and rural working-class, do not base their culture on the written word: as we know in schools, they prefer always *not* to write a letter, and often prefer not to receive one. If our children have a great deal of lively oral training in conversation and drama, and if they are singing, saying, reading aloud and hearing poetry and songs, then we may feel we have begun our task adequately. Of course reading books is a great joy, and an activity without which civilisation would be impossible: but many people would profit from reading less, and a third of the books in public libraries could be burned without anyone being deprived of anything except an anodyne. The careful study of a long book such as *Moby Dick* or *The Decline and Fall of the Roman Empire* requires special kinds of stamina and ability: only a minority can read a long work with profit, and the G.C.E. pretence that such works are read widely by children is a deception, while training for an examination itself is largely one in taking short cuts. (Of course, I suppose, it might be argued that without the exam nobody would read anything 'hard' at all.) The effort of teaching children to respond to one good poem, or one good short play, or to make up stories or dialogue of their own is of much more value than effort spent on getting them to read such a book as *Guy Mannering*, which is dull; or an illustrated classic, which is worthless; or a 'true' escape story, which is probably superficial in its treatment of character (and has, as T. R. Barnes once pointed out, that 'air of unreality' of some 'true' war stories.) The reading habit is not worth having at any price, and, rather than feel bound misguidedly to labour through dull 'classics', we should feel bound to give our children oral fluency and articulateness above all. We can, after all, read them good poetry and prose, to make them responsive. It should not be our concern merely to raise bookworms who will later bore only through pulp.

Nonetheless we must teach children to read, and assuming that they are being well trained in speech, oral composition and drama, we want them to read a good deal if possible, in order to develop their powers of being articulate in speech and writing; powers of vocabulary, sentence structure, spelling and all such skills. But obviously to this end we must not divide 'reading' from 'literature'—the content of what we read is inseparable from its effect on 'the whole man': if literature is good writing, then it is good reading, too: poor matter for 'reading' and literature for 'Eng. Lit.' will only produce bad writing and bad reading habits. If we teach reading by using dull works or rubbish we may be malforming a child's taste for the word. Even in teaching the mechanics of reading we are, willy-nilly, making it more possible, or less possible, for the child to develop powers of sensibility. To give a child boring readers or boring text-book passages may cramp his capacity to symbolise and frustrate his relish for words. Enid Blyton and 'Biggles', on the other hand, provide the effortless distractions of a lazy daydream: life is not like that, and in suggesting it is they are disabling—it is not our function to disable children for life, and we should have nothing to do with such fiction, unless we are to demonstrate, as kindly as we can, its weaknesses.

Reading a story book has the advantage, above all, of giving us the experience of sharing an experience which we can talk a good deal about. Of course, drama and poetry provide the same, but the kind of short poetic drama and short poem we tend to use do not give quite as much scope for discussion of a work of art in relation to life, at the child's level. We can discuss the meaning of, say, the words 'rocks melt' in *The Turtle Dove*, or of God's request to Abraham in *Abraham and Isaac*. But the peculiar value of the novel—the reason it came into being, indeed— is that it deals at length and in complexity with manners, morals, activities of human beings in different conditions and stages of life. Thus, while a Chinese poem by Po Chu-I may give a child the experience of being an old man, in imagination; while in a spontaneous drama he may become an escaped negro in imagination; if he has read *Huckleberry Finn* with his classmates, he will be able to discuss events that happen in the book—murder, deceit, sheltering a negro, a feud, punishment, the river, steam-boats, different ways of living, the duties of parent to child, God and morality; and he will be really discussing with his fellows the nature of civilisation itself, in a way controlled by his imaginative experience. But we must remember that a novel is of value *because it is an imaginative work*—a work of symbolism, not a treatise.

Whatever librarians or committees say, we must accept that in dealing imaginatively with aspects of civilisation the novel is a pre-eminent form among long books; and that some novels will be better than others—as some minds are more subtle and finer than others. Some novels, indeed, will have the effect on us of misleading us, of giving us false impressions of what human beings are like, even of undermining our sense of identity, either because the novelist is unable to be honest, or is lacking in common humanity, or is day-dreaming, or merely finds that bad writing pays. The novel is much more dangerous than 'non-fiction', but the best novel has the power to change our whole beings, to refine our feeling and understanding, to develop our hold on life.

Perhaps at this point, then, we may briefly state our maximum aims in the teaching of reading, and then, in the light of what has been said, consider the content of the work. At the centre of what I have been saying is the problem of quality—which books to choose. The maximum aims then should be:

1. To teach every child to read aloud from a book, using the best possible material, and training him to understand what he is reading above all. (This will overlap, of course, with work in poetry and drama.)
2. To teach every child to read silently to himself. (Novels, poetry and drama included.)
3. To read aloud to our classes a number of short stories, poems or extracts from a longer work (e.g. *Pickwick Papers*), setting a standard of reading aloud so that children whose speed of reading seldom keeps pace with their appetite for the 'story' may respond to a few complete prose works read well, and heard complete, every year.
4. To accustom children to seeking pleasure from books, to respect

books, to be interested in the use and care of books, and to go on after school life wanting to possess and read books.

5. To train children to use a library, know how to find a book using the common classification systems, and know how to seek information in a library.

6. To train children to read well enough to make short 'reviews' of books they have read, either orally or in writing; to discriminate between authors and books; and to be able to make a précis of a book or a chapter.

7. To train a child to read a book so as to bring what he remembers of it to a class discussion of the book; to exchange his opinion of it with others, and to balance both their opinion and that of the teacher against his own; to have some sense of the relation between books and life and of the deeper symbolism of fiction.

Dictionaries (*The Pocket Oxford Dictionary*) should be available at the child's side during all this work; and the habit of pausing to record a new word in an exercise book, with its meaning, should be encouraged. Skeat's *Concise Etymological Dictionary* should be in the classroom.

Ths success of all this work depends entirely upon the quality of the books chosen for (1), (2), (3), and (7). I am aware that the final choice will depend upon the teacher's own taste, limited by the conservatism of most publishers. But I feel that much more can be done by demonstrating the qualities of a few touchstones rather than by giving another of the long lists found in most books on English teaching. Certainly the touchstones may help us excise a few of the titles which appear time after time as 'children's classics'. For instance, a most useful list published by Coventry City Libraries of editions of 'the Children's Classics' contains the following:

> Ainsworth, W. H., *Windsor Castle*.
> Brontë, Charlotte, *Jane Eyre*.
> Dickens, Charles, *The Cricket on the Hearth*.
> Gaskell, Mrs E. C., *Cranford*.
> Kingsley, Charles, *Hereward the Wake*.
> Thackeray, William Makepeace, *The Rose and the Ring*.

Are we convinced that any effort we make to get children to read them is justified by their quality as literature, even leaving aside the question as to whether they are enjoyable or not?

We need, certainly, to be very careful indeed in choosing our touchstones—those works to which we can give complete assent as being good books for young people. Most of the novels we regard as 'classics' belong to years immediately before 1870,[1] and to a mid nineteenth century which had its own peculiar limitations in attitudes to children, and in its ways of addressing children. To many nineteenth-century writers childhood appeared as a state of innocence from which maturity was a fall into corruption: and many works about childhood are using it as a measure of human goodness. Thus the child became, as it were, a tool of penetrating moral incisiveness in an age of confused values—in Henry James' *What Maisie Knew*, Mark Twain's *Huckleberry Finn*, and, in a different way, in *Treasure Island*. The edge is less sure, under the pressure of a nostalgia which becomes self-pity for the adult fallen man, in such works as Dickens' *David Copperfield* and Stevenson's *A Child's Garden of Verses*. But yet another movement throughout the nineteenth century was away from the sentimental view of childhood which followed the didacticism of Isaac Watts —and from childhood used to falsify problems of adulthood, as found in *Little Lord Fauntleroy*. Lewis Carroll, obsessed with childhood innocence in a way which differs only by a hair's breadth from perversion, produced an anti-didactic fantasy which embodies that symbolism, such as we find in nursery rhymes, which explores and comes to terms with our deepest fears of loss of identity. Water de la Mare brought this power into our own century: but the power has remained a largely poetic one. In English prose, as yet, there has been no succession to *Hucklebery Finn* and *Alice in Wonderland*, no representative rendering of the child's sensibility of today and embracing our recognition of the inward problems children have to deal with. Freud led the way to the discovery that children have severe problems of anxiety over identity, sex and

[1] E.g. Louisa Alcott c. 1868; Robert Ballantyne c. 1856; Richard Blackmore c. 1869; Richard Dana 1840; Charles Kingsley c. 1866; R. Stevenson 1888. In the *List of Editions of Children's Classics* published by Coventry City Libraries only the following appear outside the nineteenth century—Bunyan, Barrie, Frances Hodgson Burnett, Cervantes, Defoe, Kenneth Grahame.

death. We come increasingly to see how bravely they work by symbolism on problems of love and hate. Here, to be sentimental is to show hate oneself—as Barrie does:

—When was I born?
—At midnight, dear.
— I hope I didn't wake you, mummy.

(from the film version of *Peter Pan*)

This note on children in literature, brief and unsatisfactory though it is, will suffice to help me state our problem. Here we are with the fourth generation following the 1870 Education Act: we are giving them authors whose language habits on the whole are foreign to them, perhaps more so than those of many Elizabethan writers, even. We are backing up our contest against the corrupting effect of their environment with books that are often foreign to their sensibilities. We often mistake their surface sophistication for maturity and give them books before they are old enough for them:[1] and in so doing we fail to provide them with training for 'the whole man' when they most need it. Along with this we fail to see that what we do not supply, commercial sources will. If the nineteenth century 'classics' ignore the sexual, because their writers wished to avoid the vibrations consequent upon human love, then we are leaving our children exposed often to forms of titillation of their anxieties about sex. And finally, in failing to realise all these difficult problems, concerned simply to 'get them to read', it is obvious that the schools are exposing children to influences (such as those of journalists who happen to have written a 'true' story about war) which worsen the situation, and develop in them habits of responding to language which do not help, and may hinder, them in their need to draw on imaginative symbolism from books.

Which books provide the most helpful touchstones in choosing reading matter for our children? Perhaps first we should consider

[1] This most valuable and important point is made by Mr Douglas Brown in an article on *Treasure Island* in *Young Writers, Young Readers*, edited by Boris Ford (Hutchinson). See also here *Poor Monkey, The Child in Literature*, Peter Coveney, Rockliff, 1961.

what we are not seeking in books. I have said how important seems to me the development of oral capacities in the secondary modern school, and in a sense all our other work should help us place reading as part of our language culture. Our work in developing powers of talking clearly, of imaginative creative power in drama and composition, and in responding to and enjoying poetry, ought to give language a more solid value to our pupils, before they come to read well enough to read superficially. Anyone who has a sensitive response to language should find the sensational writer (and many of the children's favourite authors quoted in the table above are sensational writers) too painful and embarrassing to read. If we have a healthy relish for words well used, we shall dislike this kind of thing, for instance:

...a blasphemy of the human shape. She was dressed, they now saw, in a single garment, a kind of smock or shift, torn, stained brown, reaching half-way down her thighs: below it, her shanks were wizened, like an old man's, and her spindly legs moved jerkily, as she felt her way along the frayed rope that led to the privy. She turned her head this way and that, as if feeling for the sun: the blind eyes still roved about her hopefully, the head was cocked as if still expecting some faint sound from the world. The small developing breasts under the shift were a last cruel flourish of mockery; for by their evidence, their shy promise, she was, in all her horror, in all her degradation, a girl of thirteen on the bright edge of womanhood...Mrs Bannister prayed...that she might not vomit...

NICHOLAS MONSARRAT, The Story of Esther Costello

or this:

At that moment it happened. Hornblower heard the impact of the bullet, saw the force of it half roll her over. He saw the puzzled look on her face, saw the puzzled look change into a grimace of agony, and without even knowing what he was doing he sprang to her and knelt beside her. A bullet had struck her on the thigh; Hornblower turned back the short skirt of her riding habit. One leg of her dark breeches was already soaked with blood, and while he was gathering himself to act he twice saw the blood pulsate redly—the great artery of the thigh was torn...He thrust his fingers into her groin, unavailingly, the folds of the breeches balking his attempt to apply pressure to the artery...

C. S. FORESTER, Lord Hornblower

Reading

Notice, in both these, how lacking they are in reticence and economy—that reticence and economy which selects from imagined experience the few salient touches that *place* it:[1] one's nose here is rubbed in the lot. Every powerful word at the writer's disposal is used to belabour the reader's shocked imagination: 'blasphemy', 'wizened', 'horror', 'flourish of mockery', 'degradation', 'vomit', 'grimace of agony', 'puzzled look'—these are the stock-in-trade signals of the thriller-writer, however much more skilfully used here than by the general run of them. And note too the way in which disgust and physical hurt are coated with powerful sexual suggestion: 'stained brown', 'half-way down her thighs', 'privy', 'small developing breasts under the shift', 'shy promise', 'he thrust his fingers into her groin...' Both represent a neurotic kind of writing, because it is a kind of writing which does not know what it is doing—and the last thing it is doing is enlarging sympathy. What seems like sympathy ('a girl on the bright edge of womanhood', 'he sprang to her and knelt beside her') is really masking an attack in unconscious hate on an imagined woman to whom the reader has attached his feelings, and now he is to have them tortured, to a degree he perhaps hopes will be a satisfying one. Such writing arouses anxieties around primitive sadism. C. S. Forester's book covers this by respectability—it is snobbery with violence. Monsarrat's book ostensibly has a theme exposing an inhuman fraud, like Henry James' *The Bostonians*. But his book, because its appeal is based on hate, is nearer the thriller or even the popular press than the author would like to think. Yet 1 % of Modern School boys say this writer is 'their favourite author', having read *The Cruel Sea* in school.

Our approach to reading, then, needs to be controlled by and related to our careful work with poetry, and by our developing a rich complex of oral and imaginative composition, in which we encourage sincerity above all, and not the exploitation of feelings. It is no use having standards in the one and not in the other. With this background in mind we need to be searching continually among works of English prose for new 'classics'—or to revalue

[1] See below, p. 178, from *Huckleberry Finn*, where the hideousness of a corpse's face is given by the negro's comic 'Doan look at his face: it's too gashly'.

the old ones. We should be prepared to find that parts of the Authorised Version or myths in translation, or the contemporary account of the martyrdom of Thomas à Becket, may be better 'reading', and even more relevant to the needs of the present day sensibility than many nineteenth century novels. Yet at the same time we must recognise, too, that the development of interest in the long story is a natural one for a growing child, and that the development of the novel is one which belongs to English society since, say, 1750, for reasons that go with changes in the English identity which are not only irreversible but make for greater human potentialities.

The novel, as D. H. Lawrence said, illumines many secret places of life—the unspoken workings of the mind and being. The long story of manners and morals gives the growing child not only a more satisfying experience than poem or play can give at the same age, but at the same time gives a most important opportunity to discuss an imaginative experience in all its aspects with his fellows. The value of this is greater in our time, when we have so few opportunities for creative symbolism at large, and because the themes of the greatest novelists have been largely those concerning the uniqueness of each individual life, in a society which has become more and more complex, impersonal and indifferent to the individual. To have thought and felt this problem through some good novels is almost an essential qualification for a member of a democracy. And all I have said depends upon the experience being that of a *work of art*—an imaginative experience in a prose form.

I have pointed out that the mid-nineteenth century is the source of many books considered as children's 'classics' and I question whether this is the best period of English prose. Our selection from this period needs revision, certainly. The period is one of a verbal extravagance in writing that is quite different, say, from that of Shakespeare and the Elizabethan period. The latter had its roots in the vital vernacular of the common people and their habits of metaphorical, moral investigation of life—in sermon, saw, song, local tale and 'gossip speech'.

The verbal exuberance of the mid-nineteenth century is best

represented by that of Dickens (few escaped his influence), who, although he takes in a great deal from the vernacular, writes in the study, and is on the people's 'side', rather than among them shoulder to shoulder, as the Elizabethan writer could not but be. Don't mistake the point: Dickens has great compassion for the common people, but his language is not theirs. Even George Eliot, despite her feeling, as with Mrs Poyser, for local idiom, invents her own idiomatic language even for such characters, and writes for middle-class educated readers. Both write essentially for readers with a great deal of time and stamina to spare. In lesser hands Dickens' verbal extravagance becomes tedious: here is R. M. Ballantyne in *Hudson Bay*, for instance:

The ceaseless din of plates, glasses, knives, forks, and tongues was tremendous; and this, together with the novelty of the scene, the heat of the room, and excellence of the viands, tended to render me oblivious of much that took place... Who were, and who were not, the gentlemen of the committee, was to me a matter of the most perfect indifference; and as no one took the trouble to address me in particular I confined myself to the interesting occupation of trying to make sense of a conversation held by upwards of fifty pairs of lungs at the same time... The redfaced gentleman, now purple with excitement, then rose, and during a solemn silence delivered himself of a speech, to the effect that the day then passing was certainly the happiest in his mortal career, that he could not find words adequately to express the varied feelings which swelled his throbbing bosom, and that he felt quite faint with the mighty load of honour just thrown upon his delighted shoulders by his bald-headed friend.

This kind of hyperbole, belonging to an age of rich Christmas-cake prose, springing from Dickens' fantastic powers of the gab, would seem to me the most unsuitable prose possible for children. In the first place it has an air of display—'fancy' ways of saying things are used to create 'style': 'the excellence of the viands', 'a matter to me of the most perfect indifference' (nothing can be 'most perfect', for perfect is perfect), and so on. Secondly, the sentence structure is unnecessarily complex (Dickens delighted in this). Thirdly, the wit is that wit of playing upon cliché and debunking the bourgeois pretensions of social conduct. This Dickens developed marvellously from the eighteenth-century writers, but the mode ends up in the adolescent rag spirit of W. S. Gilbert (cf. *Bab Ballads*), in a facile destructiveness in which values are almost spitefully torn up. Here 'the happiest in his mortal career', 'adequately to express the varied feelings that swelled his throbbing bosom', are expressions deliberately inflated to suffer the jeer implicit in 'his bald-headed friend', 'red-faced' and so on. It goes with a kind of assumption of superiority, and a cruelty (even Dickens had this) which make it, I suggest, undesirable for children.

The effect of dwelling on such prose is to make children write in a style which makes them seem like old men, and they do it to please teachers who think this is 'style'. The following is the kind of writing (it was written by a boy and quoted in *The Use of English*, Vol. 2, No. 1) based on concepts of 'English style' derived from nineteenth century literature:

Reveille the next morning was at 6.15 a.m. and we arose like the proverbial larks. We hastened to the ablutions where we washed or took a shower while the more unfortunate of the cadets who were approaching manhood had imposed upon them the additional task of removing the stubble from their chins. Naturally there were one or two cadets who were loth to leave their beds and who lingered as long as possible but these were dealt with severely by the early risers, who intimated that such indolence was indesirable...The breakfast we received that morning—although not attaining the standard of home breakfasts—was appetising and delectable. It was apparent that the meals given to some of the cadets did not satiate their Gargantuan appetites and frequently additional helpings were required. Information on this score can be gleaned from 'Going up again?'—implying a return visit to the counter—and synonymous phrases.

Here 'satiate their Gargantuan appetites' is the same kind of phrase of display, vulgar circumlocution and ironic superiority as in Ballantyne's 'excellence of the viands'. It is such habits which vitiate the speech of nearly all educated Englishmen: and they belong to the smoking room of the nineteenth century, of the upper middle class club, not to the people, and certainly not to the sensibility of the child of today.

There is also something immature about such prose: it lacks guts and goes with a lack of warm feeling and a sexlessness which make it remote from our children's needs. This brings me to a delicate point. We can deceive ourselves, unless we look carefully at what they write themselves, about what is 'fit' for them to read. Children's awareness of love and death, as I have tried to say in dealing with poetry, is profound but inexplicit; and they cannot deal with such matters directly. Yet their preoccupations cannot be dealt with by giving them matter which is without all reference to passion and sexual love. There are stages at which the sexlessness is appropriate—*Huckleberry Finn* and *Treasure Island* are ideal at this moment. Young children have infantile anxieties about sex (sadistic fears of it as a kind of 'eating'): their way out is to find that it is a way of expressing relationship between individuals, and leads towards procreation and fulfilment. Sometimes we are led to think otherwise by the superficial sexual knowingness commercial culture has imposed on our children. This has produced kinds of stock reaction to any love-story—manifestations of anxiety, really, like the jeer or the wolf-whistle. Yet the child needs to contemplate love in a realistic way. So at fourteen or fifteen *Wuthering Heights* is a perfect book in that it deals with love in a symbolic way, exploring the inner conflict of love and hate, and primary need. There is passion, but no explicit dealing with sex. The symbolic drama renders the 'togetherness' of Cathy and Heathcliff as something triumphant. To the child of early adolescence it is a marvellous romantic tale, and makes implicitly the profound point that our relational needs in which we find our identity may be more important than life itself. Love here is a greater human potentiality than what is often popularly meant by the word 'love'. But what child brought up on *Diana* and *Marty* can take in the implicit point of *Wuthering Heights*?

For the complex within which we train reading is both a verbal and spiritual malaise of our time. I have remarked in schools two extraordinary features of behaviour—and they have been the more extraordinary because of their acceptance as normal. One was the cat-calling and raucous laughter with which any school audience greets salacious humour in a film (e.g. a joke about double or single beds). The other was the behaviour of some children, of, I suppose, fourteen, watching a cricket match on the grass in front of the school offices. A boy lay next to a girl, embraced her, kissed her full on the mouth, stroked her breasts, and thighs under her skirt. Nothing remarkable, perhaps, at the age between 14 and 20 when 'there's nothing but wronging the ancientry or getting wenches with child', and most of us have behaved so, at, say, sixteen. But—*the caresses were not meant*: this is the realisation which dawned after watching this extraordinary scene: they were copied from the cinema. This explained the lack of all sense of a need to seek privacy for love-making, of behaving so among half-a-dozen others, the extraordinary *panache* of the methods of kissing, the lack of any sense of doing anything unsanctioned (the children were quite aware that they could be seen by others) and the fact that the petting was accompanied by no tenderness or expression of any real affection. It was mimicked sexuality. The children were imitating behaviour they had seen on the screen—and that behaviour was sex depersonalised and de-emotionalised to a schizoid degree for the purposes of commerce. This destructive trend has become worse since.

Some knowingness is given to the child through his reading matter. The first six favourite magazines of boys at secondary modern schools in the W. H. Smith–Harrap survey were:

John Bull	5·30	
Eagle	5·00	% who said
Buchan's Football Monthly	4·60	this was their
Tit-bits	4·30	favourite paper
Picture Post	3·40	
Reveille	3·10	

We will assume for the moment that the first five are respectable. The sixth represents a significant new feature of our time: 'spicy' matter to hold an adult public, which is widely read by children. We may assume that if *Reveille* is the favourite magazine of 31 out of a thousand boys (11–16), many more in fact read it. What do they find in a typical issue? I will quote at some length to convince the reader that we live, and read, in a very strange era:

Front-page: cheese-cake picture of a girl in a bathing suit pressing her thighs against a rock and stretching back in the swallow-dive position.

Text: '*Fair Sex*ercise'. This lovely member of the fair sex is...As she does her arms stretch, any man would willingly bend the knee before her.'

Article: '...she is only one of the women pilots in Turkey's "Glamour squadron"...All of them are trim, shapely girls between twenty and thirty. And, like all the other women in the different sections of the Turkish defence forces, THEY ARE DISTRIBUTED EQUALLY AMONG THE GENERAL UNITS. THERE IS NO SEX SEGREGATION.' (Capitals in the original.)

Joke: 'All marriages are happy. It's what happens afterwards that causes all the trouble.'

Review: 'Shocked by bras and stockings': review of a book by a woman who had renounced her vows as a nun, after 28 years. She was shocked by 'a very realistically modelled bust bodice' which emphasised what in her youth was 'decorously concealed'. Following these hints the review selects from the books the account of how in the convent 'discipline' meant inflicting pain on oneself with a scourge made of thin waxed cord with little knotted tails attached: or a metal one with slender snake-like tails; or bracelets of steel, wide-linked and studded with points.

Article: *Hush Hush Sin list for Britain.*

U.S. Airforce in Britain has a Sin File—a directory of brothels and picking-up places of ill repute. Fewer than a dozen places in the whole U.K. are listed: these are places where 'incidents' have taken place, 'anything from a fight to a V.D. case'. A far bigger Sin File is kept by the U.S. Sixth Fleet which lists the business addresses of prostitutes...from Barcelona to Istanbul...In Beirut nine out of ten of the easy girls are diseased...drug dens, etc.

Cartoon: (alongside): Three girls with bosoms protuberant to a deformed extent, two men, caption, 'I see Spring is bursting out all over.'

Article: 'As she neared the edge he slipped behind her, drew his revolver, and shot her just behind the ear.'

English for Maturity

Caption: 'Love is the effort a man makes to be satisfied with only one woman.'

Question: I have been happily married for 24 years...he is going back to the woman he was engaged to 30 years ago. *Ans.* He will be happy at first. Then the 'holiday feeling' may wear off. One day he'll probably look back in anguish.

The magazine ends with another large cheese-cake figure in the time-worn piece of mock leopard skin. On close inspection the magazine contains the weariest of themes belonging to those journals which have catered for half-educated popular taste for nearly a century. Some of it, in a tit-bit form, is even good and sound—moral, and healthy—scientific information, *Round the World Alone*, advice on make-up. But *Reveille* is bought for the hints about 'the facts of life' such as I extract above—hints which provide the child with a frightening, *and frightened*, knowingness before his time, arouse in him anxious feelings about sex, and encourage him to deal with these by denying his needs for love and relationship. 'Love is the effort a man makes to be satisfied with one woman': the tone of the writing conveys the depersonalisation of sex played on by commerce: essentially, it is diseased.

It would of course be unfair to accuse the proprietors of such a paper as *Reveille*, or the distinguished people of taste who own the *Daily Mirror*, or the respectable directors of the *News of the World* or any other Sunday paper of even an unwitting responsibility for corrupting the young. Indeed, some of these people claim, as those responsible for the *News of the World* did claim before the Royal Commission on the Press, that their paper, like the Old Testament, was a record of punishment, and therefore highly moral in effect. As teachers we need only concern ourselves with the incidental effect of such matter on children, since they cannot escape it. As Richard Jay says in his essay in *Young Writers, Young Readers* on the Harrap survey, that *Reveille* has soared into the first six favourite magazines of modern school boys since 1940 reveals the choice of parents visited upon the children.

The effect of the continual play on the themes of depersonalisation in sex and the denial of our need for dependence (our need to

174

express tender feelings in love) is not to cause 'immorality' but, since it conflicts with our deepest needs, to divert energy and undermine our capacity to feel real. So it is only possible to consider with alarm the effect on the heart of things in our life of the stream of debasement coming from Fleet Street. For the effect may be read in the faces lining the wall of every youth club: many youth seem threatened with having no real feelings left except the hollow, de-emotionalised ones of the world of Cliff, Elvis, Tommy, and their successors—and of their 'romantic' papers. We have not sufficiently considered how much disruption of the texture of our society has been caused by abandoning such powerful cultural influences to the money-makers. They operate well within the law—once, as with horror comics, the law has been put in the book—but there is a sense in which the subtle implications, and the essential effect in persuading us we are less than human, are more sinister than open obscenity. Certainly, of course, worse than open eroticism: and it is ironic that public authorities will debate for days about whether a statue should wear a *cache-sexe*, while the prurient muck-raking of the Sunday papers lies about the parlour for their own children to absorb.

What can children of eleven to fourteen imagine of the brothel? What picture of marriage do they get from their reading matter ('every morning I wake up with a jerk—this is him')? What strange awareness do they get of perversions and sexual disease? The knowingness, for some, must be a terror which they hide under knowing behaviour, such as petting, and wolf-calls: for the whole atmosphere of such reading material emerges from a symbolism which is developed out of fear of life in the body, and a horror of relationship—even of being human.

Yet is it this profoundly disturbed cultural background which we must take into account—in which tender children's minds are subjected to emotional disturbance caused by matter appropriate to a middle-aged, mentally sick *voyeur*, a Leopold Bloom. Joyce's rendering of Gerty Macdowell's view of life, in *Ulysses*, in the language of *Peg's Paper*, and of the sordid onanistic act which takes place in that 'Siren' chapter is a penetrating comment on our commercial culture: it is manic compensation for weakness.

To turn to matter specifically printed for children: the inculcation of the reading habit combined with the commercial needs of Fleet Street to keep presses running and to seek new vehicles for advertisers (who are turning over fast to television) has produced a new kind of comic for children in the last ten years. When I was a boy I spent many Saturday afternoons on the hearthrug eating a bar of chocolate and reading *The Wizard* and *The Magnet*. The latter contained one story of, I suppose, 10,000 words, and the magazine is well described by George Orwell in his essay on boys' weeklies in *Inside the Whale*. *The Magnet* is dead, though *The Wizard* survives, a paper of short stories and cartoons, offering at least a choice between pieces of *reading* matter, however badly written. *The Magnet* could be studied as representing the provision in a limited way for boys' needs: I remember it as being very funny at times, full of prejudices (against some foreigners, for instance) and yet so impossibly unreal as to make one aware that one was indulging in a fantasy; no boy really ever cried 'Yarooo!' and 'I say, you chaps'—at least not in my circle.

But there was a recognisable connection between reading *The Magnet* and *The Wizard*, and reading Richmal Crompton, John Buchan, and other books. The same is not true of the lurid new comics. These have put on such an educational face that many teachers are deceived. But they simply do not encourage the habit of reading at all. They present stories so simplified, for the purposes of drawing, that nothing is left but the most sensational moments (AAARGH!), and a sequence of indefinite grimaces, mostly of agony. The prototype was *Eagle*. It may be of interest here to examine one of the imitators launched in recent years, only to fail. *Junior Express* for instance, had the format of *Eagle*, and 'an educational bias'—*Wulf the Briton*, *Secret Flight 9X* (given the appearance of a true-escape story—for don't they use these in school?), *Evans of the Broke* (patriotic-historical), *Atomic Icebreaker*, *Lumberjacks in Canada* (geography: to please Lord Beaverbrook, too), *Montezuma's Gold* (Aztecs—History—Geography etc.). The concessions to child taste are *Gunlaw* (Western), *Rocky Roll* (comedy), *Doomed Planet* (space) and *Men of the Mounties*. The fare is not only somewhat jaded by age, but also thin in word: perhaps there is hope in the possibility that the comics will, like the newspapers, become not-comics, lacking in all possibilities of providing satisfaction, even by violence, and bring on their own end. Can the movement towards the lowest common denominator go on for ever? Are the failures of the *Junior Express* and the *Junior Mirror* a portent?

Here is the typical language of the picture comic: again these extracts are from *Junior Express* in its first issues when it was probably sailing close to the educational wind, as it were). Here is the language even of the 'respectable' comic:

Ancient Briton:

What plot are you hatching now, you licker of Roman boots? Speak! That scar! Where did you get it?...But the arrow flew wide...and as I ran to recover it...AAAH!...My brother staunched the wound... Cassander! I am your brother Tegeus...

Wild West:

Your brother's crazy going after those crooks on his own—he'll be killed for sure...(*thinks*) I'm no squirrel—but if I can reach that branch...Phew! It's as slippery as butter...(*minutes later*) Come on Chester—let's help the Marshall with the last round up! I reckon those guys back there will be glad to get into a nice warm jail...

Evans of the Broke:

(*As the big seaman leaps Teddy acts*) AAAH!...Lieutenant Evans sir, look. It's a sea-leopard. A sea-leopard is a rare specimen. There's many a museum who'd like that beauty. Got him! We'll tie it up and tow it... (Suddenly a whale appears) Look out! (!) It's breaking the floe! Help! Hurry! Those men won't last long if they fall into the icy water! The weight of that leopard thing is holding us back. Quick, she's cracking up fast...(Will Evans succeed in his rescue bid? More adventures in the white wilderness next week!)

It seems doubtful whether such dull words are ever read at all except when a picture puzzles a 'reader'—they can so be taken for granted. Any child of average intelligence writes better (see p. 122) because he writes with interest and so his words have rhythm: the chief charge one may make against such picture comics is that, written by jaded and very poor writers, they present a jaded and very poor picture of life's possibilities, and all they do with their minor sensationalism (on which their sales depend) is to divert energy which could be better used, as in reading books, and cause children to make nonsense of what they do read. However many clergymen or educationists are enlisted by Fleet Street to lend respectability, these comics only create bad reading habits.

With the words of the comic in our mind let us turn to a great touchstone in children's reading, *Huckleberry Finn*. As we read this we may gather courage in the face of a difficult situation and commercial depreciation of taste. After all, we hold the trumps:

Boggs comes a tearing along on his horse, whooping and yelling like an Injun, and singing out: 'Cler the track, thar. I'm on the waw-path, and the price uv coffins is a-gwyne to raise!' He was drunk, and weaving about in his saddle; he was over fifty year old, and had a very red face. Everybody yelled at him, and laughed at him, and sassed him, and he sassed back, and said he'd attend to them and lay them out in their regular turns, but he couldn't wait now, because he'd come to town to kill old Colonel Sherburn, and his motto was, 'Meat first, and spoon vittles to top off on.'

He see me, and rode up and says: 'War'd you come f'm, boy? You prepared to die?'

Then he rode on. I was scared; but a man says: 'He don't mean nothing; he's always a carrying on like that, when he's drunk. He's the best-natured old fool in Arkansaw—never hurt nobody, drunk nor sober.'

Boggs rode up before the biggest store in town and bent his head down so he could see under the curtain of the awning, and yells:

'Come out here Sherburn! Come out and meet the man you've swindled! You're the houn' I'm after, and I'm a-gwyne to have you, too!'

...By and by a proud-looking man about fifty-five—and he was a heap the best-dressed man in that town, too—steps out of the store, and the crowd drops back on each side to let him come. He says to Boggs, mighty calm and slow—he says:

'I'm tired of this; but I'll endure it till one o'clock. Till one o'clock, mind—no longer. If you open your mouth against me, only once, after that time, you can't travel far but I will find you.'

(Everyone tries to persuade Boggs to give up cursing, and to shut him up, but to no avail.)

...here comes Boggs again—but not on his horse. He was a-reeling across the street towards me, bareheaded, with a friend on both sides of him a-holt of his arms and hurrying him along. He was quiet, but was doing some of the hurrying himself. Somebody sings out:

'Boggs!'

I looked over there to see who said it, and it was that Colonel Sherburn. He was standing perfectly still in the street, and he had a pistol raised in his right hand—not aiming it, but holding it with the barrel tilted towards the sky...when they see the pistol the two men jumped to one side, and the pistol barrel come down slow and steady to a level—both barrels cocked. Boggs throws up both of his hands, and says, 'O Lord, don't shoot!' Bang! goes the first shot, and he staggers back clawing at the air—bang! goes the second one, and he tumbles backward onto the ground, heavy and solid, with his arms spread out...

Colonel Sherburn he tossed his pistol onto the ground, and turned around on his heels and walked off...

Mark Twain achieves a clarity which goes with the artist's 'terrifying honesty' by using Huck as a medium. The child sees life without flinching, without being encumbered by the blinkers of 'sivilisation', such as we come to wear as we grow older: 'but they tore open his shirt first, and I seen where one of the bullets went in.' This may be compared with the extract from C. S. Forester above. Huck's details present us with human reality: the 'gashly' is not here exploited merely to arouse anxiety. In the lively simple language of the Boggs episode we have a profoundly disturbing account of man's inhumanity to man: 'Folks can be awful cruel to one another,' as Huck says elsewhere, and 'You feel mighty free and comfortable on a raft.' Boggs is drunk, over fifty, he is 'sassed' (sauced), a braggart ('Are you prepared to die?'—cf. 'O Lord, don't shoot!'), yet 'never hurt nobody'. Colonel Sherburn, who later faces a mob intent on lynching him and laughs in their faces, kills a man who is barely sober, in cold blood; yet he warned Boggs, he is a law unto himself, and, in such a dissolute, rough, community, one feels his pioneer dignity: 'A proud-looking man', 'the crowd drops back on each side to let him come'. Rather than a Western roughhouse we have a drama of two contrary states of the human soul. No can could fail to respond to this, once he has read it himself with attention, or has had it read well to him, or fail to be disturbed, so that, without knowing it, he is puzzling in his being—which is right? Whether he identifies himself with Huck, or Boggs, or Sherburn, he will suffer equally—there is no easy way out by way of a day-dream: for this is how men behave. Yet the whole is a fantasy. But one's mouth goes dry at that, 'and the pistol barrel come down slow and steady to a level—both barrels cocked' (the latter being one of those details which the boy Huck had time, and the eyes, to notice). The rhythm, the dramatic use of tense ('here comes Boggs again...'), the observed and economic detail ('had a very red face') spring from Mark Twain's profound humanity and from his creative concern to explore hate in symbolism, and consider how men might overcome it.

One of the most superb moments in literature is the discovery of Huck's father, dead:

Another night, when we was up at the head of the island, just before daylight, here comes a frame-house down, on the west side. She was a two-storey, and tilted over considerable. We paddled out and got aboard—clumb in at an upstairs window. But it was too dark to see yet, so we made the canoe fast and set in her to wait for daylight.

The light began to come before we got to the foot of the island. Then we looked in at the window. We could make out a bed, and a table, and two old chairs, and lots of things around about on the floor; and there was clothes hanging against the wall. There was something laying on the floor in the far corner that looked like a man. So Jim says:

'Hello, you!'

But it didn't budge. So I hollered again, and then Jim says:

'The man ain't asleep—he's dead. You hold still—I'll go en see.'

He went and bend down and looked, and says:

'It's a dead man. Yes, indeedy; naked too. He's been shot in de back. I reck'n he's ben dead two or three days. Come in, Huck, but doan' look at his face—it's too gashly.'

I didn't look at him at all. Jim throwed some old rags over him, but he needn't done it; I didn't want to see him. There was heaps of old greasy cards scattered around over the floor, and old whisky bottles, and a couple of masks made out of black cloth: and all over the walls was the ignorantest kind of words and pictures, made with charcoal.

Reading

There was two old dirty calico dresses, and a sun-bonnet, and some women's underclothes, hanging against the wall, and some men's clothing, too. We put the lot into the canoe; it might come good. There was a boy's old speckled straw hat on the floor; I took that too. And there was a bottle that had had milk in it; and it had a rag stopper for a baby to suck. We could 'a' took the bottle, but it was broke. There was a seedy old chest, and an old hair trunk with the hinges broke. They stood open, but there warn't nothing left in them that was any account. The way things was scattered about, we reckoned the people left in a hurry and warn't fixed so as to carry off most of their stuff.

We got an old tin lantern, and a butcher knife without any handle, and a bran-new Barlow knife worth two bits in any store, and a lot of tallow candles, and a tin candle-stick, and a gourd, and a tin cup, and a ratty old bed-quilt off the bed, and a reticule with needles and pins and beeswax and buttons and thread and all such truck in it, and a hatchet and some nails, and a fish-line as thick as my little finger, with some monstrous hooks on it, and a roll of buckskin, and a leather dog-collar, and a horse-shoe, and some vials of medicine that didn't have no label on them; and just as we was leaving I found a tolerable good curry-comb, and Jim he found a ratty old fiddle-bow, and a wooden leg. The straps was broke off of it, but barring that, it was a good enough leg, though it was too long for me and not long enough for Jim, and we couldn't find the other one, though we hunted all around.

This passage is a perfect touchstone in choosing reading matter for children. It is about death, change, transience, the ugliness of sleaziness and the way the sins are visited upon subsequent generations, about the horror of human 'civilisation' at its worst; about pain, and about the at times meaningless-seeming incessant impulse of humanity to live; about our pathetic attempts at manic gaiety. It is about the consequences of the break-down of identity and relationship. There is a corpse—'Something laying on the floor in the far corner that looked like a man...' Yet all this is done at the level of a boy's eye, looking for useful objects; the horror is thrust back, placed by a sure and bounding vitality: 'doan look at his face—it's too gashly.' Compare this with the quotation above from Monsarrat: there is no dwelling here on the sordid, for sordid's sake—but the abyss is, really, deeper: old greasy cards, whisky bottles, a couple of masks, words and pictures of the ignorantest kind (wonderful expression—how unpious, how superbly disdainful—how one would love to hear Huck's comments on *Reveille*!), a sun-bonnet(!),—and 'a bottle that had had milk in it: and it had a rag stopper for a baby to suck'. The horror of a baby, out of all this greasy, purposeless orgy, dead in the flood, unwanted in the seediness, the 'nothing of any account'—Huck! Of course, the baby was the Huck that once was, in such surroundings! But Huck is free ('You feel mighty free and comfortable on a raft')—free from 'sivilisation'—and yet the thought need never come to the surface: 'we would 'a' took the bottle, but it was broke.'—Huckleberry has hand and eye on life, and living. And so the hilarious list of hooks and medicine, fiddle-bow and wooden leg—the flotsam and jetsam of music, science, war, enterprise. Well—what more does it amount to, life, civilisation? The boy and the negro, runaways both, collecting *what might come good*, have triumphed over all the paraphernalia of dissociation, in their very vital and human relationship, as human brothers (Huck disrupts the whole accepted morality of slave-ownership—and we need not suppose slavery, as treated here, has gone from the earth).

The passage is most poignant and profound: yet it is unnecessary even to say so to children, or to make explicit what I have made explicit. *Huckleberry Finn* is the perfect story, for it is about men and the life they lead, in the hands of an artist's imaginative power. The river, the thunderstorm, the lights of towns at night on the shore are poetic symbols, as such things become to the imaginative child. And such a book is the tool in our hands in teaching the reading habits that make for creative gains in life.

How shall we handle such a book? It seems to me that the correct way round to tackle our problem is to say, 'Here are a few books we feel every child should experience—how do we bring child and book together?' This is not a literary problem, but a problem inseparable from reading: one's first experience of a tale, like one's first love, helps to make or unmake one's capacities for developing one's powers.

First, we must be sure to choose books for the right age of a child's *being*—not reading age. Children are always younger than we think; though their reading powers may be behind or in advance of their age, their sensibilities usually seem to lag behind their apparent sophistication, and do not match mere improved reading ability. The choice will depend on the teacher who knows his children, but I give a considered list below.

There are several ways of tackling reading matter, and it is again up to the teacher to choose between them. The main problem is the very considerable differences in reading ability as between pupils. To improve actual reading we need practice lessons. 'Reading round the class', one hopes, has gone, and pupils are nowadays divided into groups according to their reading ability, each group having a novel suited to its reading age. Within these groups readers may be divided as between characters, with a narrator for the descriptive paragraphs. For this reading work in groups I would suggest the use of well-written books of the second order: those which, although they are not great books, provide an adequate and exciting story, of some imaginative power—I am thinking of such books as *The Otterbury Incident* by Cecil Day Lewis, *The Bird of Dawning* by John Masefield, and *The Family from One End Street* by Eve Garnett—the kind of book (with some reservations) published in Heinemann's *New Windmill Series* and some of the other more enterprising publishers' lists. I give a list below.

Of course, a great deal of this reading work in groups should be more than mere 'reading', and, rather, collaborative work on 'programmes' of poetry and prose for class presentation, or presentation to the whole school. The Authorised Version and scientific, geographical or historical books are appropriate to such reading work, and it is inseparable from both drama and choral speaking, from training in oral composition, and the use of reading in all other subjects in which English is used. The concern in reading practice is to train the child first to make sense of words, of phrases and sentences, and then of whole paragraphs and to be able to use his voice to help convey the meaning to others. I have not discussed speech training in this book, as I have no knowledge of it: there are exercises one may do, and no doubt we need to learn more about how sounds are made. Some children cannot make some sounds at all, and need to work with a speech therapist. But most of the work in speech training is combating laziness. This one must, of course, do all the time, setting the best example oneself. Fundamentally, good reading or speaking aloud depends on goodwill, on trying to make others understand what is being said or read. I don't discuss the teaching of backward readers here (but see *English for the Rejected*). There are several books on this work with the unfortunate minority, and Mr A. E. Smith has an excellent note in his *English in the Secondary Modern School*, where he suggests that with such children reading needs always to be very closely linked with activities and projects such as breeding rabbits and so on. But there is surely here also a problem of relating reading to deeper interests. It has always seemed to me that hundreds of teachers will attend a course on backward readers while comparatively few show interest in problems of creative English and literature. At the same time psychometric psychology seems to have generated an over-confidence in 'grading and such 'scientific' approaches to teaching reading, while too little attention is paid to what his reading offers the child in terms of symbolic *content*.

To return to our novels for children. We have two lists: works we feel a child, every child, ought to experience; and a more general list of good books to read and read from. Let us consider first ways of giving the experience of the great books to the child. We may:

1. Read them the book aloud, in a kind of dramatic performance (this is not to say this should be done theatrically). We may read *a*. whole short stories; *b*. a novel serialised; or *c*. extracts from a novel to whet their appetite for reading it themselves. By this means the teacher is setting a standard of choice, of understanding, and of reading and delivery. He communicates, too, his excitement. (If he has none, then of course he can't do it at all.)
2. Direct silent reading. This may either be reading of the selected classic or from a selected list of books. We must provide disciplines in an age which has none. Left to himself in a library between rubbish, picture-books, or good books Gresham's Law will operate and the child will choose rubbish (you and I do it in the common room or dentist's waiting room, and they have less stamina).

Reading

Enjoyment of reading demands effort and concentration and we must provide the conditions: a period a week of silence with the injunction to *read a book*. The children should have dictionaries and a book in which to write notes and notes on words of difficulty or interest. The discipline should be one of reading fiction. The flicking through encyclopedias which passes for 'library work' in many schools is a waste of time.[1]

3. Such periods of reading should be followed by class discussion; or by the writing of 'reviews' or the keeping of a book diary, and sometimes the investigation of an author's other works, his life, letters, biography and so on.

Huckleberry Finn, I would suggest, lends itself to a combination of (1) and (2). The first few chapters might be read by the teacher and then discussed in class: did they like this story? Or the teacher could read Chapter 5 first (*Huck's Father—The Fond Parent—Reform*), and discuss with them the morality of parents and children: for Huck is the means to an imaginatively controlled discussion of many such matters—and this is what we should seek in such books for 'close study'. And so the teacher could go on, selecting episodes for reading aloud—Huck's disguise as a girl, the Boggs episode, the island, the feud, the deception over Peter Wilks. Everyone of these is far more exciting than any Western, and more meat than 'spoon vittles'.

The kind of questions, oral or written, one asks about such a book as *Huckleberry Finn* should be about the meaning of the story, and contrived in such a way as to show how puzzling over a book makes it more enjoyable: this is the power of good reading. Take for instance the smallpox episode (pp. 93 ff. in the Puffin edition). Huck feels he must give up Jim to the law of the white folks because Jim is a negro and property. 'I says I *got* to do it.' Along come two men in a skiff and ask Huck about the man on the raft: 'Is your man black or white?'

'I didn't answer up prompt. I tried to, but the words wouldn't come. I tried, for a second or two, to brace up and out with it, but I wasn't man enough—hadn't the spunk of a rabbit. I see I was weakening; so I just give up trying, and up and says:
    'He's white.'

[1] I heard recently of a primary school which when allotted £450 for reading books ordered *The Encyclopaedia Britannica*.

I have heard teachers complain about Huck because he is un-grammatical and spells wrongly: he does, but in this he presents a challenge—for his 'wrong' grammar gives a syntax that is more lively than normal syntax, and his wrong spelling a richer texture of vernacular (far richer than stock 'Western' American). Huck's idiom is the fine use, by an artist, of the very free language habits of our own children. Can we embrace it? In the episode just quoted the masterly power of Mark Twain is shown, as through-out the book, in inverting morality by the simplest touches so that we may examine it. The child reader can be asked, what is Huckleberry trying to 'brace up' and say? The child may reply first—that Huck is trying to say that he hasn't got a negro on board: he's trying to summon up courage to hide Jim. But he *isn't*; Huck says, 'I gave up trying and says, 'He's white".' Consternation in the class perhaps. What then was Huck trying to do? To give Jim up. Why? Because people thought 'niggers' were property. (You remember someone says in the book when a boiler blew up, 'Anyone hurt?' 'No mum: killed a nigger.') What is it then that makes Huck go against his 'conscience'? His love for Jim. Must we always obey our conscience? Here, surely, conscience dictates the thing that everyone thought was right, merely out of force of habit. And so on.

Huck lies to the men: he says Jim is his father. They offer to tow the raft. Huck says 'Everybody goes away when I want them to help.' 'Well, that's infernal mean. Odd, too. Say, boy, what's the matter with your father?' 'It's the—a—the—well, it ain't anything much.' And so he encourages them to think it is small-pox (though he never lies) and they make haste to leave Huck and his 'pap'. Huck says: 'They went off and I got aboard the raft, feeling bad and low, because I knowed very well I had done wrong.' Why does Huck have such terrible doubts? Because he has sheltered a negro. Is he wicked then? No, we feel pleased. But we hate the men. Have they done anything wrong? Not really, because Jim hasn't got smallpox—it was just a clever trick of Huck's. But they are mean because they thought they were leaving a sick man out of fear of catching smallpox themselves— it is like the story of the Good Samaritan. Huck is 'better' than they are, even more so because he doesn't know it; and, although he says, 'So I reckoned I wouldn't bother no more about it, but after this always do whichever come handiest at the time,' he doesn't do what is handiest, but what is best.

Such a discussion shows how a discussion of social and personal morals may emerge from, and be controlled by, the discipline of reading. And, as it arouses the child's passionate sense of justice and injustice, it may be an experience which clinches the child's awareness of how exciting a book can be. The moral meaning of a book can be taken without any such explicit commentary as mine above. Here are two pieces on George Orwell's *Animal Farm* by pupils of twelve. I quote them by permission of Mr Kenneth Fell and the Editor of *The Use of English*: the book had been read aloud to the pupils with no comment, and these are answers to school examination questions.

1. Mr Jones was the original owner of Animal Farm, he was a cruel tyrant and was hated by all the animals. Napoleon was the pig ruler of Animal Farm, he was a hypocrite and a story teller, he worked the animals to the bone and became a crueler more cunning tyrant than even Jones.

   Boxer was a big strong horse but he had little intelligence, and always believed in everything that Napoleon said or did. He worked till he nearly dropped to make the Windmill but in the end was wickedly killed because he was too old.

   Benjamin was the old donkey who did not take part in the revolution and did not believe that any good would come of it. He just worked and was the same as he was in the old days he was the wisest of the animals and it was he who realised that Boxer was going to his death.

   Mr Whymper was the man that Napoleon imployed to see to biusness deals. He was a thin strip of a man and none of the animals liked him.

2. It was sometime after the hated slave driver Mr Jones had been driven from animal farm, and that morning the pigs, who had appointed themselves as cheifs of the farm, found a chest of Mr Jone's, which was full of cloths. Soon, the pigs were seen to be practicing their first steps on two feet, and a couple of weeks after that Napoleon came out of his house, strutting on two legs, and clothed in Mr Jones' Sunday best. After him came the other pigs,

though with less imperous clothes. It was rumoured also, that Napoleon had ordered the changing of the animals legend which now reads, 'But some are more equal than others.'

Here children have gained those insights which give such satisfaction in reading a good prose work. Of course, there are dull patches in every book: we need to skip, and the teacher will know when to stop, to withdraw, to pass on to something different. There need be no hurry—*Huckleberry Finn* will provide at least a term's work if a form takes to it, for close study: and we should aim at depth of response, not quantity of books done. With the better classes, of course, the work may be helped by readings aloud by more able pupils, dramatisations of episodes, and even the use of a character as a mode for invention by word of mouth, in drama, and writing. An author lives with his characters for months and years, and, in a sense, for life—so can we.

BOOK-LISTS AND PRACTICE IN READING

Having come so far, I am in some difficulty when it comes to suggesting lists of books for the teaching of reading in the secondary modern school. The problem is a most intractable one. There is only a limited amount of money available for each school and each teacher: some choice has to be made. The range of reading ability is from age eight to eighteen. Teachers' own tastes will differ—and what is perhaps more important, their methods will differ. Some of us may be satisfied with our abilities to convey the gist and pith of a book by a dramatised reading; others will prefer to work carefully chapter by chapter, by exegesis. And we shall apply this to different classes according to their size, mental age, emotional age, and stamina. Then, again, we live in an age of changing values—values changing both for proper reasons, because sensibility is changing; and for less desirable reasons, because of various suspect methods of promotion by publishers and reviewers. By which I mean that quite undeserved reputations, such as are hailed every now and then by the periodicals, are investments, and none of us escapes being taken in by such promotions. Thus there is a great difference between one man's conception of what makes a 'classic' and another's; and even more between their notions of why they encourage other people to read books at all.

Thus an all-inclusive book-list is, I think, not much to my purpose. Readers can find such a list in Mr A. E. Smith's book on *English in the Secondary Modern School*, or in Miss Rosemary Beresford's *What Shall I Read?* (The latter, however, contains some lofty stuff, even for grammar school children, such as the novels of Ivy Compton Burnett, which baffle the present writer.) The school library must, of course, contain a very catholic selection, but I would insist that the 'classics' should be there, if only to imply values, or because they may be taken out by accident. There is a helpful list issued by the National Book League, which also has a travelling sample school library. Its catalogue list, however, reveals some of the odd blindnesses and weaknesses in the standards of judgement exhibited by such official productions. From this catalogue, for instance, my touchstone *Huckleberry Finn* is missing altogether, and so are the books of E. Nesbit, also *Typhoon*, *Great Expectations*, *White Fang*, and *The Secret Garden*, while Thomas Hardy is represented only by *Our Exploits at West Poley*. Edward Thomas, by the way, is also missing from the poetry, though room has been found for *Under Milk Wood*! There is also a useful inclusive list in *Four to Fourteen* by Kathleen Lines, and other lists may be obtained from the School Library Association.

Reading stamina nowadays is low, and teachers of English feel an urgent need to deepen whatever reading capacities they are forced by the law of the land to give their pupils. With many children it may be a matter of merely introducing them to a habit; with others we feel, with some resignation, that it is enough if they have once in their lives enjoyed a book. But the deepening, where deepening can be done, is generally thought of as working through substantial prose works in class. The choice of these works, judging by many school store cupboards and publishers' lists, is made by standards formed fifty years ago in the old standard schools, when adventure stories, such as those of Ballantyne and Henty, tended to go with an atmosphere of imperial responsibility belonging to the Boer War. Good solid reading is still often thought of as a means of widening a child's geographical, and perhaps anthropological, interests in empire-building; or, at most, leading-colonies-towards-self-government. 'Biggles' books are the culmination of this genre, though they certainly lead to no ideals of self-government: colonials and foreigners are treacherous to Captain Johns, and must be kept in order by a clean right to the jaw, for the most part. The line, no doubt, belongs to the development of education in the State schools using public school values—values by which it would be impossible even to understand what is going on in (say) present-day Africa. At best, the choice of much matter for school children's reading carries on the general uplifting principles inherent in the old concepts of standard education: that literature only has value if it inculcates ideals of bravery, endurance, fortitude, and so forth: this is expressed in the universal use of books such as *Kon-Tiki*, or the prevalent use of war stories, which are in any case sometimes merely respectable covers for crude violence. In America the use of story books to inculcate the values of conformity and patriotism is deeply entrenched.

We do not, of course, read novels, books of fiction, primarily to learn about foreign countries, or to become adventurous or courageous: we read to become more aware of life and the world, and to develop in imagination our capacities to deal with it. Children know this, and in their own reading they turn avidly to fantasy—'William' books, 'Biggles' books, Enid Blyton. They turn to these out of hunger for fantasy: fantasy which they know from their experience of words since babyhood to be an essential part of their growth. The trouble is, of course, that they are betrayed: the prose of Enid Blyton is day-dream at its most bloodless and flaccid—the writer appeals so widely simply because she has never grown up herself, and so she can offer nothing but regression to a magical denial of reality. Her books are without form or rhythm, without the contest with difficulty of any kind, and she reduces experience to the level of the coddled vegetable. Unfortunately, this is the ethos of many homes, in our subtopian era, and so such a writer as Enid Blyton makes the perfect chronic delusion for the childhood which is spent in an atmosphere of atrophy of spirit.

Yet there is also a kind of betrayal in what the school too often provides. First, we do not make sufficient recognition that the child we are dealing with is probably better able to deal with oral than written literature: that is, that we have a duty to *read a great deal of prose and verse* to the children. This naturally determines in part our choice of books—and extends the range at the same time. Failure to provide for the child's fantasy needs is in giving children, with all the authority of the teacher, books which are essentially day-dream at a not much higher level. This is true of many of the widely used travel, escape, autobiographical, and war books (such as *Reach for the Sky*, by Paul Brickhill). The object seems to be to 'get on the side of the child' by giving him matter about his own time, which perhaps, say, links up with a film. But essentially the books are often, as symbolism, impoverished: they are written by journalists 'about' Africa, or fighting, or are books 'about' the sea by raconteurs, and, as treatment of human experience in words, not of great value.

While such books should be in every school library, and while reading of much of this kind of book may not do much harm— we have all had our orgies of Jeffery Farnol and P. G. Wodehouse, just as we had orgies of eating huge amounts of cheap nougat or locust beans—yet with the less able child something is missing if there is no more substantial fare in his small diet of reading. No other agency than the school will enrich his creative life; Enid Blyton has become a very rich woman simply by providing for the child's desperate needs for prose dealing with—'about' —the human heart and mind. Except, of course, that 'provide' and 'deal' are just what she doesn't do, in any nourishing way.

Dealing with the human heart and mind is the province of the artist. The journalist who has to deal with human experience in a travel or war book frequently does so in a commonplace way which has no 'inner' symbolic depth. Where the artist is concerned, it is pretty well irrelevant what a book is 'about': Conrad's books are not really 'about' the sea, but about the integrity of a Captain Macwhirr, or the moral squalor in egocentricity of a Mr Verloc. Children, of course, like books to be 'about' this, that, and the other: they have a hunger for information about human life in Africa, or the ends of the earth: but the chief hunger, we must always bear in mind, is for answers to inner questions of identity, and, with the child, 'what will adult life be like?' They must be given answers to these questions in 'felt' symbolic terms, through the hands of the sensitive and responsive artist. If we do not do this essential work we are betraying them to a habit of reading which, leaving them untrained in taking in the essential wisdom of prose writing, will merely open them to those predators, in Fleet Street, the advertising worlds, and commercial publishing who have exploited the growth of literacy at the expense of sensibility.

Yet the concern with giving our children something effective by way of imaginative prose brings a further two problems. One is of length merely—the prose work is by its nature an expansive form, and the structure of the shortest novel is complex enough for adults to find it difficult to discuss a novel with any relevance. The other problem is that of adult sexual passion. In poetry the latter can be dealt with in ways children may assimilate—and I have allowed for this in my anthology, *Iron, Honey, Gold*. In poetry the passion is suspended in the inexplicitness of the verse structure. But it is the nature of prose to be much more explicit, and while D. H. Lawrence pronounced that a child reader of his novels dealing with sex would simply be bored, it is likely, that, under the pressure of the frightened knowingness of the child's culture in the 1960s, a child might be disturbed and made unhappy by a reading of such an essentially well-meant work as *Lady Chatterley's Lover*. I think the child, however 'knowing', can only take the explicit rendering of adult sexual passion in detail in prose as something which makes it anxious. The child needs more the opportunity to explore love and hate by symbolism, questions of identity and relationship, and the values involved. It is to these that Henry James limits his protagonist Maisie, in his very great novel *What Maisie Knew* about the child in the midst of the failure of love. Such a work as *Wuthering Heights* seems to me perfect for children, simply because it explores love at the level of a deeper wisdom, as a matter of the whole being and psyche, rather than at the level of what has come to be meant by 'love'. The passion in *Wuthering Heights* transcends the sexual, which it is never explicit about. This is not to excuse us from tackling human love: we fail if, in a world of knowingness and depersonalisation, we deal with life only in terms of single-sex adventure books or asexual books such as *Treasure Island*. Much can be done by judicious cutting which yet does not emasculate. I have compiled an anthology of short stories by such writers as Hemingway, T. F. Powys, Lawrence, Scott Fitzgerald, and James Joyce. But only the teacher himself knows how far he may, and dare, go in handling the aspects of human love about which his pupils desperately need wisdom.

Of course, it is not only wisdom about love for which our

pupils starve: they also want to explore death, pain, and the ceaseless struggle to live with others in the give and take of the human community. Here, for instance, is the prose of the insight, the wisdom, of the artist: it is from the terrible passage in *Le Feu* (*Under Fire*), by Henri Barbusse, when the soldiers discover Cocon's dead head: 'When you hear of or see the death of one of those who fought by your side and lived exactly the same life, you receive a direct blow in the flesh before even understanding. It is truly as if you had heard of your own destruction. It is only later that you begin to mourn.' The relevance of this to Lawrence's profound remarks about the 'real feelings' felt by the body (in *A Propos of Lady Chatterley's Lover*) will be appreciated by those who know it; and, as the artist's perception of the whole being in which we live, it is a piece of wisdom that could be taken by the child and applied to all that may happen to it in life, including falling in love. As Lawrence said, 'it is only afterwards that the feelings are recognised by the mind': it is this kind of wisdom about the flux of our experience that we aim to give by the teaching of reading and the fostering of creative symbolism.

If we approach making a booklist in this frame of mind, we shall find that we can vindicate many of the accepted children's classics. We shall also need to delete many that remain on the publishers' lists and in the school cupboards from sheer inertia. Some we may delete because they are too emotionally adult and overdone, such as *Jane Eyre*; others because they do not deserve attention as art, such as *Gallions Reach*. But we shall also see that there is no occasion to inflict poor adult taste on children— neither from 'practical' considerations nor because of a lack of good simple creative writing. Why give them the Monsarrat kind of stuff? Certainly we may ask, why do such writers as Raymond Chandler find their way into school CSE syllabuses? What value to children can be the commercial exploitation of language used to arouse the phantasies and emotions of anxiety and insecurity?

I propose to give two lists here. One is a list of books which seem to me to be works of art, and from which teachers might select the fifteen or so they will try to use with their best classes as they grow up through the school. Many may seem pious gestures: but we must allow for the possibilities, in some places, and at some times, of exceptional stamina in teacher or pupil; of developing techniques, and of the wider use of energetic *reading to* children. If, for instance, classes ever come to be reduced in size, say, to twenty pupils, some of my higher gestures would come within range. The second list is a general one of books which have sound virtues in their dealing with life as experience: these could be the core of a selected class library from which children drew for directed silent reading: or, of course, they too can be read aloud to them.

BOOKS FOR CLOSE STUDY

First year

Bunyan, John, *The Pilgrim's Progress.*
Carroll, Lewis, *Alice in Wonderland; Alice Through the Looking-Glass.*
Defoe, Daniel, *Robinson Crusoe.*
De la Mare, Walter, *Collected Stories for Children.*
Dickens, Charles, *Oliver Twist* (Broadstream Books, C.U.P.).
The Golden Ass of Apuleius, school edition.
Greek authors, retold by Rex Warner, *Men and Gods.*
Homer, *The Odyssey*, trans. E. V. Rieu (Penguin).
Kipling, Rudyard, *The Just-So Stories.*
Marryat, Frederick, *Children of the New Forest.*
Swift, Jonathan, *A Voyage to Lilliput.*
Twain, Mark, *Tom Sawyer.*

Second year

Conrad, Joseph, *An Outpost of Progress* (short story).
Dickens, Charles, *David Copperfield; A Tale of Two Cities.*
Graham, Angus, *The Golden Grindstone.*
London, Jack, *The Call of the Wild; White Fang.*
Orwell, George, *Animal Farm.*
Slocum, Joshua, *Sailing Alone Around the World.*
Twain, Mark, *Huckleberry Finn; The Prince and the Pauper.*

Third year

Brontë, Emily, *Wuthering Heights.*
Butler, Samuel, *Erewhon.*
Conrad, Joseph, *Typhoon; The Secret Sharer* (short story).
Dickens, Charles, *Great Expectations.*
Falkner, J. Meade, *Moonfleet.*
Gorki, Maxim, *Childhood* (Broadstream Books, C.U.P.).

Melville, Herman, *Moby Dick* (abridged by L. E. C. Bruce).

Twain, Mark, *Life on the Mississippi* (first half); *Roughing It* (Broadstream Books).

Fourth year

Austen, Jane, *Northanger Abbey; Pride aud Prejudice.*

Collins, Wilkie, *The Woman in White* (abridged).

Conrad, Joseph, *The Shadow Line*; *The End of the Tether; The Nigger of the Narcissus; The Secret Agent* (school edition); *Youth.*

Dickens, Charles, *Hard Times.*

Hardy, Thomas, *The Trumpet Major*; *Tess of the D'Urbervilles.*

Jefferies, Richard, *After London.*

Mark Twain, *Pudd'nhead Wilson* (Broadstream Books).

Also short stories as in *People and Diamonds*, I–IV.

Such a list I do not offer as The Great Classics in which all our children's noses must be rubbed. I offer the list as an aid, an instrument, to creating, with as many of our children as possible, a taste for reading the best prose written in English. I offer it to back up the teacher who wishes to give the secondary modern pupil a glimpse of the inheritance. A teacher who battles his way along, reading aloud, discussing, upholding such books as he chooses by personal preference from that list can feel some assurance that he is doing good, in terms of expanding the capacities of soul of a new generation.

There need to be added to this list some titles to bring it up to date. Here the problems are again of length and adult passion, for the novel, in recent decades, has come to explore adult passion deeply. At the same time it has thrown off less by the way (as the nineteenth century did supremely) for children. Thus the future of reading in the secondary school is a matter of proposing to publishers that they experiment, not only with children's books (as for instance, the Heinemann list of readers and the Methuen 'Reluctant Readers' list have so enterprisingly done) but with children's editions of adult works of distinction, abridged by page and paragraph. Here is a list of such possible editions, of both modern works and old works which, now the age of respectability is gone, we should bring, perhaps sometimes cut, to offer their robust wisdom to our pupils, who have so little offered them that is positive and creative at large.

Reading

Preparing such possible editions raises questions of bringing to our young readers the essential qualities of twentieth-century prose at its best: but they are questions which should not be dodged by turning to the work of mere journalists, or looking for authors for children among fashionable names. We must give a touch of the best, or strive to give it, and not just give an indiscriminate reading habit. Yet, to make access to the best, while rewarding, is hard work, simply because it requires the disturbance and readjustment of our attitudes to life.

So we need to back up our exploration of 'the best' books with as much reading as we can manage in bulk, on books which, though they cannot perhaps be called 'great', are creative, honest, well written, and offer something of a wider light on life's possibilities. So, we can now suggest a larger list from which the teacher can draw books which he enjoys himself.

[1] Now in a school edition edited by the present author, published by Heinemann.

My allocations to year are approximate. I find in discussing the problem of reading with other teachers that differences in conditions are such that what one teacher considers suitable for the first year, another will find successful only in the fourth year. It is worth remembering all along, perhaps, as Douglas Brown has pointed out, that we too often give children books that are too old for them. Figures, e.g. (1–4), indicate age-range.

First year

FICTION

Broome, Dora, *Fairy Tales from the Isle of Man.*
Bond, Michael, *A Bear Called Paddington* (1–3).
Canfield, Dorothy, *Betsy.*
Clarke, P. *Twelve and the Genii* (1–2).
Fuller, Roy, *Savage Gold.*
Grahame, Kenneth, *The Wind in the Willows.*
Grice, Frederick, *Severnside Story* (1–2).
Grimm, the brothers, *Household Stories.*
Hergé, *King Ottokar's Sceptre* (1–4).
Kästner, Erich, *Emil and the Detectives.*
King, C., *Stig of the Dump* (1–3).
Lynch, Patricia, *The Turf-cutter's Donkey.*
Macgregor, R. J., *The Secret of Dead Man's Cove.*
Manning-Sanders, R., *A Book of Giants* (1–4).
Masefield, John, *Jim Davis* (1–3).
Norton, Mary, *The Borrowers.*
Pearce, Philippa, *A Dog so Small, Tom's Midnight Garden, Minnow on the Say*
Poliakoff, *Coco the Clown.*
Prøysen, Alf, *Little Old Mrs Pepperpot* (1–3).
Serraillier, Ian, *The Silver Sword* (1–4).
Sewell, Anna, *Black Beauty* (1–2).
White, E. B., *Charlotte's Web* (1–2).
Wilder, Laura Ingalls, *By the Shores of Silver Lake.*
Williamson, Henry, *Tarka the Otter* (1–4).

NON-FICTION

Maeterlinck, Maurice, *The Life of the Bee.*
Sangster, Lord George, *Seventy Years a Showman.*

Reading

FICTION

Second year

Aiken, Joan, *The Wolves of Willoughby Chase* (1–4).
Alcott, Louisa, M., *Little Women* (1–4).
Anonymous, *Legends and Folk Tales* (O.U.P.)—any of this series.
Bullen, F. T., *The Cruise of the Cachalot*.
Burnett, Frances Hodgson, *The Secret Garden*.
Cooper, Fenimore, *The Deerslayer*.
De la Mare, Walter, *Told Again*.
Denison, Muriel, *Susannah of the Mounties*.
Garnett, Eve, *The Family from One End Street*.
Grice, Frederick, *Bonnie Pit Laddie* (1–4).
Irwin, M., *Still She Wished for Company*.
Lewis, Cecil Day, *The Otterbury Incident* (1–4).
Masefield, John, *The Bird of Dawning*, (1–4); *The Box of Delights*.
Nesbit, E., *The Wouldbegoods; The Railway Children*.
Ransome, Arthur, *We Didn't Mean to Go to Sea*.
Seligman, A., *Voyage of the Cap Pilar*.
Severn, David, *The Future Took Us*.
Thompson, Flora, *Lark Rise to Candleford*.
Tschiffely, A. S., *A Tale of Two Horses*.
Van der Loeff, A. R., *Avalanche*.
Wells, H. G., *The First Man in the Moon; The Invisible Man; Short Stories*.

NON-FICTION

Durrell, Gerald, *New Noah*.
Fabre, J. H., *The Mason Wasps*.
Heyerdahl, *The Kon-Tiki Expedition*.
Nansen, F., *Farthest North*.

FICTION

Third year

Buchan, John, *The Thirty-Nine Steps; Greenmantle*.
Collins, Wilkie, *The Moonstone*.
Cousteau, J. Y., *The Silent World*.
Doyle, Conan, *The Lost World*.
Garnett, David, *Pocahontas*.
Haggard, Rider, *King Solomon's Mines*.
Karazin, N., *Cranes Flying South*.
Kipling, R., *Many Inventions*.
Morse, E., *Chang*.
Pearce, Philippa, *The Strange Sunflower*.

199

Picard, *The Mermaid and the Simpleton* (1–3).
Reeves, James, *The Pillar-Box Thieves.*
Shaefer, Jack, *Shane*
Tschiffely, A. S., *Tschiffely's Ride.*
Uttley, Alison, *A Country Child.*
Wells, H. G., *The Time Machine.*

NON-FICTION

Frank, Anne, *The Diary of Anne Frank.*
Grimble, A., *A Pattern of Islands.*
Scott's Last Expedition (John Murray).
Wong, J. S., *Fifth Chinese Daughter.*

Fourth year

FICTION

Barstow, Stan, *Joby.*
Bell, Adrian, *Corduroy; Silver Ley.*
Childers, Erskine, *The Riddle of the Sands.*
Cleary, Beverly, *Fifteen.*
Forster, E. M., *The Machine Stops; The Celestial Omnibus.*
Hardy, Thomas, *Under the Greenwood Tree; The Woodlanders.*
Lee, Harper, *To Kill a Mockingbird.*
Hemingway, Ernest, *A Farewell to Arms; For Whom the Bell Tolls.*
Hilton, James, *Lost Horizon.*
Hughes, Richard, *In Hazard; High Wind in Jamaica.*
Lawrence, D. H., *Tales* (some, e.g. *A Sick Collier, Samson and Delilah*).
Melville, Herman, *Billy Budd.*
Sillitoe, Alan, *The Loneliness of the Long Distance Runner.*
Waugh, Evelyn, *Scoop.*
Wells, H. G., *Kipps; The History of Mr Polly; The War of the Worlds.*

NON-FICTION

Baldwin, James, *The Fire Next Time.*
Braithwaite, E. R., *To Sir With Love; Paid Servant.*
Measham, D. C. (ed.), *Fourteen.*
Stapledon, Olaf, *First and Last Men.*
Smith, Emma, *Maiden's Trip.*
Thomas, Helen (widow of Edward Thomas), *World Without End.*
Wordsworth, Dorothy, *Journal.*
Yevtushenko, Yevgeny, *A Precocious Autobiography.*

Reading

Picture Books

For use with less able readers.

First Year

Ardizzone, Edward, *Johnny the Clockmaker* (1–3).
Hewett, *The Little White Hen.*
de Jong, Meindert, *The Last Little Cart.*
Zion, A. and Graham, M. B., *Harry the Dirty Dog.*

Second Year

Erbele, *Peter and the Mouse* (1–2).
Calhoun, *Witch of Hissinghill* (1–2).
Herman, F., *The Giant Alexander* (1–2).
Standon, A., *Tin Can Tortoise* (1–2).
Wildsmith, Brian, *The Rich Man and the Shoemaker* (1–2).
Williams, Ursula Moray, *Gobbolino, the Witch's Cat.*

If the 'close study' of such books as are in my first list is secure at the heart of our work in reading, then all our other work in handling books follows from it. It will provide a stimulus for home reading—borrowing from the school or local library. With the close study of those great works which excite both teacher and pupil may go activities which help provide a guide, starting from the known good works among the shelves of lesser works. This work may be encouraged by such things as a Reading Club, which invites 'literary' people to give it talks, on writing, reviewing or printing books. If one has experienced the excitement a great book can give, one is the more anxious to learn to use books properly and well, and there should be lessons in school on the care of books. Of course I have dealt with maximum, 'A' stream, possibilities. But our work with lower streams should follow by implication: the important thing is to give these readers whose preoccupation with the mere mechanics of reading prevents their enjoying a large-scale work the taste of such works by reading *to* them. Then they can search for a book they can read, of some quality, so they may feel they can read a good book.

Of course, no school is complete without a library, and this should by now no longer need saying. Children should be taught how to use the normal systems of classification, how to find a book, how to put a book back in the correct place, and so forth. But a library is only opened to a child (except as a source of time-passing distraction) if he is given a sense of values to carry to the shelves. In every library the best books ought to be there: and behind every child there should be the experience of a class library (i.e. books from my second list, with others added). This should be his library for directed silent reading, and it should contain both the books listed above for close study, in adequate and handsome editions, and those books used in groups as readers. Work from this background library (as far as fiction is concerned) may be devoted to the following:

1. Browse among the fiction shelves and find (*a*) a book that interests you from a cursory glance; (*b*) a book by an author of whom you know or of whose work you have already read something.

   Be prepared to say in writing or by word of mouth why you have chosen the book, or why, after reading it a short while, you rejected it.
2. Class discussion of such stories, comparison of authors and books.
3. Simple written pastiche of some authors: e.g. Buchan, Bunyan: and of pupils' own popular reading books.
4. Investigation of author's biographies, how many works they wrote, where and when they lived, and so on.

Dictionaries and other reference books such as the *Concise Dictionary of National Biography* (up to 1900) should be available.

Such reading work as I have outlined here puts the comprehension of the artist's words at the fore—that is the pleasure of reading. This reading activity should lead to the reading and comprehension of non-fiction: reading for investigation. This work is best done in collaboration with other subjects, if not actually by teachers of other subjects, though this is seldom done in practice. The English teacher will concern himself to teach the following skills of reading for investigation:

1. The ability to read a set of instructions aloud so that they make sense to a listener.
2. The ability to read instructions and repeat the gist of them from memory.
3. The ability to read a page of, say, a scientific book or a book on geography and give an account of its content orally.

4. To write down in two or three sentences the gist of a paragraph in such a book.
5. To indicate by one question what the author attempts to answer in that paragraph.
6. To read a newspaper and give, after making notes, an account of its contents, including a list of the more important news items in order of their importance. (A great deal of our reading work of this kind should be done using periodicals and newspapers, for these are the forms of reading matter which surround our children in their environment, and it is a discriminating approach to these that we wish to train.)
7. To be able to use a library index, a book index, and the main reference works such as an encyclopaedia, *Keesing's Contemporary Archives*, a large dictionary, to make an investigation into a subject, e.g. *The History of the Suez Canal*, and make notes on it for an essay.

But it is obvious that such work really belongs to the other 'subjects' and the subject teacher. Our main effort is the reading of prose as art. Some of the books I give in my general bibliography will help with reading work of all kinds and with 'reading to investigate' (see p. 254).

CHAPTER 11

Drama

Nowadays hardly anyone means the same thing by the word 'drama', or 'dramatics'. This has something to do with the present uncertain state of the theatre in England. There is an impassable crevasse between the work of the teacher who is trying to give his pupils the experience of the mediaeval verse play *Abraham and Isaac* and the work of the producer of the latest exploitation of violence and cruelty for its own sake in the commercial theatre, or on film or television. The whole problem of drama and its value is bedevilled by the decline of habits of symbolising. In schools what is meant by 'drama' may include a kind of imaginative composition, elocution, a training for the specialisations of the naturalistic stage, or the 'school play', which is often a piece of window-dressing.

Rather than plunge into a largely negative account of the state of contemporary drama let me try to suggest what is valuable to a child as dramatic experience. To a child, drama has the same function as it had in adult communities where drama had not fully emerged from ritual—drama, that is, without an audience, in which all are performers and participants. It is to children still the *dromenon*, the 'thing done', in which they are fully and gravely caught up, and do not play merely for amusement. George Thomson quotes the account given by a reciter of the Homeric poems (in *Aeschylus and Athens*), and this is the spirit in which a child participates in drama:

When I am describing something pitiful, my eyes fill with tears, when something terrible or strange, my hair stands on end and my heart throbs...and whenever I look down from the platform at an audience, I see them weeping, with a wild look in their eyes, lost in wonder at the words they hear...

The words they hear—is a significant phrase: even in such a degree of 'voluntary suspension of disbelief'—weeping, with a wild look

—it is the *words* at which the audience is 'lost in wonder'. And this is the condition of children watching *Punch and Judy* or taking part in one of their own children's games. They know this is 'play-acting', that 'it is made up of words', but at the same time it is a serious activity, not just 'passing the time', because it is a form of symbolising which gives strength to the inner life.

As infants, children show an immense capacity for dramatic activity. A child imitating an engine *becomes* an engine, as Mark Twain portrays in the famous fence episode from *Tom Sawyer*:

Ben was eating an apple, and giving a long melodious whoop at intervals, followed by a deep-toned ding dong, ding dong dong, for he was personating a steamboat. As he drew near he slackened speed, took the middle of the street, leaned far over to starboard, and rounded-to ponderously, and with laborious pomp and circumstance, for he was personating the *Big Missouri*, and considered himself to be drawing nine feet of water. He was boat, and captain, and engine bells combined, so he had to imagine himself standing on his own hurricane-deck giving the orders and executing them...his right hand meantime describing stately circles, for it was representing a forty-foot wheel...

By such symbolic enactment a child learns to deal with life. If we examine children's games—those games they have preserved over many centuries—we find there is a search, through these embryonic forms of drama, for a coming to terms with the most disturbing things in the inward life. The traditional games provide the fantasy experience of violence and fear:

> WITCH: Your feet are too dirty.
> MOTHER: Can't I cut them off?
> WITCH: The blood would run all over the floor.
> MOTHER: Can't I wrap them up in a blanket?
> WITCH: The fleas would hop out.

They contemplate death:

> Ashes to ashes and dust to dust
> If God won't have you, the Devil must,

and sexuality:

> The wife made a pudding
> She made it nice and soft
> Up came the husband, cut a slice off
> Taselum, toselum, don't say nay
> For next Monday morning is our wedding day...

From anthropologists we know that these games are descendants of rituals performed by adults at significant times—at funerals, weddings, initiation ceremonies or fertility rites. In a simple little game such as *Draw a pail of water*, for instance, we have a reference to the ancient ceremony of well-dressing, and behind it elements of worship of the springs of fertility, initiation and the ritual dance. In the children's games the long past of the ritual and its verses, the primitive depths, are suspended in a vigorous dancing rhythm and an economy of haunting melody. They enable the children to share the mock experience of the feared thing—the death, the violence—and to emerge feeling satisfaction—a triumph is felt over the inner fear. (These points are made at greater length in the present writer's book on *Children's Games*.)

Lady Alice Gomme, who collected the children's games at the end of last century, recognised their dramatic qualities:

There must be some strong force inherent in these games that has allowed them to be continued from generation to generation, a force potent enough to almost compel their continuance and to prevent their decay. This force must have been as strong or stronger than the customs which first brought the games into existence, and I identify it as the dramatic faculty inherent in mankind.[1]

This 'dramatic faculty inherent in mankind' is shown today, I feel, at its best in children. Children have this capacity to enter imaginatively and directly into the creative working out by symbols of aspects of our most troubling experience. The adult is largely in the hand of 'distraction from distraction by distraction', of an impoverished symbolism and a sensational culture, his environment lacking creative opportunities and his work often unsatisfying. Increasingly we try to solve 'inner' problems in

[1] *Dictionary of British Folk-Lore, Part I: Children's Games* (D. Nutt, 1894), p. 514.

'outer' ways—as by more acquisition of material comforts. In this situation culture tends to become merely delusional or merely one of low-level hedonism.

This disabling culture is epitomised in the rhythm-less prose of Enid Blyton for children, and in the unreal romantic fantasies of adolescent papers. Beside these, traditional verse has qualities of unflinching sincerity, those qualities which belong, in the highest sense, to drama:

> My father said
> That if I did
> He'd bang my head
> With the teapot lid.

If children need to experience violence and fear, then, some might argue, we can let them read the horror comic: after all, they like *Punch and Judy*. And here we come to further points about children's dramatic faculties. Many people would censor from *Punch and Judy* the gallows, coffin and ghost, just as they leave out the more disturbing nursery rhymes such as the frightening verses of *Old Mother Hubbard*, or *The Old Grey Goose*. They feel safest with little Noddy, whose experience rules out everything mysterious, discomforting and troublesome: in Toyland every difficulty may be overcome by some such device as a jolly magic rubber, and everything is tractable.

Unfortunately life is not like that, however much suburbia hides what it can under its delusional home decor and the arcadian shrubs in the ideal garden. People die; they are ruined by changes of fortune; happiness is often shattered as soon as grasped by sickness or other circumstance; we have to strive all our lives with problems of identity and relationship, with guilt, jealousy, and fear over inner conflicts between love and hate. In this, even in normal family life, are our satisfactions. Of course the middle-class suburban mother, with television and a clean cosy home, will protest that such disturbances as jealousy have never troubled little Johnny, who is happy the live-long day with his Hornby trains and his Wild Western outfit, playing in the garden by himself. But give little Johnny a chance to write a story or a poem and we discover a proclivity for extraordinary violence, or the evocation of a sad and disturbing loneliness. Fears of weakness and loss of identity trouble children deeply: as indeed they trouble all of us deeply. Unfortunately we have lost much of our cultural help in coming to terms with these. But children preserve some elements of symbolism in their own games, and in traditional culture that remains, such as *Punch and Judy*.

Mr Punch is about the dangers of annihilation the child feels to be in sex. His stick is phallic. He is the talion father whose lust may destroy the mother, and he kills the child (as children may desire to kill brothers and sisters). He dies, but is resurrected, with much clowning—the kind of buffoonery that accompanies death in all folk drama. He kills everyone, including those we most fear, constable, hangman, Authority. Having killed his wife, he goes off with Polly. He is our own aggression, taken to its ultimate extremes (raping mother, killing baby). At the end Punch defeats even the Devil. And his flouting buffoonery yet brings no actual retribution: his is the triumph of art and symbolism over the deeper threats of annihilation in the psyche. Punch is the triumph —*and the child audience knows it all the time*—of the wooden painted doll, the verbal play, the buffoonery, the song, over fears belonging to inner reality. In this sense Mr Punch is infinitely superior to the child's experience of the film, the television and the horror comic. Never for a moment does the child forget he is watching *puppets*, though even at just over one year old he can become involved in the play. He knows that the fantasy is in his own heart and head: the dreadful wrongness of the bad film, bad television programme and the bad comic is in their pretending that *this is really happening*.

From this discussion of the traditional drama of childhood, descended from adult ritual drama, what may we deduce for the school and the classroom? First, that children have a natural sense of the dramatic, without the exercise of which they cannot grow up. This natural sense emerges in such activities as dressing up, playing mothers and fathers, and rhyme-games. We may also deduce that the word, poetry, dance, movement and music are the essential elements of their traditional drama, and that drama is utterly 'non-realistic' (no child bothers, as Mark Twain shows, to enquire whether he could stand on his own hurricane deck). We may see, too, that puppets provide a satisfying kind of 'objective correlative' for the dramatic experience, to maintain a distance of symbolising, non-realism. If we compare infra-red photographs of children watching a horror film with one of some watching *Punch and Judy*, we see the former cowering and the latter 'serious' or roaring with laughter. Although *Punch and Judy* is very disturbing, the child emerges with a sense of relief and elation, as we do from watching a true tragedy, rather than feeling 'drained' or with anxiety aroused. We also may deduce from children's own dramatic culture that a spontaneous element is fundamental, and that there are certain traditional, archetypal symbolic patterns which belong to poetic drama and ritual. This traditional aspect is neglected too much today, perhaps.

Work based on these deductions may have affinities with the work I have suggested as the ways for developing powers of imaginative composition. The purpose of our dramatic composition will be similar. The difference is in the way drama, the *doing*, involves more than the words themselves, though the words must be central to the experience. Drama involves bodily movement, group movement, music and song, and spectacle. And I think it is important to think of drama as belonging to the spoken or sung word and not properly to the written word at all. The writing down of drama is merely a means to provide actors with parts and to make it possible for the play to be reproduced—it is significant that Shakespeare was careless about the printing of his plays. Punch and folk-plays were never written down, and the *commedia dell'arte* always improvised to a synopsis. Plays are not written for the purpose of reading: Shaw's essential weakness is that his plays are written for reading, however much they 'go' on the stage.

The preserved or written play, like Punch and the children's dramatic game, provides for us a work which is a pattern, an embodiment of a traditional or created wisdom—and we must recognise the necessity for marrying the dramatic spontaneity of the child with the discipline of performing a work of literature created by minds superior to our own or embodying a folk-wisdom—submitting ourselves thereby to a refining experience of art.

If we regard drama thus as an important art experience, particularly in the growth of the child, we shall see that much of the work which is done in the name of drama in schools today is useless. We must have standards of speech and movement, but for the work which seems to me appropriate in school those standards and methods which belong to our professional 'realistic' theatre seem utterly foreign, as does the kind of vocal gymnastics called elocution. Movement and mime surely need to spring from the capacity either to enter into an imaginative experience or from the producer's capacity to make a movement-pattern which enhances the symbolism of the work of art. Good speech comes from an understanding of the words spoken and the desire to convey them to an audience. Some training will help both: but one has seen too often the difference between a child who has entered into the person of the Virgin Mary and reads the *Magnificat* in such a way as to bring tears to one's eyes, and the 'produced' child gawkily mincing about and elocuting good words as though they were some parrot-learnt incantation for making an audience clap. Above all, most texts used for drama in school are worthless.

We must abjure altogether, I think, the school play intention and the old-fashioned kind of 'ham' dramatic training. The public performance of a play invites two possible reactions. If Shakespeare is done, there is an air of 'You're not supposed to enjoy it, it's educational'. On the other hand one find teachers, parents and the older pupils urging the abandoning of standards for 'fun', to make money for school funds, or to please parents with a bad play. As T. R. Barnes has said in the *Journal of Education*, the choice of modern plays is mostly between rubbish and 'intelligent drivel' by such writers as Anouilh and Fry: and, I would add, between plays which are fundamentally negative or sentimental and those which have serious intentions but fall into cleverness. The failing of most available plays is in not really providing any essential drama at all—they have no essential creative symbolism to offer.

The professional kind of dramatic training is for the kind of

Drama

play from which the following extract comes. I use it as an example of a particular kind of highly artificial convention of naturalism. When most of us think of 'acting' or 'drama' we think of this kind of thing:

RALEIGH: (*he tries to raise himself, and gives a sudden cry*)
            Oh—God. It does hurt.
STANHOPE: It's bound to hurt, Jimmy.
RALEIGH: What's—on my legs? Something's holding them down—
STANHOPE: It's all right old chap; it's just the shock—numbed them.
            (*Again there is a pause. When* RALEIGH *speaks, there is a different note in his voice.*)
RALEIGH: It's awfully decent of you to bother, Dennis. I feel rotten lying here—everybody else—up there.
STANHOPE: It's not your fault, Jimmy.
RALEIGH: So—damn—silly—getting hit (*Pause*) Is there—just a drop of water?

This is from *Journey's End*, a moving play about the 1914–18 war. Here the character Raleigh comes to realise he is dying. The whole effect depends upon language which, as unemotional and commonplace as possible, enables the actor to show a man playing down his deeper feelings. Raleigh is keeping a stiff upper lip: but his language gives nothing of the inward flow of feelings. This is, of course, a highly artificial convention which is belied by being called *naturalistic*: people just do not talk like this, as a tape-recorder will reveal—this dialogue is highly contrived. The emotions dealt with are powerful, but undefined by the words spoken: everything has to be done by the actor simulating reality. This simulation cannot define an experience, and the feelings the actor must simulate are not given definition in the stage directions. It is because of this failure of definition that the naturalistic stage and cinema have come to the end of their respective tethers in dustbin-drama and cinerama: the modern audience's expectations are not of dramatic symbolism. Children themselves have more to offer from their intuitive dramatic sense. The child miming an imaginative fantasy will mime an archetypal experience, an imaginative concept—say of old age, or kingship, or stealth: he will not be trying to convince an audience of the validity of an individual portrayed in a 'real' state of emotion. Note how the stage direction in the above, 'a different note in his voice', is the only indication we have (or the actor can give) that Raleigh now knows he is dying. In any case such technical subtleties are beyond children.

The difference may perhaps be made clearer by considering how children would enact this:

ISAAC: A mercy, father, why tarry ye so?
Smite off my head and let me go;
I bid you rid me of all my woe,
That is all I pray.

My dear father, I you pray,
Let me take my clothes away.
Fear shedding blood on them today
At my last ending.

(*Abraham raises his sword but an angel appears and grasps the point of the uplifted weapon.*)

ANGEL: Abraham, my servant dear!
ABRAHAM: Lo, Lord, I am already here
ANGEL: Lay not thy sword in no manner
On Isaac, thy dear darling...

Here the action is formal, ballet-like, and what is being enacted is a poem about submission to God's will. The humanity of the poem goes with the individual grief and struggle of Abraham and Isaac as characters: but the actor does not need to convince us that these are 'real' characters in this situation; there is no need to, as the poem itself—the words themselves—develop an amazing dramatic power, concentrating our attention on the suffering of the two protagonists at the centre, and towards this climax. We are relieved from the preoccupation with realism by the rhyming verse, and the formal movement: as with children watching Punch, we can enter into the fantasy, knowing it is symbolism. Groans, writhings, faltering voice, tricks of shuddering, or rolling eyes, to convey feeling on the part of Isaac or Abraham, would obviously be out of place: the main effort of the actor is to speak the poetry as effectively as possible, and in so doing subject himself to a deep experience, which, if he has any dramatic faculty (all children have it) will seize upon him and give his gestures and facial expression those undefinable qualities which emerge from entering into an experience. All the producer has to do is to move his actors, make sure they can be heard, that they understand what they are saying, that they know their cues, that they keep still, and subdue everything to the experience—the poem—which is being enacted. And of course to bring all the resources of the other departments of the stage—music, lighting, stage carpentry and costume, to bear on the enacted experience, too.

Drama is bound to dislocate timetables and requires a tolerant environment. The best work in drama—classroom exercises in free dramatic invention—is untidy and noisy. In order to justify all the difficulties of dramatic work we must be firm about what we intend by the experience of drama in school.

In practical terms in school, I suggest that the best aims (allowing for great differences between schools, classes and teachers) would be as follows:

1. The development of free imaginative acting, as a form of imaginative composition, as a classroom activity.
2. The translation of such imaginative dramatic compositions into written drama, which can be repeated and tidied up in formal production.
3. The acting of scenes from good plays or whole short verse dramas in class and in assembly or maybe the miming of folksongs or stories in music (such as *Peter and the Wolf*).
4. The creation of 'programmes', plays, puppet plays, operettas for performance to the school.

Free imaginative acting can be taught like free oral or written composition. Here, however, we are concerned with more than verbal organisation and may not be working in words at all, but in the use of the body to explore experience. Such work in mime has the same kind of value as dance, in bringing the body into play as part of the whole intelligent being. A good deal of nonsense has been written on this subject, some of it no doubt based on some of D. H. Lawrence's less fortunate explicit pronouncements, and shades off into uplift. But Lawrence was right in insisting that the 'real emotions' belonged to the body, and were only 'recognised by the mind', and that one of our weaknesses in living is a lack of

wholeness, in the togetherness of body and mind, and the capacity
to allow experience to be 'felt in the blood and felt along the heart'.
Significantly, a training in relaxation has made a great difference to
many women's ability to give birth without pain. And to be quiet
is a faculty which becomes more and more inaccessible to us:
Adrian Bell, in his Introduction to his remarkable anthology *The
Open Air*, writes of a quietness in an old countryman which seemed
to belong to another age than ours:

Near me sat the only other person who was alone; he was either a
tramp or odd-job man, middle-aged and somewhat wizened. His
belongings lay in a bag at his feet: his hand held a short clay pipe to his
mouth, and he sat, while forbearing yet to take the final draught from
his glass, staring at the counter before him with wrinkled eyes and a
tight little smile as of one gazing gratefully at a good fire...He seemed
the embodiment of the constant fatalistic living thread of our history;
that power of quietness in him went back from generation to generation, born of the earliest arts of life, of the inherited intuitive knowledge of the best way to live within the framework of natural law.[1]

The whole passage is worth reading: it is evocative of something
we, in our age of 'drive', have lost.

Children could be encouraged, then, to be still, first, and as the
task belongs more to physical education than English, it might
well be done, in the gymnasium, and combined with other such
work, and dancing. (The book *Leap to Life* by Wiles and Garrard
is interesting on this work.) But this kind of dramatic training is
another subject: certainly one often wonders what kind of grace
and gentleness is possible in the children one sees, ungainly,
mawkish and destructively full of nervous energy, on their way
home from school. A ride on any school bus is enough to convince anyone of the futility of our education: here is humanity
at the opposite extreme from the rough graciousness of the
peasant dance, or the strange euphoria of the savage at his ritual.

The training we give in the use of the body for expressive
purposes should not model itself on the usual forms of training
for the professional naturalistic theatre, for forms of 'ham'. For

[1] *The Open Air, An Anthology of English Country Life* (Faber).

the highly artificial convention of our stage requires a training in the imitation by the body of generalised emotions: showing fear, horror, grief, happiness: walking like a criminal, a gentleman, through snow, and so on. The reason for this is that in the naturalistic play, and in the common stock of bad plays belonging to the decadent English theatre of Victorian England and the West End (with some few notable exceptions), the emotions which the dramatic work is rendering are not defined in the words of the dialogue, as I have said above, but are indicated in the stage directions. In an amateur play I saw the direction once, '*Felicity looks at Polonius with the light of adoration in her eyes.*' The adoration should have been in the text, in the words spoken—which would have defined the emotion for the spectator in the gallery. But the fact is that, though the actress would simulate 'adoration', she couldn't in fact put 'adoration' as a 'light in her eyes', and from a half-crown seat in the gallery you would in fact see nothing except that the actress was 'registering' something we might with luck take to be 'adoration'. Even if you could see her face, in a film close-up, your reaction, even conditioned by the context and the words that (in this case) followed ('Would you care for some tea?') —you would not have a defined reaction: the actress's movement and tricks of expression, and montage would give you a general emotion but not a definite one. I suggest an experiment: take a few pieces of film, or a few photographs of different human faces in different moods, and show them, without text, to a group of adults or children. Ask each to write down what the faces are 'saying': the answers will all be different. On the stage, or screen, facial expression needs to be carefully qualified by adequate words. Greek actors wore masks: the emphasis was on the definition which the words, music, gesture, dance gave in the dramatic experience. Of course we have some fine actors, who can make you weep with a shrug of the shoulder or by raising an eyebrow: but unless the text of the play emerges as the paramount defining element the reactions of the audience will be in terms of that betraying lump in the throat together with a generalised feeling of emptiness and exhaustion which seems to me to be the effect of the experience of drama in film. From a stage tragedy, such as

King Lear, when we can hear the words, and see the minimum necessary enactment of the play in terms of grouping, pattern, movement, gesture, light, colour, costume—we emerge, rather with a sense of elation, having been involved deeply in the imaginative experience of the symbolic work of a great and sensitive mind.

Such an experience is rare in our theatres, because the producers and actors are so intent on drawing attention to themselves.

Shaw, writing for 'reading', is one of the worst offenders in leaving emotional definition to the actor's acting. In the passage quoted below, for instance, there is nothing at all in the way of definition in the dialogue: everything is left to the actor, and the actor's imagination.

(*This is the signal for the breaking up of the party. Anderson takes his hat from the rack and joins Uncle William at the fire. Titus fetches Judith her things from the rack. The three on the sofa rise and chat with Hawkins. Mrs Dudgeon, now an intruder in her own house, stands inert, crushed by the weight of the law on women, accepting it, as she has been trained to accept all monstrous calamities, as proofs of the greatness of the power that inflicted them, and of her own wormlike insignificance. For at this time, remember, Mary Wollstonecraft is as yet only a girl of eighteen and her vindication of the Rights of Women is still fourteen years off. Mrs Dudgeon is rescued from her apathy by Essie, who comes back with the jug full of water. She is taking it to Richard when Mrs Dudgeon stops her.*)

MRS DUDGEON (*threatening her*) Where have you been? (*Essie, appalled, tries to answer but cannot.*) How dare you go out by yourself after the orders I have given you?

Essie: He asked for a drink—(*she stops, her tongue cleaving to her palate with terror*).

JUDITH: (*with gentler severity*) Who asked for a drink? (*Essie, speechless, points to Richard.*)

RICHARD: What! I!

JUDITH (*shocked*) Oh Essie, Essie!

RICHARD: I believe I did. (*He takes a glass and holds it to Essie to be filled. Her hand shakes.*) What! Afraid of me?

ESSIE: (*quickly*) No. I—(*she pours out the water*).

RICHARD (*tasting it*). Ah, you've been up the street to the market gate spring to get that. (*He drinks.*) Delicious! Thank you. (*Unfortunately, at this moment he chances to catch sight of Judith's face, which expresses the most*

*prudish disapproval of his evident attraction for Essie, who is devouring him
with her grateful eyes. His mocking expression returns instantly. He puts down
his glass; deliberately winds his arm round Essie's shoulders; and brings her
into the middle of the company...)*   *The Devil's Disciple*

For this kind of play, the actor has to be prepared to act being
'threatening', 'appalled', 'with tongue cleaving to palate with
terror' (this couldn't be seen from the front row of the stalls),
'devouring him with her grateful eyes', 'mocking expression',
etc. This kind of play really demands a training in the kind of
expression seen on the face of the boy in Millais' *Bubbles* or in the
eyes of Landseer's dogs; it makes its effect by emotional blurring
rather than defining. But this passage represents the kind of drama
we are used to, and it is difficult for us to respond to other possible
modes, not least essentially symbolic drama.

Where we need to begin, perhaps, is in making the child feel
his imagined experiences in the body, and this is where we may
start in school. The training in the highly artificial face-making,
'registering', of the naturalistic theatre is of no value to us, any
more than is that theatre's trick of real-seeming speech, as in the
dialogue from *Journey's End* above. What we require is the capacity
to imagine *with the body*, and the skill to enact dramatic poetry.
(For I would go as far as to say that non-poetic drama is mostly
out of place: though of course a play may be in prose and still
have poetic qualities.)

First then we may begin with exercises in the spirit of the remarkable booklet, *Story of a School*, by Mr L. A. Stone (HMSO):
a study of the illustrations in that will suggest the kind of free
work we should aim at. Miming singly, or as a class, the children
should be encouraged to become possessed by an imagined experience and express it in movements of the body: these will become, in fact, stylised and even formal. But they will express a
kind of pattern imposed on the experience, just as a free imaginative composition is the imposing of a verbal pattern. The experience must be there first, of course, and here much depends on
the teacher, in providing an adequate stimulus. He may use a
poem or a story (e.g. the opening of *The Jungle Book* by Kipling),
or tell a story of his own, or read a child's story. Children respond

magically, even at sophisticated ages, to the story of the Nativity. The aim is to achieve what Mr Stone achieved:

After the Sermon on the Mount, Christ was persuaded by Peter...to rest, and there was something beautiful in the way in which this young lad *took the arm of the imagined figure*, quietly propelling it down the hall and *talking to it* with an air of real sincerity. In the Crucifixion Scene they *imagined the procession to Calvary*, and so strongly did they identify themselves with the crucifixion that we, as onlookers, *were forced to see the Cross* which was only there by their imagination. *In fact, so strongly did they portray the scene that we were inclined to doubt the wisdom of allowing them this experience.* *Story of a School*, p. 17

I have italicised the significant phrases: the last shows the spirit of care in which this work must be done. But the training is manifestly one in what Mr Eliot has called the capacity for the Higher Dream—in having visions, and thus a most valuable means to the apprehension of possible experiences other than our own.

Of course, with less able children the miming will often be dissociated and full of violence. Under the influence of television a good deal of tedious rough-house will show itself, just as black v. white 'Cops and Robbers' is driving out the more complicated and subtle boys' ritual chasing games. But no child is utterly unresponsive to the well-chosen imaginative stimulus, unless he is mentally sick. The book *Leap to Life* has some interesting things to say about ways of developing dramatic work from the initial unregulated developments.

From this initial work of bringing children by mime to enter into imaginative experiences, it is possible to go on to spoken dramatic invention. Here children can perform singly, or in pairs or groups: the less able children seem to function better by working in groups. And here, too, it is possible to develop the sense of entertainment on the one hand, and concentration, listening, on the other, by having class criticisms of performances. Some of the performances may be in the nature of charades: or others could be the enactment of something to do with folksongs or poems known to the class, for them to guess the reference. The imaginative stimulation depends upon the teacher, to keep things going, and to keep the work from sinking into the duller levels to which children have been reduced by the popular culture imposed on them, for our popular culture saps everyone's imaginative resources. It would be unwise to give here, I think, a list of 'subjects': but they should, I am convinced, be far-fetched, romantic, Biblical, or extraordinary subjects rather than mundane ones. Of course, when working in groups the children will often reproduce Wild Westerns, Enid Blyton, TV serials and so on: an important part of the teacher's work is seeking to help children transcend their dull old favourites, by providing more exciting material. There is, after all, no shortage of exciting situations in the stories in the Bible, Chaucer's *Canterbury Tales*, mediaeval drama, Shakespeare, Ben Jonson, Greek tragedy, and myths. If the teacher can gain a knowledge of children's own dramatic games and know the great drama in his own language he will never run short of ideas. And he will see that what excites children are those situations around simple and fundamental features of human life —death, loyalty, concealment of stolen goods, defying authority, aggression, treachery and love—those elements of the symbolism in poetic drama which interested the Elizabethan audience so deeply. The Robin Hood ballad, the wooing of Anne by Richard III over her husband's body, the murder of Duncan, the hiding of Mak's sheep in the cradle, the sacrifice of Isaac, the betrayal by Judas,—these are what satisfy children most, and shall outlast Hollywood and Television House.

And now, quite naturally, we have reached a point at which we need to write down the dialogue of any dramatic piece which has emerged from the free mime into spoken spontaneous drama. This will make not only an exercise in writing, but it will also convey the point of the dramatic text, which is a reduction from a spoken art, and a means to recreate it again and again. We will probably find that, once written, the dramas lose some of their spontaneity, and so we come to see that the work of the playwright is a skilled art-work. And so we turn to scenes from plays, or whole verse plays (e.g. *Noah's Deluge*), and perform them in the class-room, attempting to involve everyone in some capacity. The great practical problem in drama, of course, is the poor reading capacities of members of the lower streams, and the fact that 'parts' too often go, in despair, to those who can read best. The answer is, perhaps, group work with those forms who will never get much beyond the stage of dramatic invention: to develop the use of percussion or 'effects'; crowd work; the use of pupils for stage managing, and other ancillary tasks: or, indeed, to give the audience work to do, as in W. H. Auden's *Dance of Death*. Such a piece of contemporary verse drama, despite its limitations, suggests new ways of handling speech dramatically, with percussion, even jazz, accompaniment, and involving everyone in simple forms of action and speech. Parts of Mr Eliot's *The Rock* and even *Sweeney Agonistes* (with slight bowdlerisation) might be most effective in a similar way. It is a pity there are so few simple modern verse plays of this kind suitable for schools.

The problem will always be the amount of work involved in staging. Here one solution may be to use puppets, if the art and woodwork departments will collaborate: with puppets we can concentrate on the reading of the script, cues, and the music or singing, and so produce a play, once we have the puppets made, in a short time. The danger with puppets is that they may come to be too much of a preoccupation in themselves. And there will come a time when children themselves become dissatisfied with what puppets can express, and obviously need to use their bodies.

But the staging of plays, and the poetry programmes I have suggested, are perfectly feasible if we make simplicity the keynote. Often, again, in the provision of schools with stages, the planners have inevitably followed the naturalistic Landseer–Millais tradition of naturalistic spectacle and 'meaningful expression' and provided a picture-frame proscenium opening. I don't propose to give plans for a stage here, but obviously something very flexible and simple is the best provision: a raised platform with adequate depth, doors leading on to it, a curtain grid with movable rails, curtains across the front of the whole, lighting fixtures, and a very large number of rostrums in store, to create different levels. (The En-Tout-Cas Company make a very adaptable form of nest of rostra, the Leicestershire Unit Stage, £33.) The whole stage, if it is a simple one, can be taken down or ignored in favour of an arena in the centre of the hall. But the provision of a school stage should be for daily and weekly work of all kinds, not to provide Hippodrome-style equipment for the annual performance of *Lady Windermere's Fan* or *The Monkey's Paw*. (It seems surprising that more schools are not provided with a classroom with a stage like the Mummery at the Perse School, Cambridge. See *The Use of English*, pamphlet by C. Parry.)

The final stage of our work will be the writing and producing of a dramatic performance, if possible with music: one knows that this is possible in secondary modern schools, in varying degrees, and all the work I have tried to suggest should lead towards it. Ideas for plays, and scenarios, will have emerged at the second stage, and it is only one step further to writing down a dialogue which has already been improvised on the lines of a scenario. Whatever is attempted should not be 'naturalistic', but according to the patterns of poetic drama, play-in-music, or towards the popular forms of pantomime or even musical or 'music hall'. Perhaps the most effective work will be done round those festivals which retain their power of inspiration even today—Christmas, Easter, May, Midsummer. From what I have said it will be apparent, I hope, that it is the English teacher who must hold the language-art, the play-in-words, to be the governing feature of any dramatic performance. He must insist that everything is subordinate to that, and that simplicity is the keynote. All grouping, movement, lighting, instructions for music, must emerge from the dialogue itself, and indeed, working these out with older forms is a valuable exercise in comprehension.

The weakness of the naturalistic stage, in which the definition of emotion is left to the interpretation of the actor, and of the 'producer's' or 'actors'' theatre, is that we find in every stage production a large amount of 'business' which is nothing to do with the play at all. Sometimes this is carried to fantastic lengths, as when, in a Cambridge production of *The Merchant of Venice*, during Portia's speech about 'the quality of mercy', the judge was made to play with a yo-yo. And one has seen productions of *The Tempest*, a play deliberately set by the poet in the bare context of a desert island, in which the quantities of sea-weed, ornamental pool, lobsters and other aquatic paraphernalia were the object of incessant 'business' by Caliban and Ariel, so that one could hardly pay attention to the verse.

'Business' on the stage should relate to the meaning of the play, and each movement or act of a character or group of charaters should be controlled by the producer in relation to that meaning, which is primarily the meaning of the words. In *Murder in the Cathedral*, for instance, the meaning concentrates round the nature of martyrdom, and in the scene of the actual murder the grouping must suggest in the priests the normal attitude of churchmen, offering argument at the normal plane of living in the 'real' world: while Thomas embodies and enacts a contemplation of eternity and acceptance of God's will that is out of time. And Thomas embodies, too, this message for the audience. Thus in the exchanges here (stage directions mine):

> (*In the Cathedral. Enter Thomas and Priests, from auditorium perhaps, in monastic costume, with rosaries, Thomas with a simple crook and mitre.*)

PRIESTS: (*variously*)
> Bar the door. Bar the door.
> The door is barred.
> We are safe. We are safe.
> They dare not break in.
> They cannot break in. They have not the force.
> We are safe. We are safe.

> (*Thomas walks to altar while priests run across to bar 'doors'. Thomas turns at altar and raises hands.*)

THOMAS: Unbar the doors; throw open the doors;
> I will not have the house of prayer, the church of Christ
> The sanctuary, turned into a fortress.
> The Church shall protect her own, in her own way, not
> As oak and stone, stone and oak decay;
> Give no stay, but the Church shall endure.
> The Church shall be open, even to our enemies. Open the door!

PRIESTS: (*These lines may be spoken by two priests who stand each side of Thomas in suppliant posture.*)
> My Lord! these are not men, these come not as men come, but
> Like maddened beasts. They come not like men, who
> Respect the sanctuary, who kneel to the Body of Christ,

But like beasts. You would bar the door
Against the lion, the leopard, the wolf or boar,
Why not more
Against beats with the souls of damned men, against men
Who damn themselves to beasts. My Lord! My Lord!
(*Pause while Priests lower heads, recognising his stubbornness.*)

THOMAS: (*Quietly, coming forward, addressing audience. Chorus kneels.*)
You think me me reckless, desperate and mad.
You argue by results, as this world does,
To settle if an act be good or bad.
You defer to the fact. For every life and every act
Consequence of good and evil can be shown.
And as in time results of many deeds are blended
So good and evil in the end become confounded.
It is not in time that my death shall be known;
It is out of time that my decision is taken
If you call that a decision
To which my whole being gives entire consent.
I give my life
To the Law of God above the Law of Man.

(*Turns, returns to altar, kneels, stands, commands.*)
Unbar the door! unbar the door!

In this exchange the priests should probably be moving, at first, rapidly about the acting area, seeking to keep the besieging knights out, to protect the archbishop, to act according to the normal human response to such a situation. Only Thomas remains still, with the stillness of one who has apprehended the 'still centre' of peace with God. This again would be symbolised by his relation in the pattern to the altar, and his position upstage at the altar. The priests shout: Thomas (as the verse demands) speaks contemplatively, and quietly, except when he commands 'Open the door!', and shows thereby that to achieve the 'wink of heaven' is to achieve great strength and power. The 'message' is made clear if Thomas addresses the audience, who obviously identify themselves with the priests in their urgency for safety, when he comes to the lines, 'You think me reckless...' Here the priests will be resigned, hearing, as it were, the words of a courage which sets this world at nothing, and kneel or stand bowed, below Thomas.

When later the knights enter they should appear to be drunk, as if with worldly power, and this should for a moment disturb the priests again ('To the roof! To the crypt!'), leaving only Thomas untouched by fear. The knights' lines ('Where is Becket the Cheapside brat?') obviously demand chanting, which makes Thomas' subsequent quiet verse the more effective ('It is the just man who...').

A production of this scene based on 'business' developed from such an approach would be balletic, a matter of simple grouping, based at every stage on the progress of the verse.

As one tries to visualise mediaeval verse drama it becomes obvious that such formal, balletic movement was the nature of popular and folk drama. The interpretation of such a play as *The Towneley Second Shepherds' Play*, the play of Mak the Sheepstealer, depends entirely upon our studying its poetic meaning. It also shows a highly developed popular stagecraft, in terms of poetic drama: in such a incident as this, for instance, which is one of high comedy (I quote from a version of the play I have prepared for a collection of short verse dramas for secondary school use):

> (Mak has stolen a sheep, and, knowing that the shepherds will be seeking it, he and his wife have hidden it in the cradle. The shepherds enter and search his house, but find nothing. His wife has been groaning as if in the after-pains of childbirth.)

2nd SHEPHERD: Sir, Our Lady give it joy,
    Is your child a boy?

MAK: Any lord might enjoy
     This child for his son.
    When he wakes up he skips; it's a joy to see.

3rd SHEP: In good time be his steps and may he be happy.
    But who were his gossips, his midwives, tell me?

MAK: (*aside*) The devil sew up their lips!

1ST SHEP: (*Aside to the others*) Listen hard: here's a lie.

MAK: Sir, God thank them well
    Parkin, and Gibbon Waller, and our tall neighbour
    John Horne: they were all here during labour
    Till you came, making a great row, didn't stay for
     Meat as well...

2nd SHEP: Mak, friends we will be, for we are all one.

MAK: We? No, I'm holding back, me: for me comfort
there's none.

(*aside*) Farewell all three. We'll be glad when you've
gone.

(*The* SHEPHERDS *go.*)

3rd SHEP: Fair words there may be, but love there's none,
This year.

(*They walk gloomily on. Suddenly* SHEP 3 *stops in his track.*)

1st SHEP: Gave you the child anything?

2nd SHEP: I swear not one farthing!

3rd SHEP: Fast again will I fling.
You wait for me here.
(*He returns to Mak's door.*)
Mak! We forgot the child's gift—come and unbar.

MAK: (*aside*) Ah, now they'll find the theft—I thought we
were clear!

3rd SHEP: The child mustn't be bereft, the little day-star.
Mak, by your leave, let me give the little dear
But sixpence.

MAK: No! Get away! He sleeps.

3rd SHEP: I think, yes he peeps!

MAK: When he wakes up he weeps
I pray ye get hence.

3rd SHEP: Give me leave him to kiss and to lift him out.
What, the devil is this? He has a long snout!

I have made the text a little obvious, for children, and added the
stage directions. But the quality of the piece is to be seen in the
way it dictates its own stage business: it is a remarkable combination of the ability to convince us that the incident is happening,
and of poetic comedy. The set, obviously, cannot be naturalistic,
because the shepherds need to move about, out and in the cottage,
with ease. Yet there must be a door, a cradle, a bed, and a table,
and we do and should feel we are there, in Mak's hovel. When
Mak describes the antics of his son (born a few hours before) he
must obviously leap like a sheep. When the shepherds shake
hands with Mak they would possibly smell their hands afterwards
surreptitiously, to see if they could smell sheep. The asides can be
sheer pantomime, but are none the less effective for that—the
comedy of being found out is something we shall have experienced

deeply as children. Thus the suspense when the shepherds pause on, 'Gave you the child anything?' is great, and develops into comedy as Mak and his wife try to keep up the fraud against all odds, eventually trying to make out the sheep is a changeling. The speed of exchanges is again dictated by the speed of the verse (the 'sleeps—peeps—weeps' rhyme suggesting a rapid pushing and pulling of the coverings over the sheep). And while Mak is a part for such high skill in comedy as that of Charles Chaplin, it is also a part that could be played by a child—because it invites imaginative 'entering into' the character, it is simple, and is a matter of enacting the poetry, simply.

Such a programme of dramatic work as I have tried to suggest here needs amplifying by considerable experiment. The main difficulty—and perhaps the main reason for the indifferent work widely done—is the shortage of texts which are good poetry or prose, or drama with sound content. I can only suggest, in the absence of a book to recommend, that teachers search themselves in unfamiliar places—say among mediaeval plays in modern English, to find a version of the *Towneley Second Shepherds' Play* as above, or try the *Norwich Passion Play* (a mediaeval verse play), W. B. Yeats' *Calvary*, the Falstaff episodes from *Henry IV Part I* and perhaps some versions of plays by Hans Sachs and Japanese No Plays. Mediaeval verse plays put into modern English are most useful, for instance, Maurice Hussey's *Chester Mystery Plays* (Heinemann) and John Allen's *Three Mediaeval Plays* (Heinemann). *The Norwich Passion Play* may be obtained from the Maddermarket Theatre, Norwich. Suitable plays of Yetas' include *The Land of Heart's Desire*, *The Pot of Broth* and *The Resurrection*. Parts of T. S. Eliot's *The Rock*, and his *Murder in the Cathedral*, are suitable. Use might be made of the libretto to the opera *Peter Grimes*, with a subsequent visit to a performance; certainly we should make use of *Let's Make an Opera* and *Noyes Fludde*, also by Benjamin Britten. The gramophone records of Ravel's *L'Enfant et les Sortilèges* might also be very useful for introducing children to a very beautiful operatic work. Perhaps *Porgy and Bess*? Use might also be made of such folk-plays as the *Symondsbury Mumming Play* and the *Revesby Plough Play* (in *The Poet's Tongue*). I have not mentioned Shakespeare, though I think much could be done in the modern school with *Macbeth*, and with the Dogberry and Verges scenes from *Much Ado About Nothing*, and other pieces suggested by these two choices.

Our work in drama is not to be separated from our work in poetry, or from the work of the school in music, towards the creation of a new popular audience. It is not generally felt, certainly not with any disturbance, what a philistine public ours in England is. And I have discussed earlier in this book what the consequences are in our ability to cope with life. For any significant cultural development the training of a new audience for drama, poetry, opera and music is imperative. In passivity and stagnation we lag even behind America. There, to take music for example, while the receipts for 'spectator sports' in 1954 were 220,000,000 dollars, some 50,000,000 dollars were spent at the concert music box office. One wonders what the parallel figures are in England: certainly not a proportion of 22 to 5—more like 100 to 1! In America, paradoxically, the great growth of mechanical means of reproducing music has led to a great interest in contemporary music: 1,451 compositions by 238 contemporary composers are available on 2,520 recordings. And now this musical activity takes the form of a 'cultural explosion' in the form of interest in opera and the play-in-music. There are 444 producing groups in 45 states, and the number of opera workshops in schools and colleges has doubled in recent years.

We may take all these figures with a pinch of salt, but they still reveal that, with our commerce-dominated West End Theatre; the dreary naturalism of local amateur drama; our obsession with the emotionally trivial such as Gilbert and Sullivan; and our neglect of live music-making, we are making little movement towards the symbolising activity in poetry, drama and opera which we need so much for the inward life. In the schools not half enough is done, as yet, towards providing for an active creative leisure. Youth on leaving school plunges into a cultural desert —yet this seems to draw the attention of state concern, as through the Arts Council, hardly at all. Meanwhile it is left to local pioneers such as the marvellous Aberdeen children's theatre, and John English's Cannon Park Centre, to show the way to the future.

CHAPTER 12

Drills

My theme in this book has been that the only means by which a child develops an adequate ability to use English is by reading a great deal, having a delight in the word, and writing a good deal, without being overburdened by worry about particulars. For the more we feel we *want* to do something, the more we are able to seek the means, and a child who has delight in the word will come to stages at which he will welcome direct instruction in punctuation, spelling, grammar and vocabulary. There is no short cut in this matter: text-book exercises have the opposite effect to that intended, unless used to help overcome difficulties found in the course of what I have called the Real Work; we cannot begin with them. But certainly we do need some drills, to help children remember points about their work which will enable them to increase their powers of language, points which they will bear in mind as they read and write, to their advantage.

Let us remember that the main aim is developing the ability, the hard task, of symbolising experience, and developing thought and feeling through words. This task is a matter of arranging words in an order which corresponds to the best order in which we can represent our experience. To do this we select words from our inherited language patterns: and in order to make our meaning clear and definite we are helped by obeying what seem to be rules of punctuation, spelling, and linguistic usage. Of course at times in order to render experience which no-one has attempted to explore before we may need to break all the rules, as Shakespeare frequently does ('But me no buts and uncle me no uncles') and as James Joyce and other writers in our century have done: '...just a wisk brisk sly spry spink spank spirit of a thing theresomere, saultering. Salterella come to her own. I pity your oldself I was used to.'

And indeed English has increasingly, since Shakespeare's

time, broken away from an orderly regimen, in order to cover and include more complex and various experience. At the same time, of course, the development of printing and a literate culture has meant standardisation of spelling and punctuation. But as far as grammar and the use of words is concerned we should accept (despite the arguments that come to us from some scholars and linguists) that the very vitality of English comes from its *not* being subject to a formal structure which would give each word a single particular grammatical function. The very ambiguity of our language, its metaphorical and poetic strength, our habits of extending the function of a word, all these make for greater definition of experience: they also make for less order and neatness, much to the chagrin of those who make up the rules of grammar and who suppose that the rules are the primary principles of language. Of course they are not primary rules—children often speak perfectly grammatical English, figuratively rich, functionally complex, meaningful even in its errors, yet without knowing one grammatical precept, or law of punctuation. A writer seldom, if ever, makes a grammatical analysis of a sentence, or needs to look up a point about punctuation as he writes: what he has to do is to read over his work as though he were a reader with limited powers of taking in the meaning of words and thus assure himself that what he has written is the best way of saying what he has tried to say and cannot easily be misunderstood.

The chief rule then is that writing or speech should be clear and not confusing: but again, we must recognise that it is confusion in thought and feeling which make for muddled language.

We must distinguish, too, before we can see the value of drills, between different kinds of error. Often a child has in fact achieved something which it then becomes a waste of our time to endeavour to teach in the abstract. If a child writes thus:

is wife looked so sad that Mr Owl could not help saying what is the matter she pointed to the dead baby owl and started crying again oh dear oh dear she sobbed I loved that one so much she is so pretty i wish he was alive again that night she laid an egg in the nest she felt something crack it was a baby owl it cheaped so much that it woke Mrs Owl she screamed so loud that it woke Mr Owl what is all this noise about he said look look she said. look at the new baby she said Mr Owl looked there in the nest was five little owls what a beuty he said

She has done the following things: 1. she has written about twenty sentences, some quite complex, and nearly all without fault; 2. she has written a good deal of direct speech; 3. she has written sentences in such a way as to give an orderly and logical sequence to events.

Her faults are these: 1. the absence of punctuation; 2. misspelling of two words—'cheaped' and 'beuty'; 3. the use of careless expressions from everyday speech: 'started crying', 'in the nest was five little owls'.

In fact this is a very literate child, whose errors are those of visual memory: she has not yet taken in sufficiently from her reading the point of full stops, capital letters and inverted commas. But these are not 'grammatical' errors, and will not be put right by a teaching of structure. A child who can write a complex sentence such as: 'His wife looked so sad that Mr Owl could not help saying, "What is the matter?"' is not suffering from a weakness in 'grammar' or the ability to handle words.

But obviously, in order to punctuate, she needs to know what a sentence is, or rather where a sentence ends. If we give her a textbook exercise she will gain, perhaps, a few technical terms in a rather mechanical and uninteresting way: on the other hand there is a good deal of exciting material in her story—and if we correct it *so that it looks like a proper book* the point will be driven soundly home. For the point is largely a *visual* point rather than anything to do with the putting of her imaginative experience into words.

So we can say to her, virtually (of course the teacher puts this kind of thing in his own words): you have written what we call sentences. They are good sentences, and when you read your story to me I can hear them, because you pause at one or two places—for instance like this: 'what is the matter—she pointed to the dead baby owl and started crying again—oh dear/oh dear/she sobbed' and so on. Why do you pause at those places? Because you have said something which you feel is complete—you've said that bit, and then you pause before you say the next bit. That helps us to see where we have got to. But when I look at your book I don't know where to pause as I read it. Of course I can pause in the right places if I work out what it means, but I don't want to have to do that—I want to follow your story straightaway when I read it first time, because I want to enjoy it first time. Now! So that I can see where to pause, you must help me by putting in full stops and commas. Otherwise I might read 'she said Mr Owl looked there' instead of "Look at the new baby," *she said. Mr Owl looked. There,* in the nest,' and so on.

At this point, the child requires two straight drill lessons, based on her work, on punctuation and on what, roughly, is a sentence?

Her spelling mistakes, too, will be accumulated into a list which the teacher uses for spelling drill. These drills are not means to develop powers of handling language (for this child has that power already) but of making her writing more accurate and easier on the reader. The power of handling language must be there first and does not come by means of the drills.

PUNCTUATION

All the rules of punctuation should be gone through in the secondary school again: the only book the teacher requires being the excellent one by G. V. Carey called *Mind the Stop* (Cambridge University Press). Children's writing will provide plenty of examples to be written on the board or duplicated, discussed in class, and then written out correctly by the pupils. On the whole it will be a matter of punctuating the unpunctuated. The first two sentences of the child's story quoted above would give scope for three lessons: one on the full stop, one on the comma, and one on the punctuation of direct speech. These impressions could be consolidated by the examination with the class of the punctuation of a poem or of a page in a story, in order to impress on the children that if they are puzzled about a problem of punctuation, they should sit down and read a book until they see their kind of difficulty solved on the printed page. And that punctuation is only necessary to help the reader make sense more easily and correctly of what we write. Very often a paragraph or poem may be perfectly understandable without any punctuation, and some writers deliberately avoid punctuation because it would limit the meaning of what they write to something less ambiguous—and so less full —than they intend.

But the question is bound to arise—how do we know when to put a full-stop and when to put a comma, colon or semi-colon: what is a sentence? Thus punctuation inevitably leads us to consider grammar.

GRAMMAR

The best use of words is learnt by reading, and by living in an environment of well-spoken English: the only grammatical errors in the piece of writing above come from careless speech habits—'there was five', 'she started crying'. Correction of such errors is best done by giving the correct usage in a discussion of a pupil's work, and adding weight by reading or writing out a number of further examples of correct usage of a related kind:

> there were three ships came sailing in,
> there were crowds of people in the streets,
> there was only a pound of apples on the tree,
> there was a crowd at the entrance,
> there were thirty children in the class,
> there was a class of thirty children,
> 'You naughty kittens!' and they began to cry...

The meaning of 'there was five' is clear in the child's story— though in another context the error might cause misunderstanding But 'she started crying' makes sense: all one can say about this is that it is not very good English, and some English is better than other English. 'She started crying' has more the sense of 'she started (to do something), crying,' and so is imprecise. 'She started to cry' is perfectly good English, and so is 'There's no need to start crying,' though simply 'There's no need to cry' is better because it uses fewer words. Inevitably class distinctions creep in here. 'Don't you start-a-crying', is working class speech, as is 'I have got a book' as compared with 'I have a book' which is upper-class and 'educated' (*Librum habeo*, that is). We must be careful not to stamp on 'common' expressions where they have vitality e.g. 'Well, what have you got that I haven't got?' has rhythmic vitality.

Incoherence, it seems to me, is better tackled by dwelling, in a 'correcting' lesson, on the *good* way to say what is to be said, using clear and meaningful writing from children's work or books, rather than on endeavouring to explain the 'rules' underlying the correct use. The latter is too abstract a process for most of our pupils, and it is one a writer seldom, after all, uses. This is not to say one should not deal with sentence structure at all: some teaching of sentence structure is an aid both to the close reading of poetry and prose and to writing. The problem is to decide how much of such analytical grammar one can and should teach in the modern school. Since it is a fallacy to regard this as the *basis* of good writing, the revival of clamour to teach formal grammar or linguistics in order to improve literacy shows a failure to understand how literacy is developed.

Rather than develop this discussion about grammar at length, I will refer the reader to a very good article in *The Use of English* by Mr A. A. Evans, Deputy Director of Leeds University Institute of Education, and to the books given in the Bibliography (p. 254 ff.). Mr Evans points out that some of the grammar taught comes from attempts to prune and train the living growth of English usage to 'a grammatical system based on Latin grammar' and he shows how valueless are many attempts to bring English under orderly concepts of case, gender and so on. He goes on:

Grammar can be a fascinating study for middle and upper school pupils (i.e. the grammar school) of a high verbal intelligence, but to the others it is puzzling and largely irrelevant: if they cannot perceive the inconsistencies and inaccuracies, it is only because they are not mature enough to grapple with the abstractions...(yet)...the textbook devoted entirely to grammar is still extensively used. It is started at too young a level before a child can grapple with abstract concepts...and before he has acquired sufficient practice and fluency in written language, a sufficient thrill in shaping phrase and sentence, and an adequate knowledge of words. Intelligent pupils can repeat definitions of parts of speech, recognise them in sentences, and fill up gaps with the correct words, but the fact that so many pupils can do this and yet write ungrammatically shows that there is no real connexion at this stage between correct writing and that superficial knowledge of grammar which they have acquired.

The Use of English. Vol. 5, Nos. 1 and 2

These points would seem to me incontrovertible and to apply even more strongly to the secondary modern school pupil than they do to grammar school pupils of whom the writer is speaking. Grammar with us needs to be no more than the discussion of the functions of words in actual sentences, and always in sentences written by the pupils themselves, or ones which they have met in the poems or prose they are reading. And grammar can be limited to teaching in this way the following functions of words:

What do we mean by a *sentence*?

A sentence has a *subject* and what we call a *predicate*. This may be merely a *verb*, or be made up of a *verb* and *object*.

But we cannot say all we need to say simply in sentences such as 'Tom hit Bill', and to *subject*, *verb*, and *object* we add a great many different kinds of adjuncts. These tell us more about the *subject* or the *object*, which will nearly always be *nouns* or *pronouns*, or about the *verb*. These adjuncts, if they are used in connexion with the verb, tell us when things happened, where, how, and so on, and will be *adverbs*. In amplifying the *nouns* they tell us what these things, or persons, were like, and will be *adjectives*. Sometimes the adjuncts are not simply single words, *adjectives* or *adverbs*, but groups of words, *phrases* and *clauses*, which are *adverbial clauses* or *adjectival clauses*.

Hardly any more grammar than this is needed, except perhaps a few lessons dealing with *singular* and *plural*, *past*, *present*, and *future*, and a few other names of parts of speech such as *article*, *preposition*, and *conjunction* (defined by example rather than by an attempt to define their function): and we have four years in which to teach it. But we must realise that while a child can happily write, 'His wife looked so sad that Mr Owl could not help saying "What is the matter?"' it will be another four or five years before—if ever—she can say what all the parts of that sentence are (could the reader?), and we should forego ambitions to enable her to parse the sentences she can so ably write: what would it profit her anyway?

With a few terms at our disposal, such as those in italics above, we should be able to talk about the English of poetry and prose both in our 'reading in low gear' and in helping children improve their own expression. The best grammar lessons will be those given to puzzling over the meaning of poetry, for there language

is used at its syntactically most efficient: to substitute the discipline
of 'parsing' and abstract text-book grammar for the discipline
of responding to poetry is to work to create illiteracy rather than
literacy.

There is no need to choose syntactically difficult poetry either:
the simplest poetry is often the most difficult to grasp. For instance, here is a simple poem by an early American devotional
writer:

> *Upon a Spider catching a Fly.*
>
> Thou sorrow, venom Elfe:
>   Is this thy play,
> To spin a web out of thyselfe
>   To catch a Fly?
>   For why?
>
> I saw a pettish wasp
>   Fall foule therein:
> Whom yet thy whorle pins did not hasp
>   Lest he should fling
>   His sting
>
> But as afraid, remote
>   Didst stand hereat
> And with thy little fingers stroke
>   And gently tap
>   His back.[1]

Here the exploration of the syntax will be at one with the whole
response to language: the brief lines and simplicity force syntactical economy on the poet—and this makes for a figurativeness
and a finish we are not used to today, in popular writing at least.
The poem describes how a spider by its nature knows that it can
deal easily with a fly whereas it needs to be circumspect in dealing
with a wasp. This shows, says the poet, that we should know our
own strength, by calling on Nature, 'or go to pot'. But the
spider is also the Devil, 'Hell's spider', who tangles 'Adam's race'
in his stratagems and who easily bites dead the silly fly, whereas
he has to treat the pettish wasp with more respect: in any case

[1] By Edward Taylor, 1645–1729. The whole may be found in my anthology, *Iron, Honey, Gold*, vol. 1, p. 51.

only God can 'breake the cord'. The analogies are not sufficiently developed and unified, one feels, as compared with Herbert's poetry, which this resembles, but the verse has a vitality of its own.

Taking the stanzas quoted here, what are the syntactical difficulties?

Is 'sorrow' an *adjective* (i.e. sorry, sorrowful) qualifying 'Elfe', or is it a *noun*, to which 'venom Elfe' is in apposition? (I think it is an adjective.) 'Out of thyselfe' out of your own substance—that is, out of thy self, the self being the substantial body. (Compare our 'he retired into himself', which is different. Primitive peoples, apparently, talk of 'my me'.) 'For why?' = what for? Does 'whom' ('whom yet thy whorle pins did not hasp') apply to the wasp or the spider? We know it is the wasp because it is 'whom' not 'who'. What is 'left out' of the third stanza? The *subject* of the sentence: and the verbal phrase *as if you were*: it would read in prose: 'But, as if thou wert afraid, thou didst stand hereat and...' This leaves us with 'remote'—what is the force of this word? Something between an *adjective* qualifying *thou* (you seem remote) and an *adverb* (did stand remote): an example of useful syntactical ambiguity, as it emphasises the spider's cautious holding back in two ways—the way a spider will seem to be in a state of not registering the arrival of too large a prey (adjectival) the way a spider will seem to be holding himself back till the prey is exhausted (adverbial).

These syntactical difficulties we could explain just as well without using grammatical terms: the advantage of the terms is to make our account shorter and easier. The syntactical problem seems perhaps more difficult than it should because of the presence of archaic words: pettish (in a pet); whorle pins—spindle pins —its legs, like the spindle of the latch of a door which goes through the *hasp* (a noun used as a verb—as in 'hasp the door' lock the door, bolt the door).

· Forty minutes on this poem, followed by repeated readings of it, with a good form, would produce more development of the understanding of the way language works than forty days with a textbook. Herbert's poetry, some of Donne's simplest, and Gerard Manley Hopkins's simplest are excellent material for such work.

Drills

A positive method of demonstrating the function of kinds of words (here, *pronouns*) is suggested by this exercise from William Cobbett's *Easy Grammar*:

A woman went to a man, and told the man, that the man was in great danger of being murdered by a gang of robbers, as a gang of robbers had made preparations for attacking the man. The man thanked the woman for the woman's kindness: and as the man was unable to defend the man's self, the man left the man's house, and went to a neighbour's.

('Make this paragraph as brief as you can.') There is a list of books on grammar in the Bibliography, p. 254 ff.

SPELLING

Spelling seems to me merely a matter of drill, as the same words tend to be universally spelt wrongly, and as correct spelling seems to depend upon a visual picture of the word, except for those who have insufficient visual sense and who can learn best by spelling a word aloud.

Only harm can be done by giving children mis-spelt words to correct. Spelling is perhaps best dealt with on the Daily Dozen principle, in the form of tests, bees, and other competitive games. Spelling mistakes should be written out *once* and looked at: for a child to copy the word out a number of times may merely cause him to lose a sense of its shape in the tedium; and in any case children frequently go back to their original wrong spelling and repeatedly copy that, which merely confirms them in their error. (I suppose it is too much to ask that writing, spelling, copying, learning verse, should *never* be used as a punishment?)

Graded lists will be found in F. J. Schonell's *Essential Spelling Lists*. On the whole I feel teachers make too much fuss about spelling, which, like many other skills, comes by long acquaintance with reading and writing, and is not in any case the worst feature of our present state of illiteracy. (I remind myself I have only recently become able to spell 'occasional' and 'accommodation' in my own work.) It appeals as an 'educational' concern, obviously because it is a matter of right and wrong 'answers', and is the first thing a business man notices, I know. In a queer old-fashioned way we take good spelling to be the mark of 'education'. Confusions between pairs of words such as of/off, their/there, and to/too are more than visual errors: or at least the visual confusion needs to be overcome by exercises in their use in writing practice sentences—but the pairs should *not* be discussed and exercised together. A few dictated sentences containing *too*, *their* and *of* would provide opportunities for correction by discussion: but the common confusion between *there* and *their* comes from an inadequacy of understanding of the function of the word *their*, which needs to be exercised, by itself, until it is possessed, as it were.

The following list of words should be learnt by rote (the teacher will certainly be able to add to it!):

lose successful surprise amateur woollen received expense usually conscious maintenance occurred believed coming February exercise beginning business excellent foreign changeable separate acquaintance lightning noticeable committee definite existence lying until pronunciation immediately sentence mediocre occasionally accommodation preceding secretary gauge unnecessary forty quiet receipt privilege repetition Wednesday Parliament referred height similar seize college.

These are common confusions:

> to/too   of/off   there/their   practice/practise
> licence/license   prophecy/prophesy   principal/principle
> dependent/dependant   whether/weather   its/it's
> whose/who's   stationary/stationery
> cereal/serial   marshal/martial   effect/affect
> council/counsel   illegible/ineligible
> all ready/already   draft/draught

Many schools keep a book in which common errors are written and from which all teachers can draw words for 'daily dozen' exercises.

VOCABULARY

Children should be encouraged to write unusual or exciting new words in a section of their exercise books or a special word book, with their meanings, as they find them. The work depends much on the teacher's own feeling for words and his ability to convey excitement and relish. Vocabulary is extended by reading, and by hearing things read, with pauses at times on new-found words. Children should be shown how to use a dictionary in library work —not only the pocket dictionaries, but those the size of the *Shorter Oxford Dictionary* in two large volumes. Here they will find something of the history of a word, at what period it was first used, and by whom, and how its meaning has shifted and been extended. Skeat's *Etymological Dictionary* provides fascinating clues to the history of words, and *History in English Words* by Owen Barfield is a fascinating book. Regional idiomatic words and expressions should be encouraged: often they will be found to have antecedents in mediaeval poetry, or in Chaucer or in Shakespeare or Clare, and this provides for considerable interest. And in their own right they are often powerful means to exploring experience.

This point, and a related point about speech habits, were well made by Mrs Sybil Marshall writing in *The Use of English* on *Idiom in the Primary School*:

'I started business without much capital,' says an old countryman. 'I went into business with Charlie when we were both about twenty. I had one gold sovereign, but Charlie were *as bare o' money as a pig is o' side pockets.*'...This is the kind of language we are giving up in our search for a false sense of respectability...The fourteen year old son of a smallholder...was invited by his English mistress to read his essay aloud to the rest of the form. After describing in vivid detail the process of grooming a horse, he read out, 'When I have finished one side, I say "Cum uvver" and the horse stands over to let me get at his other side.'

The mistress intervened. 'Cum uvver?' she queried.

The boy eyed her with a look in which chagrin at this needless interruption was mixed only with pity for her ignorance. 'Well, Miss,' he explained, 'if I had said "Cam owvar", our horse wouldn't have understood it.' *The Use of English.* Vol. 8, No. 3

I have doubts on the possibility of extending vocabulary except by reading and by a live and vigorous flow of spoken language in the school. 'Stop talking!' is the command which has led as much as anything to the decline of our language habits under formal schooling. Now, outside the school, the vocabulary and texture of language in our popular newspapers and our entertainment becomes thinner day by day. Television has probably reduced conversation in the home, and even nowadays tends to dominate conversation in pubs and clubs where, at least, local gossip was maintained as a cultural form. In the face of this meagreness we can hardly hope to restore life to the language by a few textbook exercises in grammar, punctuation, and vocabulary.

Having said so much, I would add that there are some useful exercises in the text-books *Practice in Reading* by Denys Thompson and in his other course books. I prefer to base such work on relevant content, as in the Oxford *Reflections*, and my own *Iv'e Got to Use Words*. Other books are mentioned in the Bibliography, including Robert Swann's Test Books, which are noted for their good sense and simplicity. Drills, however, we must regard as the least effective part of our work: they have been made necessary only because our classes are too large, our training is so deficient, and because the environment is against us all the time.

It may be well to end this chapter with a quotation from *English for the English*, by George Sampson. This book was published in 1921, but when we re-read it we find it remarkably up to date. I am thinking of the 'trend back to grammar' and the new vogue for linguistics. What is perhaps needed is more creative refreshment for English teachers. Perhaps many turn to the text-books in ignorance and despair. Perhaps the hopeless condition of English teaching, so largely a matter of awful dog-eared grinders called 'English for Joy' or 'Happy Hours with Grammar for Citizens', is the consequence of attempts, in the wake of educational psychologists, to make English teaching too closely related to partial functions, 'techniques' and 'grading'. At any rate, in a recent list of Ministry One Year and Sabbatical Year Courses, among many courses, there were only two in English! And yet one centre advertises a year's course in Experimental Psychology! It seems extraordinary that after so much experimental psychology no-one should have discovered the simple fact that children only learn to use words by using words, and that order in the whole being, the complex of symbolism, thought, and feeling, is at the root of the growth of literacy.

Drills

But here I will leave the last word to George Sampson: the whole chapter, *Preliminary*, should be read, for it is as fresh today as when it was written:

Psychology is becoming the hand-maid of educational reactionaries as chemistry became the hand-maid of the war-lords. Delight in measured results means a demand for results that can be measured. The tables and curves of the psychologist are taking us back to examinations and a prescribed minimum standard of attainment—that is, just to the old demand that has already ruined the past and imperilled the future of elementary education...Elementary education has failed because we have thought too much of the children's heads and not enough of their hearts. Hearts are still out of fashion in school. In spite of its name psychology has nothing to do with the soul...

...The schools are wonderful laboratories for experiment, and teachers have already been told by persons of official importance that they will not be respected unless they make definite contributions to educational science. The art of teaching, it would appear, is not respectable...[children] will be inoculated with doses of knowledge and tested for reactions; their minds will be calibrated periodically with millimetric exactness, and their abilities neatly reduced to succinct tables and beautifully sinuous curves...And thus the juvenile mind will be docketed and disposed of, and education comfortably removed from the troublesome world of feeling.

In the universal work at text-book level; with all the concentration on the psychological bases of reading and spelling; in the reluctance of practising teachers to refresh themselves in anything but psychology, and in the deficiencies of 'education' courses, we are plunged into forgetfulness of what Sampson calls heart, soul and 'the troublesome world of feeling', from which alone true literacy can emerge. An English education based on 'basic drills' formed on 'basic psychological principles' or on an external concern with the 'structures' of linguistics, can only have partial success, for the real work, which is an art, fostering creative symbolic processes, requires disciplines which involve whole persons, and their intuitive gifts.

ENGLISH IN THE TIME-TABLE

English in the time-table depends much, of course, on each school—how much teachers of other subjects are willing to co-operate, and how much the whole school accepts education as a 'civilising and humanising practice'. Collaborations with music and art, and drama periods, too, sometimes need to be long ones, longer than the normal 30–45 minutes. But it may be helpful to give here what would seem to be the minimum:

(i) Periods for *comprehension work*, or reading in low gear. In which we include discussion of 'grammar' or how language works (for our discussion of points of linguistics is not to be separated from problems of meaning on the page).

The meaning of poetry; discussion of the point of stories; reading aloud in groups for intelligibility; oral exercises of a similar kind; giving the précis of a page of a book or the contents of a newspaper; simple lessons on grammar and linguistics (of an empirical kind).

2 PERIODS A FORTNIGHT

(ii) Periods for the silent reading of prose fiction selected by the teacher or for searching for information from the library. (And group and individual work for those who are backward in their reading.)

2 PERIODS A FORTNIGHT

(iii) Collaborative work between subject teachers—on song, opera, drama, puppetry, bookbinding, movement, literature and science, practical writing in geography, history, pig-keeping, book-binding, boat-building and other such projects.

4 PERIODS A FORTNIGHT

(iv) Active work in English as a creative activity—imaginative composition of stories and poems, orally or in writing; spontaneous drama; debates; 'interviews'; rehearsals and preparation of class and school magazines; free composition.

4 PERIODS A FORTNIGHT

(v) Spelling drills, pupil's corrections of own work, vocabulary drills, marking periods.

2 PERIODS A FORTNIGHT

(vi) Periods in which the teacher reads to the children or plays gramophone records: practice in listening.

2 PERIODS A FORTNIGHT

To vary with morning assembly which provides for these disciplines, too.

This gives the total of 16 periods a fortnight devoted to English. This seems to me the minimum, if we are to give children the adequate training of sensibility to which all are equally entitled, to enable them to have sufficient grasp of English to learn other 'subjects' well, to live well as men and women, or even to be articulate and literate enough to do their work efficiently in our industrial age.

FURTHER NOTES ON FOLKSONG

Folksong has come to life among young people, and in this there is hope for a disinterested revival: but there is also much confusion.

In illustration let me quote some experiences. Recently I went to a 'folksong' evening at a students' group, and heard a man performer sing a beautiful folksong well, to a guitar. His place was taken by a man with no voice, who had no musical sense, and sang a coarse and raucous song about a chastity belt, composed (I was told) by some students at Oxford. The audience showed no sense of distinction between the musical and poetic world of the one song and that of the other—between two utterly irreconcilable worlds of personal feelings and attitudes to life. Yet it was as if someone had got up to sing *My Name is Samuel Hall* in the middle of the Matthew *Passion*, while the audience continued to give genteel attention. A few weeks later I went to listen to a group of folksingers in the local pub: a young man sang *The Foggy Dew* quite well. But then he went on to destroy that song's directness of joy in natural love by offering to 'sing a folksong I made up recently about Lady Chatterley'. It was as if the singer in a recital of Schubert *lieder* suddenly offered the audience a snazzy number she had written over the weekend. Joan Baez ends a record with the sentimental *Plaisir d'Amour*—and reduces our inward echo of the great folksongs she has been singing to the level of the atmosphere of the *café chantant*. In a record shop, looking for folksong records for my children, I found a record labelled *Bawdy Folksongs* in the same series as *Music to Strip By* and the *Christine Keeler Story*.

I have seen old French peasants elbowed off a village square, where they had attempted to dance their gracious bourrée, by Americanised teenagers who wanted to jive. But no-one pretended there could be anything but failure to understand between the two cultures.

The apologist for 'pop' will protest that 'that is how the people like it', and that ten years ago I wouldn't have found any of the activities I mentioned going on at all. My first answer is that once the folksongs were on everybody's lips—a long while ago, admittedly: but coarseness and emotional degradation are not the inevitable taste of the people. Where one finds these things there has been a deliberate lowering of taste, and a confusion of standards. The second answer is an admission that, at times (as in Elizabethan broadsides), kinds of song have been mixed up. But there is no excuse for us to mix it so, to the detriment of good taste. When I was a student we sang bawdy songs, or crude political songs: what we didn't do was to mix these up with folksongs. When we came upon the folksongs, we were startled by their beauty and respected them, as we respected the Border Ballads and *The Ancient Mariner*, or Blake or Cotman or Mozart: we had no impulse to drag them down to the level of *Eskimo Nell*, or mix *The Seeds of Love* with *Mrs O'Frinke*.

So, though one is pleased that the folksong movement has spread so rapidly, one can discount much of it as significant cultural development, in so far as by such gross eclecticism it manifests ignorance of the true nature of folksong, and indifference to its greatest beauties. What really has been gained, except an impulse to make music which has been headed off by the entertainment industry and some image-promoters for whom folksong is but one gimmick among many?

Deliberate exploitation is another matter. Here we have to watch what happens to currently fashionable singers. Whatever their original talent, it is increasingly in the hands of promotion that intrudes *ersatz* personality between the listener and song.

Some of the ways in which folk 'stars' are promoted seem to me the most horrifying examples of subtle corruption being operated by commerce within the folksong movement. One's suspicions are aroused at once by the record sleeves:

The irrepressible *reality* of Bob Dylan is a compound of spontaneity, candour, slicing wit and an uncommonly perceptive eye and ear for the way many of us construct our capacities for living while a few of us don't...

This 'protest' theme links the young image, as over 'pop' singers from Elvis to the Beatles, with the commercial world's success-ful attempt over the last twenty years to alienate and hive off the teenager as a separate 'market' group, as an exploitable sector. Note that the true commercial copywriter offers us what we want to hear. There are those 'who constrict their lives': singers are to unchain us: but yet, we may not be of the kind to constrict ('many of us...a few of us'). Even so, let's join the unconstricted 'few'—the old ad-man's gimmick of appeal for a 'a book for the few—120th thousand...'

Throughout everything he writes and sings, there is the surge of a young man looking into as many diverse scenes and people as he can find...'I'm my own person. I've got basic common rights...every-thing I do and sing and write comes out of *me*...It is this continuing explosion of a total individual, a young man growing free rather than absurd...'

Nothing could be more nauseating than this 'build up' of a 'free' personality in terms of 'sincerity'—when the obvious intention is the exploitation of a projected persona, a pseudo-image. Such singers become mere vehicles for the projection of promotion campaigns. The real intention is given on another sleeve, 'it matters less where he has been than where he is going, and that would seem to be straight up': straight up, that is, to the 'top ten', not to any artistic height of excellence or truth. The singer is only his 'free' self in so far as he is financially successful. How very far this 'freedom' is from that of the true artist, who has nothing to answer to except the creative conscience!

Recordings
Further notes by Maurice Howarth.

'...in true folksong there is no sham, no got-up glitter, and no vulgarity.' (Sir Hubert Parry, Inaugural Address to the Folksong Society, 1898).

The vast agglomeration of worthless recordings which proli-ferate in the commercial catalogues under the title 'Folksong' has prompted me to make the notes for this edition very selective. If we are to understand, and are to make clear to others, the true

nature of folksong, neither the Victorian drawing-room 'arrangements' nor the tarted-up offerings of Denmark Street will suffice.
Both forms only hide or distort the real strength, subtlety and
humour of the song behind a mush of harmony and inaptly
applied technique, or the attempt to imitate as closely as possible
the rhythmic banalities of commercial 'pop'.

I have, therefore, based my selection upon the musical and
poetic integrity of the performers. Many of them have not been
brought up within the tradition, yet their choice of song and
method of delivery display the maturity of approach characteristic
of the best traditional singers.

The Traditional Singers

Jeannie Robertson and Joe Heaney are, undoubtedly, the
greatest exponents in this field. Their style, though archaic, represents the full maturity of a tradition once widespread throughout
the British Isles. Unlike so many singers of this school, age has
neither blurred their vocal qualities nor their memories: their
versions are full and the control of their voices so different from
the chaotic mumblings of so many singers of the revival.

Both performers use a highly ornamented style, and yet this
quality, individual as it may sound on a first hearing, gives to the
songs a timelessness and anonymity only gained from centuries of
a living tradition.

So far there are only two recordings of Joe Heaney available
in this country, but they exhibit, quite adequately, the full strength
of the still extant Irish tradition:

Joe Heaney Sings: Irish traditional songs in Gaelic and English. The
Rocks of Bawn; One Morning in June; Casadh An tSugain; The Bold
Tenant Farmer; The Bonny Boy is Young; Peigin is Peadar; Cunnla;
Caoineadh na Tri Mhuire; An Tighearna Randal; Bean an Leanna;
John Mitchel.

Topic L.P. 12T91

Morrissey and the Russian Sailor: Calleach-an-Airgid; One Morning
in June; The Good Man; Bean Phaidan; Morrissey and the Russian
Sailor.

Collector E.P. JEI 5

Admittedly, a good half of these songs are in Gaelic, and yet, much can still be gained from the pure lyricism and depth of the performance.

Jeannie Robertson and her relations the Stewarts are the Scottish counterpart of Joe Heaney (although they sing no Gaelic), and represent the flowers of the classical tradition of Scots balladry:

Jeannie Robertson: The Bonny Wee Lassie Who Never Said No; What a Voice; My Plaidie's Awa; The Gypsy Laddies; When I was no but Sweet Sixteen; MacCrimmon's Lament; Roy's Wife of Aldivalloch; Lord Lovat.

Topic L.P.   12T96

Jeannie Robertson: The Gallowa Hills; Oh Jeannie My Dear would you Marry Me; The Reel of Tullochgorm; the Yowie wi the Crookit Horn; Bonnie Lass come ower the Burn; Cuttie's Weddin.

Collector E.P.   JES 1

Twa Brothers: My Rovin Eye; Twa Brothers; Davy Faa.

Collector E.P.   Jes 4

Lord Donald: Rollin in the Dew; Haud Yer Tongue Dear Sally; Braes of Balquidder; Lord Donald; Twa Recruitin Sergeants.

Collector L.P.   JFS 4001

Scottish Ballads and Folk Songs: A Ald Man Cam Coortin Me; My Son David; The Deadly Wars; Tak the Buckles frae your Sheen; The Laird o Dainty Doon-By; Ten O'Clock is Ringing; Twa Bonny Black Een; Johnny the Brine; The Laird o' Windywas; Soo Sewin Silk; I'm a Man Youse Don't Meet Every Day; A Maiden Come from London Town; Aberdeen Street Games and Songs.

Prestige/International L.P.   13006

Lucy Stewart: Traditional singer from Aberdeenshire, Vol. 1. The Battle of Harlaw; Two Pretty Boys; Tifty's Annie; The Laird o' Drum; Doon by the Greenwood Side-o; The Beggar King; The Bonnie Hoose o' Airlie; Barbara Allen; The Swan Swims so Bonnie-o.

Folkways L.P.   FG 3519

The Stewarts of Blairgowrie: Songs of a Scottish tinker family. The False Knight upon the Road; The Rambling Irishman; The Road and the Miles to Dundee; The Baron o' Brackley; The Bonnie Hoose o'

Airlie; Brochie and the Highland Chief; The Beggar Man; Dance to yer Daddie; Whistlin at the Ploo; The Banks o' Red Roses; Mountain Dew.

Folkways L.P.   EG 3566

In comparison, England has very little to offer in the way of great traditional singers, perhaps because of the greater involvement (at an earlier period of time) of the majority of her people in 'Progress'. At any rate, most of those who remain are merely old people with croaky voices and inadequate memories. Three, however, are worthy of note: Sam Larner, a Norfolk fisherman; and Bob and Ron Copper, two Sussex publicans who sing in glee harmony.

Now Is The Time For Fishing: Songs and speech by Sam Larner of Winterton, Norfolk. Now is the Time for Fishing; Up Jumped the Herring; The Dogger Bank; Henry Martin; Butter and Cheese; The Reckless Young Fellow; Blow away the Morning Dew; All Fours; Green Broom; The Dockyard Gate; No Sir; Sea-Lore and Rhymes; The Drowned Lover; The Dolphin; The Bold Princess Royal; The Ghost Ship; Pleasant and Delightful; Maids when you're Young; The Wild Rover.

Folkways L.P.   FG 3507

Bob and Ron Copper: Two Brethren; Month of May; The Honest Labourer; Birds in the Spring; The Shepherd in Love; Threshing Song; Dame Burden; Season Round; The Innocent Hare; Lark in the Morn; Hard Times of Old England; Spencer the Rover; Spring Glee; Good Ale; Babes in the Wood; Cupid's Garden.

E.F.D.S.S. L.P.   LP 1002

Three other recordings of traditional British singers should also be mentioned supplementary to the above.

Stormy Weather Boys: Songs of Bob Roberts, Thames sailing-barge skipper. The Collier Brig; The Single Sailor; Stormy Weather Boys; Oh You New York Girls; The Grey Hawk; The Foggy Dew.

Collector L.P.   JEB 6

Street Songs and Fiddle Tunes of Ireland: Margaret Barry with Michael Gorman (fiddle) plus melodeon, vertical flute and piano. Songs: The Wild Colonial Boy; Our Ship is Ready; The Factory Girl; The Cycling

Championship; Her Mantle So Green. Reels: The Bunch of Keys; The Heather Breeze; Dr Gilbert. Hornpipe: The Boys of Blue Hill. Polkas: Maguire's Favourite; Tralee Jane; Maggie in the Wood.

Topic L.P.   10T6

The McPeake Family: Music of a Northern Irish family accompanying themselves on Uilleann pipes and Irish harps. McLeod's Reel; A Bucket of the Mountain Dew; Eileen Aroon; An Durd Fainne; My Singing Bird; The Lament of Aughrim; Carraig Dun; The Derry Hornpipe; The Old Piper; Slieve Gallon Brae; Ireland, Boys, Hurray; Cock Robin; An Coolin; The Verdant Braes of Skreen.

Topic L.P.   12T87

Industrial Song

At least three recordings are available of industrial song, and teachers should not overlook the importance of this field. However it should be remembered that many of these songs are rather different from those of the rural tradition. During the nineteenth century the songmaker was faced with entirely new modes of experience in the industrial town. His efforts to come to terms with his new social environment often produced striking music and poetry that have prolonged, in somewhat changed form, our folksong tradition, following the decline in the composition of rural song. Trying to include many more facts into his songs, he sometimes produced very clumsy, and sometimes unsingable, verses. But, at times, a rare poignancy was achieved.

A. L. Lloyd claims that industrial song is 'no worse than agricultural song' in the incidence of clumsy unsingable verses, and that all industrial songs aren't radically different from the country songs. This, he claims, shows clearly in the record called *The Iron Muse*. Lloyd considers this record specially valuable to teachers, because it is panoramic in scope and the songs are arranged in historical sequence, beginning with those from the early days of the Industrial Revolution (when miners' and textile workers' songs were hardly distinguishable from those of country workers). It goes on through pieces reflecting the struggles, disasters and triumphs of the nineteenth century, ending with songs made in mills, shipyards and mines within the last few years.

The Notes to this record are very full and historically documented. Also, the record is comprised entirely of songs made within the industries concerned, not created from outside 'on behalf of the working class'.

The Iron Muse: A. L. Lloyd, Anne Briggs, Bob Davenport, Ray Fisher, Louis Killen, Matt McGinn and The Celebrated Working Man's Band. Miners' Dance Tunes; The Recruited Collier; Pit Boots; The Banks of the Dee; The Donibristle Moss Moran Disaster; The Durham Lock-Out; The Blackleg Miners; The Celebrated Working Man; The Row between the Cages; The Collier's Daughter; The Weaver's March; The Poor Cotton Wayver; The Doffing Mistress; The Swan-Necked Valve; The Dundee Lassie; The Foreman O'Rourke; Farewell to the Monty; Miner's Dance Tunes.
Topic L.P.   12T86

The Colliers' Rant: Louis Killen, Johnny Handle and Colin Ross. Blackleg Miners; The Collier's Rant; Aw Wish Pay Friday Wad Come; The Putter; The Trimdon Grange Explosion; The Waggoner.
Topic E.P.   TOP 74

Also interesting is the following, though it contains many compositions by Ewan MacColl himself which, whatever one thinks of them, are not, of course, folksongs:

Steam Whistle Ballads: Ewan MacColl and Peggy Seeger. Wark of the Weavers; Droylsden Wakes; The four Loom Weaver; Oh Dear Me; The Coal Owner and the Pitman's Wife; Fourpence a Day; The Gresford Disaster; Will Caird; The Iron Horse; Poor Paddy Works on the Railway; Cannily, Cannily; The Song of the Iron Road; The Blantyre Explosion; The Collier Laddie; Moses of the Mail.
Topic L.P.   12T104

The North-East of England still retains much of the old traditional culture, and several young singers have emerged from this (notably Louis Killen, Bob Davenport and Johnny Handle) whose singing embodies much of the vigour and strength inherent in that culture:

Northumbrian Garland: Louis Killen with Colin Ross on tin whistle, fiddle and Northumbrian pipes. Anti-Gallican Privateer; Sair Gyeld Hinny; Keep Your Feet Still; Up the Raw; Do-Li-A; Derwentwater's Farewell.
Topic E.P.   TOP 75

Stottin Doon the Waall: Johnny Handle. The Collier Lad; Big Meetin Day; The Stoneman's Lament; Stottin Doon the Waall; Farewell to the Monty; The Day we went to the Coast.
Topic E.P.   TOP 78

Northumbrian Minstrelsy: Bob Davenport, Isla Cameron and The Rakes. My Bonnie Lad; Cushie Butterfield; Bonny at Morn, Three Ravens. Buy Broom Besoms; The Harrin's Heid; Salmon Tails; Keep your Feet Still; Children's Songs; The Bonny Lass of Benwell; Redesdale Hornpipe; Willie's Rare; Chevy Chase; Wild Hills o' Wannies; Durham Gaol; Whittingham Green Lane; Ward's Brae; O Can Ye Sew Cushions; Lads o' Alnwick; Johnnie Armstrong; Border Widow's Lament.
Concert Hall L.P.   AM 2339

A glut of records of the more popular T.V. folk-singers is available in most record shops, but these are not to be recommended as they do more harm than good. Neither are folksongs best served by 'art' singers (such as Alfred Deller, Peter Pears, and Owen Brannigan), though of course Britten's arrangements are superb in their own right. I feel that Mary O'Hara deserves a little more credit than she normally gets in the folksong world; many of her recordings are much more desirable than those of the overtly commercial groups.

The Purchase of Records

Teachers will find that the ten Caedmon L.P.s, together with some of the industrial ballad records, will provide an adequate basis for a sound library of folksong. Any of the other records listed here may be added as finances and individual interests permit.

Local record shops may be able to provide the Topic or Collector labels, but the American releases will be more difficult to obtain. The Caedmon, Concert Hall and E.F.D.S.S. series may only be purchased from The Folk Shop, Cecil Sharp House, 2 Regent's Park Road, London N.W. 1; and only by a member of the E.F.D.S.S., because of tax restrictions. All other records can be bought from this source regardless of membership, or from Collet's Record Shop, 70 New Oxford Street, London W.C. 1.

Bibliography

I give here, more or less related to the progress of my book, a list of those books which I feel have either helped me to reach the conclusions I set out in it, or which I would encourage teachers in training to read, in order to come at an understanding of what they are doing. If I were in charge of a school I should purchase all these books for a staff library: under 'miscellaneous' I have placed books which suggest and give immediate teaching material for class use, and other such books are given under headings for practical work. Some books may seem odd in their context, but they are there because I know they have helped me in my teaching.

I have also given here and there in the list one or two books which are not directly relevant, but which I have found seminal and provocative, disturbing our conceptions of what we are doing in teaching and writing. Such are *The Origins of Love and Hate* by Ian D. Suttie, and Professor L. C. Knights's *Explorations*. I have avoided giving the larger list I could have given, because I know from experience that certain of the books I give, when the better reader reads them, provoke further reading in the relevant direction—e.g. more of the writings of Leavis and Knights, and of the younger writers who have learned from them.

MAGAZINES AND ORGANISATIONS

Every teacher of English will find useful the quarterly journal *The Use of English*, edited by Denys Thompson and published by Chatto and Windus, price 17s. 6d. a year. This magazine provides reading of interest to teachers of English at all levels, and includes articles both on general matters of literature and on classroom practice.

The School Librarian is obtainable from The School Library Association, Gordon House, 29 Gordon Square, London w.c. 1.

Teachers may also like to know the following addresses: *The Poetry Book Society*, which sends its members four books of newly published poetry a year, and which aims to encourage the reading of new poetry: 4 St James' Square, London w. 1.

The Film Appreciation Dept., British Film Institute, 81 Dean Street, London w. 1, can help teachers anxious to train children to be critical about the cinema.

National Association of Teachers of English, Secretary, 197 Henley Road, Caversham, Reading, Berks.

Bibliography

BOOK-LISTS AND EXHIBITIONS

The National Book League, 7 Albemarle Street, London W. 1, has a number of touring exhibitions which may be borrowed, for the fees given below. Teachers may obtain the catalogues of these exhibitions from the League. Schools could club together to hire an exhibition, or persuade their Institute of Education, public library, or local Adult Centre, to put one on show.

Help in Reading, hiring charge £4 10s. od. (there are reduced charges for members of the League).
New Books for Children, £4.
British Children's Books, £7.
Children and Adults, £4 10s. od.
Contemporary Poetry, £4 10s. od.
Fantasy, £4 10s. od.
Have You Read This? £6.
Paperbacks for Young People, £4 10s. od.
School Library Books, Fiction, six exhibitions.
The Teaching of English, about 100 books for teachers, £3.

The above hiring charges apply for a showing of up to two weeks. Exhibitors meet the cost of ongoing carriage. The *Guide to Touring Exhibitions* is 2s. 6d.

BOOKS FOR THE TEACHER'S LIBRARY
The Background to English in Education

Arnold, Matthew, *Culture and Anarchy* (C.U.P.).
Bantock, G. H., *Education in an Industrial Society; Education and Values* (Faber).
Boorstin, Daniel, *The Image* (Penguin).
Coveney, Peter, *Poor Monkey; The Child in Literature* (Rockliff).
Henry, Jules, *Culture against Man* (Tavistock).
Hall, Stuart, and Whannel, Paddy, *The Popular Arts* (Hutchinson).
Hoggart, Richard, *The Uses of Literacy* (Chatto).
Jephcott, A. P., *Girls Growing Up* (Faber).
Lawrence, D. H., *Letters* (Heinemann).
Lawrence, D. H., various papers in *Phoenix* (Heinemann).
Leavis, F. R., and Thompson, Denys, *Culture and Environment* (Chatto).
Leavis, Q. D., *Fiction and the Reading Public* (Chatto).
MacKenzie, R. F., *A Question of Living* (Collins).
Milner, Marion, *On Not Being Able to Paint* (Heinemann).

Opie, Iona and Peter, *The Language and Lore of School Children* (Oxford).
Orwell, George, *Critical Essays* (Secker and Warburg), *Selected Essays* (Penguin Books).
Packard, Vance, *The Hidden Persuaders* (Longmans).
Royal Commission on the Press, Cmd. 7700 HMSO.
Segal, Charles F., *Backward Children in the Making* (Muller).
Suttie, Ian D., *The Origins of Love and Hate* (Routledge).
Thompson, Denys, *Discrimination and Popular Culture* (Penguin).
Thompson, Denys, *Between the Lines* (on the press) (Muller);
   Voice of Civilisation (on advertising) (Muller).
Williams, Raymond, *Communications* (Chatto).
Winnicott, D. W., *The Child, the Family and the Outside World* (Penguin).

Aims in Teaching English

Bantock, G. H., *Education in an Industrial Society* (Faber); *Freedom and Authority in Education* (Faber).
Bell, Vicars, *On Learning the English Tongue* (Faber).
Biaginni, E. G., *The Reading and Writing of English* (Hutchinson).
Eliot, T. S., *Selected Essays* (Faber).
Holbrook, David, *English for the Rejected* (Cambridge); *The Secret Places* (Methuen); *The Exploring Word* (Cambridge).
Hourd, Marjorie L., *Some Emotional Aspects of Learning* (Heinemann); *The Education of the Poetic Spirit* (Heinemann); *Coming Into Their Own* (Heinemann).
Jackson, Brian, and Thompson, Denys, *English in Education* (Chatto).
James, Sir Eric, *The Content of Education and Leadership* (Harrap).
Knights, L. C., *Explorations* (Chatto).
Leavis, F. R., *Revaluation* (Chatto); *Education and the University* (Chatto).
Legouis and Cazamian, *History of English Literature* (Dent).
Marshall, Sybil, *An Experiment in Education* (C.U.P.).
Newman, J. H., a selection, *The Idea of a Liberal Education* (Harrap).
Sampson, George, *English for the English* (C.U.P.).
Smith, A. E., *English in the Secondary Modern School* (Methuen).
Strong, L. A. G., *The Writer's Trade* (Methuen); *English for Pleasure* (Methuen).
Thompson, Denys, *Reading and Discrimination* (Chatto).
Thompson, Denys, and O'Malley, Raymond, *English for the Living* (Methuen).
Walsh, J. H., *Teaching English* (Heinemann).
Walsh, William, *The Use of Imagination* (Chatto).
Whitehead, Frank, *The Disappearing Dais* (Chatto).

Bibliography

The English Language

Barfield, Owen, *History in English Words* (Faber).

Fowler, H. W. and F. G., *The King's English* (O.U.P.); Fowler, H. W. (revised Gowers), *Modern English Usage* (O.U.P.).

Gowers, Sir Ernest, *The Complete Plain Words* (HMSO).

Grattan, J. H. G., and Gurrey, P., *Our Living Language* (Nelson).

Hayakawa, S. I., *Language in Thought and Action* (Allen & Unwin).

Herbert, A. P., *What a Word!* (Methuen).

Jespersen, Otto, *Growth and Structure of the English Language* (Blackwell).

King, Alex, and Ketley, Martin, *The Control of Language* (Longmans).

Pei, Mario, *The Story of Language* (Allen & Unwin).

Potter, Simeon, *Our Language* (Penguin).

Savory, T. H., *The Language of Science* (Deutsch).

Smith, Logan Pearsall, *Words and Idioms* (Constable).

Poetry

Adventures into Poetry (O.U.P.).

Brooks and Warren, eds., *Understanding Poetry* (Henry Holt and Co., New York).

Brown, V. V., ed. *The Experience of Poetry in School* (O.U.P.).

Central Committee on the Teaching of English in the East and West Ridings of Yorkshire, *Poetry and Children* (Methuen).

Eliot, T. S., *Selected Essays, On Poetry and Poets* (Faber).

Harris, L. S., *The Nature of English Poetry* (Dent).

Hudson, A. K., ed., *Shakespeare and the Classroom* (Heinemann).

Holbrook, David, *Iron, Honey, Gold*, (C.U.P.).

Leavis, F. R., *New Bearings in English Poetry* (Chatto).

Lewis, Cecil Day, *Poetry for You* (Basil Blackwell).

Matthiesen, F. M., ed., *The Oxford Book of American Verse* (O.U.P.).

Muir, Kenneth, ed., *English Poetry* (O.U.P.).

Opie, Iona and Peter, *Oxford Dictionary of Nursery Rhymes* (O.U.P.).

Reeves, James, *The Teaching of Poetry* (Heinemann).

Rosenthal, M. L., and Smith, A. J. M., *Exploring Poetry* (Macmillan).

Scott, A. F., *Poetry and Appreciation* (Macmillan); *The Poet's Craft* (C.U.P.).

Thompson, Denys, and O'Malley, Raymond, *Rhyme and Reason*, an anthology (Chatto).

Traversi, Derek, *An Approach to Shakespeare* (Sands).

Waley, Arthur, *Poems from the Chinese* (Constable).

Folksong and other forms of song

Alvin, Juliette, *Music for the Handicapped Child* (O.U.P.).
The Cambridge Hymnal (C.U.P.).
Clinton Baddeley, V. C., *Words for Music* (C.U.P.).
Hodgart, Matthew, *The Ballad* (Hutchinson).
Holbrook, David, *Children's Games* (Gordon Fraser).
Mellers, Wilfrid, *Man and his Music* (Rockliff).
The Oxford Book of Carols (O.U.P.).
Reeves, James, *The Idiom of the People*, *The Everlasting Circle* (Heinemann).
Sharp, Cecil, *English Folksong—Some Conclusions* (Novello).
Nettel, Reginald, *Sing a Song of England* (Phoenix House).

Oral and Written Composition

Beckett, Jack, *The Keen Edge* (Blackie).
Clegg, A. B., ed., *The Excitement of Writing* (Chatto).
Gurrey, P., *The Teaching of Written English* (Longmans).
Henderson, Mrs A. M., *Good Speaking* (Pan).
Langdon, Margaret, *Let the Children Write* (Longmans).
Pym, Dora, *Free Writing* (U.L.P.).
Q., *On the Art of Writing* (Guild Books).

Reading and the Library

Beresford, Rosemary, *What Shall I Read?* (Ginn) (with a teacher's manual).
Darton, Harvey, revised Kathleen Lines, *Children's Books in England* (C.U.P.).
Eleven to Fifteen. A Basic Booklist of non-fiction for secondary school libraries (School Libraries Association).
Fisher, Margery, *Intent Upon Reading* (Brockhampton).
Ford, Boris, ed., *Young Writers, Young Readers* (Hutchinson).
Grimshaw, Ernest, *The Teacher Librarian* (School Library Association).
Jenkinson, A. J., *What do Boys and Girls Read?* (Methuen).
Meigs, Cornelia, ed., *A Critical History of Children's Literature* (Macmillan).
Ministry of Education, *The School Library*.
Q., *The Art of Reading* (Guild Books).
The Scottish Council for Research in Education, *Studies in Reading*, (U.L.P.).
Stott, C. A., *School Libraries, a Short Manual* (C.U.P.).
Trease, Geoffrey, *Enjoying Books*; *Tales Out of School* (Heinemann).
Witty, Paul, *Reading in Modern Education* (Harrap).

Drama

Allen, John, *Play Productions* (Dennis Dobson).
Burford, Rose, *Teaching Mime* (Methuen).
Collins, Joan M., *Books and Materials for School and Youth Drama* (Dobson).
Kitto, H. D. F., Professor, *Form and Meaning in Drama* (Methuen).
Langdon, E. M., *Dramatic Work with Children* (Faber).
Stone, L. A., *Story of a School* (Ministry Pamphlet).
Wiles, John and Garrard, Alan, *Leap to Life!* (Chatto).
Williams, Raymond, *Drama in Performance* (Muller).

Drills

Carey, G. V., *Mind the Stop* (C.U.P.).
Davies, Hugh Sykes, *Grammar without Tears* (Bodley Head).
Schonell, F. J., *Essential Spelling List* (Macmillan).
Swann, Robert, *Simple Tests in English* (Methuen); *Common Sense Tests in English* (Methuen).

Miscellaneous Sources of Teaching Material and Books of Reference

Concise Dictionary of National Biography.
Holbrook, David, *Llareggub Revisited* (Bowes and Bowes); *The Quest for Love* (Methuen).
Jepson, R. W., *Clear Thinking* (Longmans).
A Literary and Historical Atlas of Europe (Everyman).
Klein, Melanie, *Our Adult Society and its Roots in Infancy* (Tavistock).
Onions, C. T., *Shakespeare Glossary* (O.U.P.).
Palmer, Mary (compiled by), *Writing and Action*, a documentary anthology (Allen and Unwin).
The Reader's Bible, issued by C.U.P. and O.U.P.
Roget's Thesaurus of Words and Phrases (Longmans).
School Library Association, *Librarianship and Library Technique*, list of recommended books.
Shorter Oxford Dictionary (O.U.P.).
Skeat, *Concise Etymological Dictionary of the English Language* (O.U.P.).
A Smaller Classical Dictionary (Everyman).
Stebbing, Susan, *Thinking to Some Purpose* (Penguin).
Thompson, Denys, *Science in Perspective* (Murray); *Practice in Reading* (Chatto and Windus).
Thouless, R. H., *Straight and Crooked Thinking* (Hodder and Stoughton).
Williams, Raymond, *Culture and Society; The Long Revolution.*

Index

Index

Index

Index